Laughter
the
Best Medicine II

A Laugh-Out-Loud Collection
of our Funniest Jokes, Quotes, Stories and Cartoons

Reader's Digest

The Reader's Digest Association, Inc. • Pleasantville, NY / Montreal

PROJECT STAFF

EDITOR
Marianne Wait

SR. DESIGN DIRECTOR
Elizabeth Tunnicliffe

CONTRIBUTING EDITOR
Doug Colligan

COPY EDITOR
Jeanette Gingold

COVER AND SPOT ILLUSTRATION
Elwood Smith

READER'S DIGEST BOOKS

PRESIDENT AND PUBLISHER
Harold Clarke

EDITOR IN CHIEF
Neil Wertheimer

MANAGING EDITOR
Suzanne G. Beason

ART DIRECTOR
Michele Laseau

PRODUCTION TECHNOLOGY MANAGER
Douglas A. Croll

MANUFACTURING MANAGER
John L. Cassidy

BOOK MARKETING DIRECTOR
Dawn Nelson

DIRECTOR OF DIRECT MARKETING
Lisa Walker

READER'S DIGEST ASSOCIATION, INC.

PRESIDENT, NORTH AMERICA
GLOBAL EDITOR-IN-CHIEF
Eric W. Schrier

ISBN 10: 0-7621-0814-2
ISBN 13: 978-0-7621-0814-5

Address any comments about *Laughter, The Best Medicine II* to:
The Reader's Digest Association, Inc.
Adult Trade Publishing
Reader's Digest Road
Pleasantville, NY 10570-7000

Previously published in 2005 as *Laughter, The Best Medicine* (ISBN 0-7621-0719-7)

Cover illustration © Elwood Smith

For more Reader's Digest products and information, visit our website:
www.rd.com (in the United States)
www.readersdigest.ca (in Canada)

Printed in China
5 7 9 10 8 6 4

Introduction

Doctor: "*I have some bad news and some worse news. The bad news is that you have only 24 hours left to live.*"

Patient: "*That is bad news. What could be worse?*"

Doctor: "*I've been trying to reach you since yesterday.*"

This familiar joke made millions of people laugh when we published it in *Reader's Digest* magazine. And every time you laugh, it's like taking a miracle pill for your health. According to doctors and scientific researchers, laughter can reduce stress, lower blood pressure, boost the immune system, improve brain function, and even protect your heart. Maybe that's why the average person laughs around 17 times a day.

When you think about humor and health, it's no wonder that we have a "funny bone," that humor is "contagious," and that laughter is "infectious."

Humor is also an "antidote" to everyday problems, like trying to make sense of a computer error. You can get angry about it, or you can respond with a joke, like this one:

ERROR: Keyboard Not Found!
Press any key to continue...

Press any key...no, no, no,
NOT THAT ONE
Press any key to continue or any key to quit...

Enter 11-digit prime number
to continue...

Smash forehead on keyboard
to continue...

Even subjects of great debate and heated discussion can be defused by humor:

"As long as there are tests, there will be prayer in public schools."

And when we're afraid of something, the best thing to do is laugh our way through it. Let's say you need an operation. You're scared. You're worried. You don't know if you'll come through it all. So your friend takes you aside, gives you a pep talk, and says don't worry unless you hear the following during the operation:

"Better save that. We'll need it for the autopsy."

"Bo! Bo! Come back with that! Bad dog!"

"Oh, no! I just lost my Rolex."

"Wait a minute...if this is his spleen, then what's that?"

Reader's Digest has always believed in the power of laughter. Our well-known magazine column, "Laughter, the Best Medicine," has appeared in every issue of the magazine for over half a century. Over the years, we have published more than 100,000 jokes, quotes, and funny stories from the more than 20 million people who have submitted them. We receive about 35,000 submissions each month and have awarded more than $25 million to our comic contributors. We never thought we were in the business of healing, but science has put us there—and we're glad of it.

As you read this book, remember to share a laugh or two with your family and friends. And keep it handy. You never know when you'll need another dose of the best medicine. Or, as Groucho Marx once said, "A laugh is like an aspirin, only it works twice as fast."

JACQUELINE LEO
EDITOR-IN-CHIEF
READER'S DIGEST

Contents

Aging Gracelessly
125

Face it—you're not getting better, you're getting older, and the sooner you come to terms with that, or incorporate Botox injections into your budget, the better.

Venus and Mars
151

Speaking of war and laughter—put together, it's called marriage. Despite thousands of years of practice, men and women still don't connect well. But it's fun to watch 'em try.

Humor in Uniform
181

The trials and tribulations of our sons, daughters, parents, and friends in the military.

All Creatures Great and Small
195

Dogs, cats, and countless common critters are all part of our everyday lives. Here's the funny stuff that happens when animals cross paths with us humans.

Word Play
217

Is English the easiest language to mangle? It sure seems so. Here are silly word plays, ridiculous euphemisms, hysterically flawed utterances, and other fun language twists and plays.

Last Laughs
241

Jest the facts: Laugh-out-loud humor we couldn't resist, plus the funniest one-liners of all time.

Life in These Times

It keeps us plugged in, turned on, and sometimes ticked off.
The ironies, absurdities, and marvels of modern-day life.

My boyfriend and I met online and we'd been dating for over a year. I introduced Hans to my uncle, who was fascinated by the fact that we met over the Internet. He asked Hans what kind of line he had used to pick me up.

Ever the geek, Hans naïvely replied, "I just used a regular 56K modem."

— ANNE MCCONNE

Kids have a greater need for speed than classroom computers can deliver. Impatient to turn in his term paper, one restless student kept clicking the "Print" command. The printer started to churn out copy after copy of the kid's ten-page report.

The topic? "Save Our Trees."

— KEN CUMMINGS

I am five feet, three inches tall and pleasingly plump. After I had a minor accident, my mother accompanied me to the emergency room.

The triage nurse asked for my height and weight, and I blurted out, "Five-foot-eight and 125 pounds."

While the nurse pondered this information, my mother leaned over to me. "Sweetheart," she gently chided, "this is not the Internet."

— M. M.

During a visit to the ladies' room, my friend Addy heard the woman in the next stall suddenly ask, "So how are you?"

Startled, Addy replied tentatively, "Fine."

The woman continued, "So what's new?"

Still confused, Addy said, "Not much. What's new with you?"

It was then that the woman snapped, "Do you mind? I'm on the phone."

— MARION SPARER

I was visiting a friend who could not find her cordless phone. After several minutes of searching, her young daughter said, "You know what they should invent? A phone that stays connected to its base so it never gets lost."

— MIRIAM SCOW

Trying to explain to our five-year-old daughter how much computers had changed, my husband pointed to our brand-new personal computer and told her that when he was in college, a computer with the same amount of power would have been the size of a house.

Wide-eyed, our daughter asked, "How big was the mouse?"

— CYNDY HINDS

Learning to use a voice-recognition computer program, I was excited about the prospect of finally being able to write more accurately than I type. First I read out loud to the computer for about an hour to train it to my voice, then I opened a clean page and dictated a nursery rhyme to see the magic.

The computer recorded: "Murry fed a little clam, its fleas was bright and slow."

— CARRIE E. PITTS

Timeless Humor from the 50's

The big electronic computer in the accounting department performed admirably until summer weather arrived. Then it practically quit. A diagnosis of the trouble revealed that the machine was extremely sensitive to changes in temperature, so the only thing to do was to move it into an air-conditioned room.

Now, as we office drones perspire and droop, we are treated to the vision of the computer operating coolly and efficiently beyond the glass wall of its private office. What was that again about men being smarter than machines?

"It's guaranteed for the life of the product, which obviously ended when it broke."

A friend of mine was enjoying his new car's powerful sound system by driving along with the volume way up. At a traffic light, he heard someone shout, "Hey, do you mind?"

Stopped next to him was a young man in an open convertible. He pointed to an object in his hand and said, "Can't you see I'm on the phone?"

— DENNIS DIGGES

When my printer's type began to grow faint, I called a local repair shop, where a friendly man informed me that the printer probably needed only to be cleaned. Because the store charged $50 for such cleanings, he told me, I might be better off reading the printer's manual and trying the job myself.

Pleasantly surprised by his candor, I asked, "Does your boss know that you discourage business?"

"Actually it's my boss's idea," the employee replied sheepishly. "We usually make more money on repairs if we let people try to fix things themselves first."

— MICHELLE R. ST. JAMES

A pastor I know of uses a standard liturgy for funerals. To personalize each service, he enters a "find and replace" command into his word processor. The computer then finds the name of the deceased from the previous funeral and replaces it with the name of the deceased for the upcoming one.

Not long ago, the pastor told the computer to find the name "Mary" and replace it with "Edna." The next morning, the funeral was going smoothly until the congregation intoned the Apostles' Creed. "Jesus Christ," they read from the preprinted program, "born of the Virgin Edna."

— ROBIN GREENSPAN

I returned from Russia after living there nearly two years. My sister decided to surprise me by creating "welcome home" signs in Russian. She went to a website that offered translations and typed in "Welcome Home, Cole." She then printed the translated phrase onto about 20 colored cardboard signs.

When I got off the plane, the first thing I saw was my family, excitedly waving posters printed with a strange message. My sister gave me a big hug and pointed proudly to her creations. "Isn't that great?" she said. "Bet you didn't think I knew any Russian."

I admitted that I was indeed surprised—and so was she when I told her what the signs actually said: "Translation not found."

— COLE M. CRITTENDEN

I purchased a new desktop-publishing program that surprised me by containing a make-a-paper-airplane option. I decided to give it a try. After I selected the plane I wanted, the software gave me a choice of accessories available for my plane, including a stick-up tail, adjustable flaps and an AM/FM radio. Out of curiosity I chose the AM/FM radio.

The program responded with a message box stating: "Come on, be serious. These are just paper airplanes."

— GREG SCOTT

Our newer, high-speed computer was in the shop for repair, and my son was forced to work on our old model with the black-and-white printer.

"Mom," he complained to me one day, "this is like we're living back in the twentieth century."

— DENISE PERRY DONAVIN

One cold night my furnace died, so I went to my parents' house. In the morning, a neighbor called to tell me that my water pipes had burst and flooded my town house and hers. I raced home—and on the way got a speeding ticket.

Then the furnace repairman arrived and told me he didn't think he had the proper fuse but would check in his truck. Meanwhile, the plumber cut holes in my bathroom wall to locate the leak.

When the furnace repairman returned, he held aloft a fuse. "I had the right one," he said triumphantly. "This must be your lucky day."

— CANDACE M. PRESTWICH

The first Sunday after my husband and I bought a new car, we parked it in the last row of the church lot, not wanting to be ostentatious. While talking with friends, my husband, Byron, accidentally hit the panic button on his electronic key. Immediately our car's horn blared and its lights flashed.

Watching Byron fumble with the button, his friend teased, "Wouldn't it have been in better taste to put a few lines in the church bulletin?"

— DONA A. MOWRY

Working as a telemarketer for MCI Communications, I made a call to a Minnesota home one evening. When a boy around eight answered the phone, I identified myself, told him I was calling for MCI and asked to speak to his parents.

As he put the phone down, I heard him yell, "Dad! Dad! The FBI wants to talk to you!"

As soon as the father answered the phone in a quivering voice, I said, "Sir, this is not the FBI; this is MCI Communications."

After a long pause, the man said, "This is the first time I am actually glad to hear from you guys."

— LYNDA CYPHER

"I'm going to prescribe something that works like aspirin but costs much, much more."

I was preparing lunch for my granddaughter when the phone rang. "If you can answer one question," a young man said, "you'll win ten free dance lessons."

Before I could tell him I was not interested, he continued. "You'll be a lucky winner if you can tell me what Alexander Graham Bell invented."

"I don't know," I replied dryly, trying to discourage him.

"What are you holding in your hand right now?" he asked excitedly.

"A bologna sandwich."

"Congratulations!" he shrieked. "And for having such a great sense of humor…"

— LOLA CANTRELL

My son, Scott, an insurance broker in Florida, loves ocean fishing and takes his cell phone along on the boat. One morning we were drifting about ten miles offshore as Scott discussed business on the phone. Suddenly his rod bent double, and the reel screamed as line poured off the spool.

Scott was master of the situation. "Pardon me," he told his customer calmly. "I have a call on another line."

— ART HARRIS

It is so rare to be offered a meal on airlines these days that I was surprised to hear the flight attendant ask the man sitting in front of me,

"Would you like dinner?"

"What are my choices?" he responded.

"Yes or no," she said.

KERVYN DIMNEY

Telephone solicitors are one of my father's pet peeves. He is especially annoyed by those who offer "free gifts" as part of their sales pitch. Late one night, Dad was in bed when the phone rang.

The voice on the end of the line said: "Congratulations, you've just won a free burial plot!"

"Great!" Dad replied. "Send it over." Then he hung up.

— D. VANCE NOONAN

The elevator in our building malfunctioned one day, leaving several of us stranded. Seeing a sign that listed two emergency phone numbers, I dialed the first and explained our situation.

After what seemed to be a very long silence, the voice on the other end said, "I don't know what you expect me to do for you; I'm a psychologist."

"A psychologist?" I replied. "Your phone is listed here as an emergency number. Can't you help us?"

"Well," he finally responded in a measured tone. "How do you feel about being stuck in an elevator?"

— CHRISTINE QUINN

One night, telephone solicitors kept interrupting our supper. When the phone rang yet again, my father answered it. By his remarks, we assumed it was his friend Ed, a notorious practical joker.

Dad kept saying things like, "Cut it out, Ed. This is very funny, but I know it's you. C'mon, stop it or I'll hang up. I'll get you for this."

When Dad hung up, my mom asked, "Was that Ed?"

"No," my father replied. "It was a salesman, and I don't think he'll call back."

— TONI M. VIDRA

I provide technical support for the computer software published by my company. One day, over the phone, I was helping a customer install a product on a Macintosh. The procedure required him to delete an old file. On the Mac there is an icon of a trash can that is used to collect items to be permanently deleted.

I told the customer to click on the old file and drag it to the trash. Then I had him perform a few other steps. As a reminder, I said, "Don't forget to empty the trash."

Obediently he replied, "Yes, dear."

— CYNTHIA KAINU

One Saturday night my boss and her family came to our house to play cards. As they were driving away at the end of the evening, I discovered that she had left her purse in a corner next to the dining-room hutch. I was about to call her house, intending to leave a message on the answering machine, when my son reminded me that they had a cell phone.

As I dialed the number, I marveled at the technology that would alert them before they had driven all the way home. A few seconds later the purse began to ring.

— PATTY DUNHAM

I'm a deputy sheriff and was parked near a motel, running radar checks, when a man approached my vehicle and asked for help. He complained that the volume on the television in the empty motel room next to his was so loud that he and his wife couldn't sleep.

No one was in the motel office. The man's wife was outside when I reached their door. That's when I got my idea. I asked her for their remote control, aimed it through the window of the empty room, and turned off the blaring TV.

— RAY ALLEN

My mother began getting calls from men who misdialed the similar number of an escort service. Mom, who had had her number for years, asked the telephone company to change the organization's number. They refused. The calls kept coming day and night.

Finally, Mom began telling the gentlemen who called that the company had gone out of business. Within a week, the escort service voluntarily changed its number.

— MARIAN BURGESS

"This man here is saying that he stole your identity,
got bored, and now wants to return it."

Just ahead of me in line at the movie theater was a woman with a cell phone glued to her ear, arguing with the ticket vendor.

"That movie can't be sold out!" she shouted. "I'm talking to my boyfriend who's sitting in the theater, and he says there's two empty seats next to him. One ticket, please."

She got her ticket.

— CLAUDIA J. WRAZEL-HOROWITZ

After I bought my mother a compact-disc player and some CDs, she was excited to discover she no longer needed to rewind or fast-forward tapes or move the needle on her record player.

Knowing she was not that technically astute, I called her a few days later to see how she was managing. "Fine. I listened to Shania Twain this morning," she said.

"The whole CD?" I asked.

"No," she replied, "just one side."

— COURTNEY DYER

A phone company representative called to ask if I was interested in caller ID. Since I'm blind, I asked, "Does it come in Braille?"

The rep put me on hold. When she returned, she replied, "I'm sorry, sir, but the caller ID box doesn't come in that color."

— ED LUCAS

My cell phone quit as I tried to let my wife know that I was caught in freeway gridlock and would be late for our anniversary dinner. I wrote a message on my laptop asking other motorists to call her, printed it on a portable inkjet and taped it to my rear windshield.

When I finally arrived home, my wife gave me the longest kiss ever. "I really think you love me," she said. "At least 70 people called and told me so."

— JARON SUMMERS

The brave new memo about the company's revised travel policy read as follows: We were no longer allowed to buy cheap tickets via the Internet. Instead, we were required to use the more expensive company travel department. Furthermore, to show how much money we were saving, we were asked to comparison-shop for fares—on the Internet.

I thought the typo in the last line of the memo summed it up best: "The new process is ineffective today."

— KIP HARTMAN

Part of what makes a human being a human being is the imperfections. Like, you wouldn't give a robot my ears. You just wouldn't do that.

— WILL SMITH in InTouch

A computer lets you make more mistakes faster than any invention in human history—with the possible exceptions of handguns and tequila.

— MITCH RATCLIFFE

"If we are a country committed to free speech," asks comedian Steven Wright, "then why do we have phone bills?"

Just think how far we've come in the 20th century. The man who used to be a cog in the wheel is now a digit in the computer.

— ROBERT FUOSS in The Wall Street Journal

Most people hate cell phone use on trains; I love cell phone use on trains. What do you want to do, read that report on your lap, or hear about your neighbor's worst date ever?

— LIZA MUNDY in The Washington Post Magazine

A modern computer is an electronic wonder that performs complex mathematical calculations and intricate accounting tabulations in one ten-thousandth of a second—and then mails out statements ten days later.

— PAUL SWEENEY

You can't write poetry on the computer.

— QUENTIN TARANTINO

You can buy anything on eBay. I bought the world's oldest globe. It's flat.

— BUZZ NUTLEY

Designer of Audio CD Packaging

Enters Hell

▶ BY STEVE MARTIN

The burning gates of hell were opened, and the designer of CD packaging entered to the Devil's fanfare. "We've been wanting him down here for a long time," the One of Pure Evil said to his infernal minions, "but we decided to wait, because he was doing such good work above, wrapping the CDs with cellophane and that sticky tape strip. Ask him to dinner, and be sure to invite the computer-manual people too."

The Devil vanished, missing the warm display of affection offered the inventor.

"Beelzebub himself opened a nasty cut on his finger trying to unwrap a Streisand best-of," whispered an imp. A thick snake nuzzled closer, and wrapped itself around the inventor's leg. "He used to be enamored of the remote-control people, with their tiny little buttons jammed together, and their enigmatic abbrevia-

tions," the snake said, "but now all he ever talks about is you, you, you. Come on, let's get you ready for dinner. We can talk about your assignment later."

As the snake led the way to the dressing halls of hell, a yearning, searching look came over its face. "How did you do it?" the snake asked. "You know, invent the packaging? Everyone wants to know."

The inventor, his feet comfortably aflame, and flattered by all the recognition, relaxed into his surroundings. "The original plastic CD 'jewel box' was just too damn easy to get into," he explained. "I mean, if we're going to prevent consumer access, for God's sake, let's prevent it! I wanted a packaging where the consumer would run to the kitchen for a knife, so there was a chance to at least slice open his hand."

"Is that when you got the idea for shrink-wrap?" said the snake.

"Shrink-wrap was nice for a while. I liked that there was absolutely no place to tear into it with a fingernail, but I knew there was further to go. That's when I hit on cellophane, cellophane with the illusion of an opening strip, where really none exists."

That night, at the celebratory dinner held once an eon to honor new arrivals, the inventor sat to the Devil's right. On his left sat Cerberus, the watchdog of Hades and noted designer of the pineapple. The Devil chatted with the inventor all night long, then requested that he open another bottle of wine, this time with a two-pronged, sideslip corkscrew. The inventor perspired, and an hour later the bottle was uncorked.

At first, no one noticed the muffled disturbance from above, which soon grew into a sustained clamor. Eventually the entire gathering looked toward the ceiling, and finally the Devil himself

CD buyers are getting a bum wrap, says renowned comedian Steve Martin.

noticed that their attention had shifted. He raised his head.

Hovering in the ether were three angels, each holding an object. The inventor knew clearly what the objects were: the milk carton, the Ziploc bag and the banana, all three perfectly designed packages. He remembered how he used to admire them before he fell into evil. The three angels glided toward the dais.

One held the Ziploc bag over the aspirin-bottle people, and bathed them in an otherworldly light. A yellow glow from the banana washed over the hellhound Cerberus, designer of the pineapple, and the milk carton poured its white luminosity in the direction of the CD packager. The Devil stood up abruptly, roared something in Latin while succubi flew out of his mouth, and then angrily excused himself.

After the fiasco, the inventor went back to his room and fiddled with the five remotes it took to operate his VCR. Frustrated, he closed his eyes and contemplated the eternity to come in the bleakness of hell, and how he would probably never again see a snowflake or a Fudgsicle. But then he thought of the nice meal he'd just had, and his new friends, and decided that snowflakes and Fudgsicles weren't that great anyway. He thought how the upcoming eternity might not be so bad after all. There was a knock at the door, and the snake entered.

"The Devil asked me to give you your assignment," the snake said. "Sometimes he gets powerful headaches. He wants you to be there to open the aspirin bottle."

"I think I could do that," the inventor replied.

"Just so you know, he likes a fresh aspirin every time, so you'll have to remove the tamper-resistant collar, the childproof cap and the aluminum seal," said the snake.

The inventor breathed easily. "No problem."

"Good," the snake said, and turned to go.

Just then a shudder rippled through the inventor's body. "Say"—his voice quavered with nervousness—"who will remove the cotton wad from inside the bottle?"

The snake turned slowly, its face contorted into the mask of Beelzebub. Then its voice deepened and transformed itself, as though it were coming from the bowels of hell:

"Why, you will," he said. "Ha, ha, ha, ha, ha!" ▲

"Bobby was caught imposing his values on another student."

Our flight was about to take off when the passenger behind me immediately launched into a loud and annoying conference call on his cell phone. "Sally, get the customer lists. Charlie, pull all the data together we have on… Bob, can you bring us up to date…" and on and on.

As the flight attendant began the preflight safety instructions, the executive's voice was drowned out by the PA system. While the safety speech continued, I heard him mutter into the phone, "Hold on a second. Some people just like to hear themselves talk."

— G. BORMAN

I recently bought a new car that had a faulty light. When, after five visits to the dealer's shop, they were unable to fix it, I tried to get it replaced by threatening to use my state's lemon laws. My calls and letters to the dealer got me nowhere.

I went to a florist, ordered a fruit basket filled with lemons and sent it to the dealer with this poem:

"When I drive my lemon, I'll be thinking of you.

Pretty soon, my attorney will too."

A short time later the dealer called and asked what color I'd like my new car to be.

— JOHN T. CARROLL

The auto auction I attended was selling cars to benefit charity. Vehicles were classified as either "Running" or "No Start." On the block was a No Starter.

It had a shattered windshield, two missing tires, a sagging front bumper, a cockeyed grille, a hood that was sprung up at an angle, and dings and dents all over the body.

Before he started the bidding, the auctioneer announced the car's year, make and model, and then read the owner's comments: "Please note—the radio does not work."

— CHICK MANSUR

Friends and I were chatting over dinner in a restaurant. A man at the next table told his cell phone caller to hold on. Then he stepped outside to talk.

When he returned, I said, "That was very thoughtful."

"I had no choice," he said to me. "You were making too much noise."

— NORM BLUMENTHAL

After we got broadband Internet, my husband decided to start paying bills online. This worked great; in fact all our bill companies accepted online payments except one—our Internet service provider.

— SARAH LIBERA

I dialed a wrong number and got the following recording: "I am not available right now, but I thank you for caring enough to call. I am making some changes in my life. Please leave a message after the beep. If I do not return your call, you are one of the changes."

— ANTONIO CURTIS

Owning a 401(k) plan is a good idea—unless you worked for WorldCom. Much of its stock has been declared worthless. There's a lawsuit in progress that's trying to recoup some money for employees.

At the litigation website, I found a number to call for more information. My hopes for a speedy resolution were dashed, however, when after dialing, I heard, "700 Club Prayer Line. How may I help you?"

— ROBERT BEATTY

Security and peace of mind were part of the reason we moved to a gated community. Both flew out the window the night I called a local pizza shop for a delivery. "I'd like to order a large pepperoni, please," I said, then gave him the address of our condominium.

"We'll be there in about half an hour," the kid at the other end replied. "Your gate code is still 1238, right?"

— MARY MCCUSKER

My mother, a master of guilt trips, showed me a photo of herself waiting by a phone that never rings.

"Mom, I call all the time," I said. "If you had an answering machine, you'd know." Soon after, my brother installed one for her.

When I called the next time, I got her machine: "If you are a salesperson, press one. If you're a friend, press two. If you're my daughter who never calls, press 911 because the shock will probably give me a heart attack."

— SUSAN STARACE BALDUCCI

I realized the impact of computers on my young son one evening when there was a dramatic sunset. Pointing to the western sky, David said, "I wish we could click and save that."

— THERESA KLEIN

"I've got to take this call."

My friend is notorious for waiting until the needle is on empty before filling his gas tank. Finally his car died on him, and we had to push it to the nearest filling station. After my friend finished pumping gas, the attendant asked if he had learned anything.

"Yeah," my friend muttered, "I learned I have a 15-gallon tank."

— EDWARD HYATT

I couldn't decide whether to go to Salt Lake City or Denver for vacation, so I called the airlines to get prices. "Airfare to Denver is $300," the cheery salesperson replied.

"And what about Salt Lake City?"

"We have a really great rate to Salt Lake—$99," she said. "But there is a stopover."

"Where?"

"In Denver," she said.

— CHRIS LEWIS

As an engineer in an upscale hotel, I was asked to repair or replace the television in a guest room. When I arrived, the couple was watching a picture one-third the size of the screen. I knew all our spare sets were in use, so I figured what the heck: I struck the side of the TV with the heel of my hand. The picture returned to full size.

"Look, honey," said the wife to her husband. "He went to the same repair school as you."

— WILLIAM W. OLLER

I was with a friend in a café when a noisy car alarm interrupted our conversation. "What good are car alarms when no one pays any attention to them?" I wondered aloud.

"Some are quite effective," my friend corrected me. "Last summer, my teenager spent a lot of time at the neighbors'. Whenever I wanted him home, I'd go out to our driveway and jostle his car."

— SHEILA MOORE

My husband, a computer-systems trouble-shooter, rode with me in my new car one afternoon. He had been working on a customer's computer all morning and was still tense from the session. When I stopped for a traffic light, I made sure to leave a safe distance from the stop line to keep oncoming drivers from hitting the car.

I couldn't help but laugh when my husband impatiently waved at me to move the car forward while saying, "Scroll up, honey."

— GEORGIA M. HARVEY

My wife was in her gynecologist's busy waiting room when a cell phone rang. A woman answered it, and for the next few minutes, she explained to her caller in intimate detail her symptoms and what she suspected might be wrong.

Suddenly the conversation shifted, and the woman said, "Him? That's over." Then she added, "Can we talk about this later? It's rather personal, and I'm in a room full of people."

— ALAN ROBERTS

Opening the box containing my new portable television, I removed the remote and turned it over to install the batteries. Molded into the device was this message: "Made in Indonesia—Not Dishwasher Safe."

— MARVIN WIER

In this battle of wits with kitchen appliances…

I'm Toast

► BY DAVE BARRY

Recently the *Washington Post* printed an article explaining how the appliance manufacturers plan to drive consumers insane.

Of course they don't SAY they want to drive us insane. What they SAY they want to do is have us live in homes where "all appliances are on the Internet, sharing information" and appliances will be "smarter than most of their owners." For example, the article states, you would have a home where the dishwasher "can be turned on from the office," the refrigerator "knows when it's out of milk," and the bathroom scale "transmits your weight to the gym."

I frankly wonder whether the appliance manufacturers, with all due respect, have been smoking crack. I mean, did they ever stop to ask themselves WHY a consumer, after loading a dishwasher,

would go to the office to start it? Would there be some kind of career benefit?

YOUR BOSS: "What are you doing?"

YOU (tapping computer keyboard): "I'm starting my dishwasher!"

YOUR BOSS: "That's the kind of productivity we need around here!"

YOU: "Now I'm flushing the upstairs toilet!"

Listen, appliance manufacturers: We don't NEED a dishwasher that we can communicate with from afar. If you want to improve our dishwashers, give us one that senses when people leave dirty dishes on the kitchen counter and shouts, "Put those dishes in the dishwasher right now or I'll leak all over your shoes!"

Likewise, we don't need a refrigerator that knows when it's out of milk. We already have a foolproof system for determining

if we're out of milk: we ask our wife. What we could use is a refrigerator that refuses to let us open its door when it senses that we are about to consume our fourth pudding snack in two hours.

As for a scale that transmits our weight to the gym: Are they NUTS? We don't want our weight transmitted to our own EYE-BALLS! What if the gym transmitted our weight to all these other appliances on the Internet? What if, God forbid, our refrigerator found out our weight? We'd never get the door open again!

But here is what really concerns me about these new "smart" appliances: Even if we like the features, we won't be able to use them. We can't use the appliance features we have NOW. I have a feature-packed telephone with 43 buttons, at least 20 of which I am afraid to touch. This phone

probably can communicate with the dead, but I don't know how to operate it, just as I don't know how to operate my TV, which has features out the wazooty and requires THREE remote controls. One control (44 buttons) came with the TV; a second (39 buttons) came with the VCR; the third (37 buttons) was brought here by the cable-TV man, who apparently felt that I did not have enough buttons.

So when I want to watch TV, I'm confronted with a total of 120 buttons, identified by such helpful labels as PIP, MTS, DBS and JUMP. There are three buttons labeled POWER, but there are times—especially if my son and his friends, who are not afraid of features, have changed the settings—when I cannot figure out how to turn the TV on. I stand there, holding three remote controls, pressing buttons at random, until eventually I give up and go

turn on the dishwasher. It has been, literally, years since I have successfully recorded a TV show. That is how "smart" my appliances have become.

And now the appliance manufacturers want to give us MORE features. Do you know what this means? It means that some night you'll open your "smart" refrigerator, looking for a beer, and you'll hear a cheerful recorded voice—the same woman who informs you that Your Call Is Important when you phone a business that does not wish to speak with you personally—telling you, "Your celery is limp." You will not know how your refrigerator knows this, and, what is worse, you will not know who else your refrigerator is telling about it.

But if you want to make the refrigerator stop, you'll have to decipher an owner's manual written by nuclear physicists. ("To disable the Produce Crispness

Monitoring feature, enter the Command mode, then select the Edit function, then select Change Vegetable Defaults, then assume that Train A leaves Chicago traveling westbound at 47 m.p.h., while Train B...")

Is this the kind of future you want, consumers? Do you want appliances that are smarter than you? Of course not.

Your appliances should be DUMBER than you, just like your furniture, your pets and your representatives in Congress. So I am urging you to let the appliance industry know that when it comes to "smart" appliances, you vote NO. You need to act quickly. Because while you're reading this, your microwave oven is voting YES. ▲

Jesus and Satan were arguing over who was better with computers. Finally God suggested they settle it: Each would spend two hours using spreadsheets, designing web pages, making charts and tables—everything they knew how to do.

The two sat down at their keyboards and began typing furiously. Just before the two hours were up, a thunderstorm knocked the power out. Once it came back on, they booted up their computers.

"It's gone! It's all gone!" Satan began to scream. "My work was destroyed!"

Meanwhile, Jesus began quietly printing out his work. "Hey, he must have cheated!" Satan yelled. "How come his stuff wasn't lost?"

God shrugged and said simply, "Jesus saves."

— LAURA MASON

Shortly after I had my car repaired, the mechanic who fixed it asked me to bring it back. I watched as he opened the hood and removed a tool he had left behind. In a conspiratorial voice I said, "If you were a surgeon, I'd sue for malpractice."

"Yeah, but if I was a surgeon," he replied, "I'd charge you for having to go back in."

— JEANIE LOVELADY

I feel inadequate when talking with a mechanic, so when my vehicle started making a strange noise, I sought help from a friend. He drove the car around the block, listened carefully, then told me how to explain the difficulty when I took it in for repair.

At the shop I proudly recited, "The timing is off, and there are premature detonations, which may damage the valves."

As I smugly glanced over the mechanic's shoulder, I saw him write on his clipboard "Lady says it makes a funny noise."

— KATE KELLOGG

My family has a tradition of naming the cruise control on our cars. We were used to hearing my father proclaim, "Take it, Max," as he flipped on the cruise control during long trips in our station wagon.

Recently, I was traveling with my parents in their new car when we hit a wide-open expanse of highway. My dad leaned back and said, "I think I'll let Tom drive for a while."

"Tom who?" I asked.

My mother translated for me: "Tom Cruise, of course."

— DANA MARGULIES

After shopping at a busy store, another woman and I happened to leave at the same time, only to be faced with the daunting task of finding our cars in the crowded parking lot. Just then my car horn beeped, and I was able to locate my vehicle easily.

"Wow," the woman said. "I sure could use a gadget like that to help me find my car."

"Actually," I replied, "that's my husband."

— KATHY BEHRENBRINKER

My 50-something friend Nancy and I decided to introduce her mother to the magic of the Internet. Our first move was to access the popular "Ask Jeeves" site, and we told her it could answer any question she had.

Nancy's mother was very skeptical until Nancy said, "It's true, Mom. Think of something to ask it."

As I sat with fingers poised over the keyboard, Nancy's mother thought a minute, then responded, "How is Aunt Helen feeling?"

— CATHERINE BURNS

The speaker at my bank's drive-through window had been broken for weeks, and we tellers had to resort to miming or writing notes to communicate with our frustrated customers. One day a sweet elderly lady whom I would see every week pulled up to the window, leaned out of her car and smacked the glass in front of my face.

"Hope this is bulletproof," she yelled.

There had just been a robbery at another bank nearby, so I was touched by her concern. "It is," I yelled back.

"Good," she continued, "because someone is going to shoot you if you don't get that speaker fixed."

— SARAH BANAKOWSKI

"I've figured out how to send e-mails and faxes, take photos, play games, and film videos, but what I'd really like to do is make a phone call."

Timeless Humor from the 60's

Students at Iowa State University proved once and for all that the computer just can't replace human calculations. They held an "IBM mixer" dance, where each student fed his vital statistics and interests into a computer and was then paired off with a member of the opposite sex who, the computer said, was most suited to him.

Imagine the chagrin of one coed who ended up with her twin brother.

— JIM CHAMPION

My sister Darlene has the courage—but not always the skills—to tackle any home-repair project. For example, in her garage are pieces of a lawn mower she once tried to fix. So I wasn't surprised the day my other sister, Jesse, and I found Darlene attacking her vacuum cleaner with a screwdriver.

"I can't get this thing to cooperate," she explained.

"Why don't you drag it out to the garage and show it the lawn mower?" Jesse suggested.

— JUDEE NORTON

After our parents retired, they moved from a busy city in Rhode Island to a small town in Maine. We didn't realize how small the town was until my sister visited the local video store. She selected a movie and told the clerk that she was going to rent the cassette under her parents' name.

The clerk looked at the title and replied, "They already saw that one."

— THERESA COUTCHER SOKOLOWSKI

Bill Gates and the president of General Motors were having lunch. Gates boasted of the innovations his company had made. "If GM had kept up with technology the way Microsoft has, we'd all be driving $25 cars that get 1,000 m.p.g."

"I suppose that's true," the GM exec agreed. "But would you really want your car to crash twice a day?"

My husband works for a high-tech company that uses a sophisticated robotic mail-delivery system. The robot makes mail stops by following a clear painted line on the hallway floor. Recently the line had to be recharged by applying special paint. While it was drying, signs were posted warning, "Please don't step on the invisible line."

— JOELLEN BADIK

The computer in my high school classroom recently started acting up. After watching me struggle with it, one of my students took over. "Your hard drive crashed," he said.

I called the computer services office and explained, "My computer is down. The hard drive crashed."

"We can't just send people

"That sounds expensive. Is there any way you could ship it without handling it?"

down on your say-so. How do you know that's the problem?"

"A student told me," I answered.

"We'll send someone over right away."

— ROLF EKLUND

My wife and I get along just great—except she's a back-seat driver second to none. On my way home from work one day, my cell phone rang as I merged onto a freeway bypass. It was my wife. By chance, she had entered the bypass right behind me.

"Honey," she said, "your turn signal is still on. And put your lights on—it's starting to rain."

— WAYNE RAY HAIRSTON

Heard on my cable company's answering machine: "We realize you are still holding. Please do not hang up, as this will further delay your call."

— EDGAR NENTWIG

A helicopter was flying toward Seattle when an electrical malfunction disabled all of the aircraft's navigation and communications equipment. Due to the extreme haze that day, the pilot now had no way of determining the course to the airport. All he could make out was a tall building nearby, so he moved closer to it, quickly wrote out a large sign reading "Where am I?" and held it in the chopper's window.

Responding quickly, the people in the building penned a large sign of their own. It read: "You are in a helicopter."

The pilot smiled, and within minutes he landed safely at the airport. After they were on the ground, the co-pilot asked how the sign helped him determine their position.

"I knew it had to be the Microsoft building," the pilot replied, "because like any computer company's help staff, they gave me a technically correct but completely useless answer."

— LINDA A. TOZER

To keep their active two-year-old from roaming onto the busy street in front of their home, my sister and brother-in-law decided to put a gate across the driveway. After working over two weekends on the project, Robert was ready to attach the lock to complete the job. He was working on the yard side of the gate, with his daughter nearby, when he dropped the screwdriver he was using and it rolled under the gate, out of his reach.

"I'll get it, Daddy," Lauren called, nimbly crawling under the newly erected barrier.

— JANICE DECOSTE

Our office building's only elevator was acting up. When I rode it to the lobby on my way to lunch, the door refused to open. Trying not to panic, I hit the emergency button, which triggers an automatic call to the repair service.

Through the speaker in the elevator, I heard the call going through and then a recorded announcement: "The area code of the number you dialed has been changed. The new area code is 810. Please hang up and dial again."

— DIANE MASTRANTONIO

Over the years I have heard my share of strange questions and silly comments from people who call the computer software company where I work as a tech support telephone operator. But one day I realized how absurd things can sound on the other end of the line when I heard myself say to one caller, "Yes, sir, you must first upgrade your download software in order to download our upgrade software."

— CARLOS MEJIA

As a promotional gimmick for my restaurant, I send out coupons offering people a free dinner on their birthdays. One day an anxious-sounding man called. "I got your card. How did you find me?"

"From a mailing list I purchased from a supplier," I told him. "Why?"

"It used my real name, and I'm in the Witness Protection Program. What's the name of the company?"

I didn't want to say it, but I had to tell him the truth: Moving Targets.

— ROY HARRINGTON

I was delighted to discover that I could play compact discs in the new computer my company had given me. One morning I was enjoying one of my favorite

My wife's car horn began to beep in cold weather and would only stop when she disconnected it. So she disabled the horn and drove to the dealership, whose garage had its door shut to keep out the cold. Outside was a sign: "Honk horn for service."

Jeff Romanczuk

CELLULAR PHONE BOOTH

MUELLER

Beethoven pieces when an administrative assistant stopped by to deliver a stack of papers.

Hearing classical music filling the air, she stopped and exclaimed, "Poor you. They put you on hold?"

— KEITH BRINTON

I thought I had finally found a way to convince Susan, my continually harried friend, that she needed to find ways to relax. I invited her to dinner and, while I was busy cooking, she agreed to watch my videotape on stress management and relaxation techniques. Fifteen minutes later, she came into the kitchen and handed me the tape.

"But it's a 70-minute video," I replied. "You couldn't have watched the whole thing."

"Yes, I did," Susan assured me. "I put it on fast-forward."

— JEAN KELLY

A co-worker asked if I knew what to do about a computer problem that was preventing her from getting e-mail. After calling the help desk, I told my colleague that e-mail was being delayed to check for a computer virus.

"It's a variant of the I Love You virus, only worse," I said.

"What could be worse?" my single co-worker asked wryly. "The Let's Just Be Friends virus?"

— ARTHUR J. ORCHEL

Roomba's Revenge

▶ BY MARY ROACH

I have always wanted and not wanted a cleaning person. On the one hand, I want very much for someone else to clean our house, as neither I nor my husband, Ed, has shown any aptitude for it. On the other hand, I'd feel guilty inflicting such distasteful drudgery on another human being. No one but me, for instance, should have to clean up the dental floss heaped like spaghetti near the wastebasket where I toss it each night, never catching on that floss is not something that can be thrown with a high degree of accuracy.

You can imagine my joy upon reading that the iRobot company of Somerville, Mass., has invented a robotic vacuum. They call it Roomba. Their website plays an animated clip of what appears to be an enlarged CD Walkman scooting across a living room carpet, sucking up conspicuous chunks of unidentified detritus. Meanwhile, sentences run across the screen: "I'm having lunch with a friend"…"I'm planting flowers in the garden." The point is that you can go out and "enjoy life" while your robot cleans up the conspicuous chunks strewn about your living room floor, no doubt rubble tracked in from the garden plot.

Roomba joined our family last week. Right away I changed the name to Reba, in order to indulge my fantasy of having a real cleaning person, yet still respect its incredibly dumb-sounding given name. As techno-gadgets go, the iRobot vacuum is surprisingly simple to use. All you do, beyond switching it on, is tell it the room size. This I calculated in my usual manner, by picturing six-foot guys lying end-to-end along the walls and multiplying accordingly.

I started Reba off in the bedroom. I was on my way out the door to enjoy life, when I heard a crash. My vacuuming robot had tangled itself up in the telephone cord and then headed off in the other direction, pulling the phone off the nightstand and onto the floor. "Maybe Reba needs to make a call," said Ed.

I couldn't, in all fairness, be annoyed, as I'm the sort of person who gets up to go to the bathroom on airplanes without first unplugging my headphones. Only the fact that my head is attached to my neck prevents it from being yanked off onto the floor. Also, it tells you right there in the Owner's Manual to "pick up objects like clothing, loose papers…power cords…just as you would before using a regular vacuum cleaner."

This poses something of a problem in our house. The corners and the floor space along the walls and under the furniture in the office, for instance, are filled with stacks and bags of what I call Ed's desk runoff. My husband is a man who does not easily throw things away. Whatever he gets in the mail or empties from his pockets he simply deposits on the nearest horizontal surface.

Once a week, like the neighbor-

hood garbage truck, I collect Ed's discards and throw them onto a vast, heaping landfill located on his desk. At a certain point, determined by the angle of the slope and the savagery of my throws, the pile will begin to slide. This is Ed's cue to shovel a portion of it into a shopping bag, which he then puts on the floor somewhere with the intent to go through it later, later here meaning "never."

I looked at the floor in our office. There were newspapers, piles of files, socks, pens, not to mention the big guys lying along the floorboards. Picking it all up to clear the way for Reba would take half an hour, which is more time than I normally spend vacuuming. It was the same sort of situation that has kept me from ever hiring an assistant.

It would take longer to explain my filing system to someone else ("Okay, takeout menus and important contracts go in the orange folder labeled 'Bees'...") than it would do to do the chore myself.

The bathroom promised to be less problematic. I lifted the hamper into the tub and put the bathroom scale in the sink, where it looked as though maybe it wanted a bath, or maybe it had a date with a vacuum cleaner.

Then I went into the bedroom to fetch Reba, who was at that moment engaged in a shoving match with one of my Birkenstocks. She had pushed the shoe across the room and under the bed, well into the zone of no-reach.

"Good one," said Ed, who has always harbored ill will toward comfort footwear for women.

I set Reba down and aimed her at the crud paved crawlspace beneath the footed bathtub. I have tried this with Ed and various of my stepdaughters, but it always fails to produce the desired effect.

The wondrous Reba was not only willing but actually enthusiastic about the prospect, motoring full bore across the tile and under the tub and whacking her forehead on the far wall. You just

can't find help like that.

The living room was a similar success. Reba does housework much the way I do, busily cleaning in one spot for a while and then wandering off inexplicably in the opposite direction and getting distracted by something else that needs doing. The iRobot people call this an "algorithm-based cleaning pattern," a term I will use the next time Ed catches me polishing silver with the mop water evaporating in the other room.

Halfway across the living room carpet, Reba stopped moving and began emitting undelighted noises. Ed leafed through the troubleshooting guide.

"It's a Whimper Beep," he said, employing the concerned baritone that used to announce the Heartbreak of Psoriasis as though it were the Cuban Missile Crisis. I turned Reba over. Wound around her brushes was a two-foot strand of dental floss. Apparently even robots have their limits. ▲

Our family took shelter in the basement after hearing a tornado warning. My husband told everyone to stay put while he got his cell phone out of the car, in case the lines went dead.

He didn't return for the longest time, so I went looking for him. I was upstairs calling his name, when I heard our phone machine click on.

"Hi," a voice said. "This is Dad. I'm locked out of the house."

— LAURE JORGES

During the mortgage closing on our summer house, my wife and I were asked to sign documents containing small print. When I asked if I should read it, my attorney replied, "Legally, you should. But here's the bottom line: If you pay your installments on time, there is nothing in there that could harm you. Should you stop paying, however, there is definitely nothing in the small print that can save you."

— MILLORAD DEVIAK

My five children and I were playing hide-and-seek one evening. With the lights turned off in the house, the kids scattered to hide, and I was "it." After a few minutes I located all of them. When it was my turn to hide, they searched high and low but could not find me.

Finally one of my sons got a bright idea. He went to the phone and dialed; they found me immediately because my pager started beeping.

— LELAND JENSEN

A solar-powered computer wristwatch, which is programmed to tell the time and date for 125 years, has a guarantee—for two years.

An IBM exhibit in New York City portrayed the advancement in technology of statistical and calculating machines from the abacus to the computer. After completing the tour, I stopped at the reception desk to ask a question. There, a distinguished elderly gentleman was keeping track of the number of visitors in the old tried-and-true method of drawing ~~IIII~~ ~~IIII~~ on a sheet of paper.

— EMIL L. BIRNBAUM

DID I LEAVE THE IRON ON?

All in a Day's Work

You put a bunch of adults together and tell them
to get something meaningful accomplished, and for
some reason, it often turns out pretty funny.

"We're considering outsourcing your job. Could you explain to this guy in Guatemala whatever it is you do around here?"

As an airline reservation agent, I took a call from a man who wanted to book a flight for two but wasn't happy with the price of $59 per ticket. "I want the $49 fare I saw advertised," he insisted, saying he would accept a flight at any time. I managed to find two seats on a 6 a.m. flight. "I'll take it," he said, then worried his wife might not like the early hour. I warned there was a $25 fee per person if he changed the reservation. "Oh, that's no problem," he said dismissively. "What's fifty bucks?"

— ANNA ZOGG

I hate the idea of going under the knife. So I was very upset when the doctor told me I needed a tonsillectomy. Later, the nurse and I were filling out an admission form. I tried to respond to the questions, but I was so nervous I couldn't speak. The nurse put down the form, took my hands in hers and said, "Don't worry. This medical problem can easily be fixed, and it's not a dangerous procedure."

"You're right. I'm being silly," I said, feeling relieved. "Please continue."

"Good. Now," the nurse went on, "do you have a living will?"

— EDWARD LEE GRIFFIN

The generation gap proved glaringly obvious at the mail-order music company where my wife works as a customer service representative. Some college students, who were working part-time inputting customer information, wrote the following notes regarding some golden oldies: "Customer is looking for two song titles: 'Shovel Off Two Buffaloes' and 'Honey, Suck a Rose.' "

— JOHN CASARES

Pulling into my service station 45 minutes late one morning, I shouted to the customers, "I'll turn the pumps on right away!" What I didn't know was that the night crew had left them on all night. By the time I got to the office, most of the cars had filled up and driven off. Only one customer stayed to pay. My heart sank. Then the customer pulled a wad of cash from his pocket and handed it to me.

"We kept passing the money to the last guy," he said. "We figured you'd get here sooner or later."

— JIM NOVAK

My fellow teacher called for help—she needed someone who knew about animals. As a science teacher, I filled the bill. "Oh," she added, "bring a net." Expecting to find some kind of beast as I entered her classroom, I was greeted instead by the sight of excited kids watching a hummingbird fly around. Rather than use the net, I suggested they hang red paper by an open door. The bird would be drawn to it, I explained, and eventually fly out. Later, the teacher called back. The trick worked. "Now," she said, "we have two hummingbirds flying around the room."

— RAY POELLET

Most people would be angry if their company was bought and the new owners replaced them with their own people. Not our neighbor Andy. "You know how it goes," he said, waxing philosophical. "Every circus brings its own clowns."

— CHRIS GULLEN

sign language

Noted at the bottom of a receipt for funeral arrangements:
"Thank you. Please come again."

— CARMELA A. HENRIQUEZ

Everyone at the company I worked for dressed up for Halloween. One fellow's costume stumped us. He simply wore slacks and a white T-shirt with a large 98.6 printed across the front in glitter. When someone finally asked what he was supposed to be, he replied, "I'm a temp."

— BRIAN DAVIS

I'm dyslexic, and attended a conference about the disorder with a friend. The speakers asked us to share a personal experience with the group. I told them stress aggravates my condition, in which I reverse words and letters when I'm tense. When I finished speaking, my friend leaned over and whispered to me, "Now I know why you named your daughter Hannah."

— CHARLES JEHLEN

My husband and I are both in an Internet business, but he's the one who truly lives, eats and breathes computers. I finally realized how bad it had gotten when I was scratching his back one day. "No, not there," he directed. "Scroll down."

— CHRISTINE AYMAN

I was on duty as an emergency-room technician when a father brought in his son, who had poked a tire from one of his toy trucks up his nose. The man was embarrassed, but I assured him this was something kids often do. I quickly removed the tire and they were on their way. A few minutes later, the father was back in the ER asking to talk to me in private.

Mystified, I led him to an examining room. "While we were on our way home," he began, "I was looking at that little tire and wondering, how on earth did my son get this thing stuck up his nose and…"

It took just a few seconds to get the tire out of Dad's nose.

— LEAH BEACK

Bad weather meant I was stuck overnight at O'Hare airport in Chicago. Along with hotel accommodations, the airline issued each passenger a $10 meal ticket, or "chit." That evening after dinner I presented my meal ticket to the cashier.

"Is this chit worth $10?" I asked.

Looking up nervously, the cashier responded, "I'm sorry, sir. Was the meal that bad?"

— HARRY ANDREWS

Working as a secretary at an international airport, my sister had an office adjacent to the room where security temporarily holds suspects. One day security officers were questioning a man when they were suddenly called away on another emergency. To the horror of my sister and her colleagues, the man was left alone in the unlocked room. After a few minutes, the door opened and he began to walk out.

Summoning up her courage, one of the secretaries barked, "Get back in there, and don't you come out until you're told!" The man scuttled back inside and slammed the door. When the security people returned, the women reported what had happened. Without a word, an officer walked into the room and released one very frightened telephone repairman.

— RUSS PERMAN

Touring Ireland's countryside with a group of travel writers, we passed an immaculate cemetery with hundreds of beautiful headstones set in a field of emerald green grass. Everyone reached for their cameras when the tour guide said the inventor of the crossword puzzle was buried there. He pointed out the location, "Three down and four across."

— STEVE BAUER

One of my friends, a musician, is always upbeat. Nothing gets her down. But when she developed ringing in one ear, I was concerned it might overwhelm even her. When I asked if her condition was especially annoying to a musician, she shook her head. "Not really," she said cheerfully. "The ringing sound is in the key of B flat, so I use it to tune my cello a half-tone lower."

— KATHLEEN CAHILL

The 104-year-old building that had served as the priory and primary student residence of the small Catholic university where I work was about to be demolished. As the wrecker's ball began to strike, I sensed the anxiety and sadness experienced by one of the older monks whose order had founded the college. "This must be difficult to watch, Father," I said. "The tradition associated with that building, the memories of all the students and monks who lived and worked there. I can't imagine how hard this must be for you."

"It's worse than that," the monk replied. "I think I left my Palm Pilot in there."

— P. J. BROZYNSKI

Some of my co-workers and I decided to remove the small, wooden suggestion box from our office because it had received so few entries. We stuck the box on top of a seven-foot-high metal storage cabinet and then promptly forgot about it. Months later, when the box was moved during remodeling, we found a single slip of paper inside. The suggestion read, "Lower the box!"

— FRANK J. MONACO

"Ah, the arbitration team is here."

Each year our company holds a training session in the conference room of the same hotel. When we were told we would not be able to reserve our usual location, my secretary, Gail, spent many hours on the phone trying to work out alternative arrangements. Finally, when the details were ironed out, she burst into my office.

"Great news, Scott!" she announced. "We're getting our regular room at the hotel!"

All eyes were on Gail and me as she suddenly realized she had interrupted a meeting with co-workers.

— SCOTT DUINK

A friend and I used to run a small temporary-staffing service. Our agency did mandatory background checks on all job candidates, even though our application form asked them if they'd ever been convicted of a crime. One day after a round of interviews, my co-worker was entering information from a young man's application into the computer.

She called me over to show me that he had noted a previous conviction for second-degree manslaughter. Below that, on the line listing his skills, he had written, "Good with people."

— JANA RAHRIG

The company where I work provides four-foot-high cubicles so each employee can have some privacy. One day a co-worker had an exasperating phone conversation with one of her teenage sons. After hanging up, she heaved a sigh and said, "No one ever listens to me."

Immediately, several voices from surrounding cubicles called out, "Yes, we do."

Jo Jaimeson

Parents are justifiably upset when their children don't get into the college of their choice. As an admissions counselor for a state university, I took a call from an irate mother demanding to know why her daughter had been turned down. Avoiding any mention of the transcript full of D's, I explained that her daughter just wasn't as "competitive" as the admitted class. "Why doesn't she try another school for a year and then transfer?" I suggested.

"Another school!" exclaimed Mom. "Have you seen her grades?"

— SHALONDA DEGRAFFINRIED

I was working as a short-order cook at two restaurants in the same neighborhood. On a Saturday night, I was finishing up the dinner shift at one restaurant and hurrying to report to work at the second place. But I was delayed because one table kept sending back an order of hash browns, insisting they were too cold. I replaced them several times, but still the customers were dissatisfied.

When I was able to leave, I raced out the door and arrived at my second job. A server immediately handed me my first order. "Make sure these hash browns are hot," she said, "because these people just left a restaurant down the street that kept serving them cold ones."

— BILL BERGQUIST

"I wrote assembly instructions for children's toys. What did you do?"

No Wooden Nickels

▶ BY DONALD R. NICHOLS

In my former position as director of corporate communication for the U.S. Mint in Washington, I fielded a lot of calls from the public. The job convinced me that what people do believe is as odd as what they don't.

Several years ago the Mint in Philadelphia had a loose hub in dies that strike pennies, and coins with double-struck profiles of Lincoln escaped quality control into circulation. Error coins are an incredible event in numismatics, particularly when they're first discovered and no one knows how many there are. These double-die pennies were going for $250 apiece.

That's when a school principal in Kansas announced over the loudspeaker that the Mint was recalling pennies and would pay $250 for each one. Hundreds of people phoned my office. A representative conversation went like this:

"The Mint makes pennies. Why would we buy them?"

"Because you're recalling them."

"We're not. If we wanted pennies out of circulation, we'd just stop making them."

"They wouldn't let you."

"But they'd let us pay $250 for a penny? Would you pay $250 for a penny?"

"Of course not." Then the clincher: "But you're the government."

Reality Check

One afternoon a woman phoned from a local Army base, identifying herself as Specialist so-and-so and declaring she had a dime with the customary profile of FDR on both its heads and tails. Private mints produce such coins for tokens at carnivals and the like; they look legitimate enough that some get into circulation.

The soldier asked if her dime was real. I explained to her what would have to happen for this coin to be from the U.S. Mint. At the end of the manufacturing process, this coin would have to escape a bag sewn shut, roll the entire length of the production floor and climb back into the press. The press would have to malfunction at exactly the same time as it did the first go-round, when it left one side of the dime blank, and again hit this one dime only on the blank side. It took a good 15 minutes to explain all this.

There followed the long silence I had come to know excruciatingly well in my job. "Oooookaaay," the woman said, slowly, meditatively stretching her vowels. "So what you're saying is, there's a chance it could be real."

In God We Trust

"Sir? I'm in West Virginia." The woman's voice was thin, weak, hesitant, intimidated. "I heard about some pennies that are worth something. And I think I have one." Right away I thought, this woman can't afford this call. I offered to call her back.

"You'd call back for sure?" she said.

I assured her I would. When I reached her I asked her to describe the penny, asked if

The $250 penny and other heads and tales from the Mint

Lincoln had two noses and chins and whether the words In God We Trust looked like they were stamped twice on top of each other. She said, "You maybe could say that."

"Well, that sounds like the penny I've been hearing about," I told her.

"You don't know what it would mean to us," she said. "Times are so hard since the last mine shut down. What do you think maybe it's worth?"

I told her where to take it to get it appraised. She thanked me, the first time that had happened in a couple of weeks, and I hung up. The phone rang with my hand still on the receiver. Before answering, I said a prayer: "God, please let this woman have just one of those damned double-die pennies."

Sight Unseen

A phone-caller had bought a coin and was suffering post-purchase doubts. The Mint had "an opportunity to reassure me"—his phrase—by examining the coin.

It was time once again to tell someone the Mint does not authenticate coins as a guarantor for private commercial transactions, but blurting that straight out seemed abrupt, too much the knee-jerk response of a naysaying bureaucrat. So I asked him what coin he'd bought.

He didn't want to tell me. That was a clue he'd bought a coin he wasn't supposed to have, likely a 1933 Double Eagle gold coin. The government at that time required Americans to surrender their gold coins for cash, which theoretically would be spent, stimulating the economy. Double Eagle gold coins from 1933 are valuable—middle-six-figures valuable—and are literally sold under the counter because it's still illegal to own them.

When I told the caller he shouldn't worry if he'd bought the coin from a reputable dealer, he said he'd rather not say where he had bought it.

"And I noticed you haven't told me your name, either," I said.

Silence.

"If you send us this coin and it's one you're not supposed to have, we'll have to confiscate it," I warned him.

More and deeper silence.

"Let me try to sum up here. You don't want to tell me your name, you don't want to tell me what coin you bought and you don't want to tell me where. So basically you'd like to hold this coin up to the phone and have me tell you it's real. Correct?"

To his credit, the man laughed. Collectors do not, in my experience, have a great capacity for laughing at themselves. He said goodbye pleasantly.

The U.S. Mint makes tens of billions of coins a year, and sometimes I felt that eventually, one way or another, if I worked there long enough, I'd talk to somebody about every one of them. ▲

On duty as a customer-service representative for a car-rental company, I took a call from a driver who needed a tow. He was stranded on a busy highway, but he didn't know the make of the car he was driving. I asked again for a more detailed description, beyond "a nice blue four-door."

After a long pause, the driver replied, "My car is the one on fire."

— DAEMIEN O'KEEFFE

"We're going to have to let you go, but I'm confident that you'll land on your feet."

Ever wonder what medical personnel scribble on those clipboards attached to the foot of the bed? Here are some incredible comments taken from hospital charts:

"The patient refused autopsy."

"The patient has no previous history of suicides."

"She has had no rigors or shaking chills, but her husband states she was very hot in bed last night."

"She is numb from her toes down."

"Patient has two teenage children but no other abnormalities."

"Discharge status: Alive but without my permission."

— WILLIAM D. J. MURPHY

Hospital regulations require a wheelchair for patients being discharged. However, while working as a student nurse, I found one elderly gentleman already dressed and sitting on the bed with a suitcase at his feet—who insisted he didn't need my help to leave the hospital. After a chat about rules being rules, he reluctantly let me wheel him to the elevator.

On the way down I asked if his wife was meeting him. "I don't know," he said. "She's still upstairs in the bathroom changing out of her hospital gown."

— PATSY R. DANCEY

My father is a skilled CPA who is not great at self-promotion. So when an advertising salesman offered to put my father's business placard in the shopping carts of a supermarket, my dad jumped at the chance. Fully a year went by before we got a call that could be traced to those placards. "Richard Larson, CPA?" the caller asked.

"That's right," my father answered. "May I help you?"

"Yes," the voice said. "One of your shopping carts is in my yard and I want you to come and get it."

— MATTHEW LARSON

During a business trip to Boeing's Everett, Wash., factory, I noticed several 747 and 777 airliners being assembled. Before the engines were installed, huge weights were hung from the wings to keep the planes balanced. The solid-steel weights were bright yellow and marked "14,000 lbs." But what I found particularly interesting was some stenciling I discovered on the side of each weight. Imprinted there was the warning: "Remove before flight."

— KEVIN N. HAW

Anytime companies merge, employees worry about layoffs. When the company I work for was bought, I was no exception. My fears seemed justified when a photo of the newly merged staff appeared on the company's website with the following words underneath: "Updated daily."

— DIANNE STEVENS

A Catholic priest I once knew went to the hospital to visit patients. Stopping at the nurses station, he carefully looked over the patient roster and jotted down the room number of everyone who had "Cath" written boldly next to his name. That, he told me, was a big mistake.

When I asked why, he replied, "It was only after I had made the rounds that I learned they were all patients with catheters."

— DENNIS SMYTH

I was halfway through a meeting with a photocopy salesman, when he suddenly mentioned his wife and children, and how contented he was. I was puzzled, but let him continue. It was only when I glanced down that I understood his reason for imparting this personal information: The table leg against which I had been rubbing my itchy foot wasn't a table leg at all!

— EILEEN GASKIN

I'm a police officer and occasionally park my cruiser in residential areas to watch for speeders. One Sunday morning I was staked out in a driveway, when I saw a large dog trot up to my car. He stopped and sat just out of arm's reach. No matter how much I tried to coax him to come for a pat on the head, he refused to budge. After a while I decided to move to another location. I pulled out of the driveway, looked back and learned the reason for the dog's stubbornness. He quickly picked up the newspaper I had been parked on and dutifully ran back to his master.

— JEFF WALL

"Since my office went business casual, I've been having this identity crisis. I mean, am I still a suit?"

"I want to try something, Caruthers— come at me like you're asking for a raise."

My husband, Daniel, had been promoted to a newly created position. He was eager to find out what his official title was, so when his business cards finally arrived, I was surprised that he seemed reluctant to show me. After some persuasion, Daniel gave me a card, naming him director of product efficiency. "Wow," I responded, "that sounds impressive."

"Not really," Daniel replied as he removed my thumb from the acronym underneath. It read DOPE.

— SANDY GERVAIS

The chef of the upscale restaurant I manage collided with a waiter one day and spilled coffee all over our computer. The liquid poured into the processing unit, and resulted in some dramatic crackling and popping sounds. After sopping up the mess, we gathered around the terminal as the computer was turned back on.

"Please let it work," pleaded the guilt-ridden waiter.

A waitress replied, "Should be faster than ever. That was a double espresso."

— BRIAN A. KOHLER

One of my pet peeves as a musician in a symphony orchestra is trying to follow the erratic beat of famous guest conductors. I didn't realize how strongly the rest of the musicians felt until we were talking to some-one from a university physics department at a reception. When I asked him what his field was, he answered, "I work with semiconductors." "So do we," I heard a colleague mutter.

— BERNARD GOLDSTEIN

During the latter stages of my pregnancy, I brought a cushion to work to make my chair more comfortable. One afternoon I returned from lunch to find my chair had been pushed to the far side of my work area.

"Looks like someone's been sitting in my chair," I commented to one of my co-workers.

Glancing down at my stomach, she said, "Looks like someone's also been sleeping in your bed."

— RUTH MALLARD

Excerpts from actual employee evaluations. Hope none of these rings a bell:
- "Works well when under constant supervision and cornered like a rat in a trap."
- "His men would follow him anywhere, but only out of morbid curiosity."
- "When she opens her mouth, it is only to change feet."
- "He doesn't have ulcers, but he's a carrier."
- "If you see two people talking and one looks bored, he's the other one."

My father began teaching business classes at the local prison through a community college. On his first night of class, he started a chapter on banking. During the course of his lecture, the subject of ATMs came up, and he mentioned that, on average, most machines contain only about $1,500 at a given time.

Just then a man in the back raised his hand. "I'm not trying to be disrespectful," he told my father, "but the machine I robbed had about $5,000 in it."

— JENNIFER JOHNSON

It was an unusually hectic evening at the emergency clinic where I work. The doctor on duty was simultaneously bombarded with questions, given forms to sign, and even asked for his dinner order.

I was in the next room, cleaning up a newly sutured wound, when I realized he hadn't given instructions for a bandage. I poked my head out the door and asked, "What kind of dressing do you want on that?"

"Ranch," he replied.

— BRENDA TODD

As a 911 dispatcher, I speak to people in various states of panic. One day, a woman called saying that a family member had fallen and needed help.

"Do you know what caused the fall?" I asked.

"No," the woman nervously replied. "What?"

— REBECCA PARKS

I work at a department store where every night at closing time one of our customer-service representatives reminds shoppers over the public-address system to finish their shopping. One evening, a woman who had recently worked at a Kmart opened the announcement by saying, "Attention Kmart shoppers…"

Quickly realizing her mistake, she tap-danced her way out of trouble by adding, "You are in the wrong store."

— MATTHEW PERENCHIO

Our copier was on the fritz so I put a note on it: "Service has been called." When the technician told me he had to order parts, I added a second note: "Parts have been ordered."

During the next five days, when we had to use an older, slower copier on the other side of the building, someone taped a third note to the machine: "Prayers have been said."

— JENNIFER HARRISON

The aquarium shop where I work has been in business for more than 20 years. One Sunday a customer called wanting to buy a larger aquarium. "And by the way, I've spent a lot of money at your store over the years," he said. "I think I should get a discount."

"Only our owner can give a discount," I explained, "and he won't be in until tomorrow."

When the customer said that he'd come in the next day, I asked him if there was anything else I could help him with.

"Sure," he said. "Where is your store located?"

— DAVID A. BILLINGTON

The squeaky wheel may get the most oil, but it's also the first to be replaced.

— MARILYN VOS SAVANT, Of Course I'm for Monogamy (St. Martin's)

You're not famous until my mother has heard of you.

— JAY LENO

The grass may be greener on the other side, but it's just as hard to cut.

— LITTLE RICHARD

A peacock that rests on his feathers is just another turkey.

— DOLLY PARTON

It was while making newspaper deliveries, trying to miss the bushes and hit the porch, that I first learned the importance of accuracy in journalism.

— CHARLES OSGOOD, Defending Baltimore Against Enemy Attack (Hyperion)

When people ask if I do my own stunts, I always answer, "Not on purpose."

— BILLY BOB THORNTON

You've got to be original, because if you're like someone else, what do they need you for?

— BERNADETTE PETERS on "Inside the Actors Studio" (Bravo)

If you can see a bandwagon, it's too late to get on it.

— JAMES GOLDSMITH

Each new patient at the clinic where I work must fill out a questionnaire asking basic health and personal-history questions. One query that inevitably gets a "No" answer is, "Do you now use or have you ever used recreational drugs?"

We were unprepared for the response of a young newlywed who wrote: "Yes—birth-control pills."

— FRANCES BOWEN

My nephew, a flight attendant, split the back of his pants one day during a flight. To save embarrassment, he decided to work in front of the beverage cart, facing forward.

The arrangement worked perfectly until he got to the last row and a passenger leaned over to him and said in a low voice, "Your fly is open."

— RICHARD F. MARKS

One of my customers at the department of motor vehicles wanted a personalized license plate with his wedding anniversary on it. As we completed the paperwork he explained, "This way I can't forget the date."

A few hours later, I recognized the same young man waiting in

"Damn it, Peterson, you've got to try and fit in!"

my line. When his turn came, he said somewhat sheepishly, "I need to change the numbers on that plate application."

— N. V. GOODMAN

While on vacation, my wife and I stopped for lunch at a diner. We sat at the counter, right next to the grill. The cook was a young man who was very busy flipping pancakes. Every so often, he would stop and hit the grill with the handle of the spatula. Finally I asked him facetiously, "Does that improve the taste of the pancakes?"

"No," he replied. "That keeps the handle from falling off."

— NORMAN SMEE

When a woman came through my cashier's line at Wal-Mart, her purchase came to twenty dollars. "That's what I had in my hand. You must be psychic," she joked.

"I am," I teased. "I knew exactly how much you wanted to spend."

The next customer stepped up and, looking at me with a big grin, pulled out a one-dollar bill.

— MELISSA MORSE

The insurance agency I work for draws business from a retirement community. Once, when applying for auto insurance for a client, I asked him how many miles he drives in a year. He said he didn't know.

"Well, do you drive 10,000 miles a year," I asked, "or 5,000?"

He said the numbers sounded high. "What month is this?" he asked. I told him it was July.

"Maybe this will help," he said. "I filled the car with gas in February."

— LYNN BEBEE

Overheard: "Yesterday I got my tie stuck in the fax machine. Next thing I knew, I was in Los Angeles."

— STEVE HAUPT

How many chiropractors does it take to change a lightbulb?

Only one, but it takes six visits.

"We need to focus on diversity. Your goal is to hire people who all look different but think just like me."

It was our new receptionist's very first job, and it showed in the way she dressed—her revealing clothes screamed "college" more than "office." As diplomatically as he could, our boss sat her down and told her that she would have to dress more appropriately. "Why?" she asked. "Are we going out to lunch?"

— CLAUDIA SMELKO & MARION ABEL

The salesman at the megastore had only one sale that day, but it was for a staggering $158,762. Flabbergasted by such a massive sale, the manager asked him to explain. "First, I sold the man a fishhook," the salesman said. "Then I sold him a rod and reel. When I found out he was planning on fishing down the coast, I suggested he'd need a boat. Then I took him to the automotive department and sold him our biggest SUV to pull the boat."

"You sold all that to a guy who came in for a fishhook?" asked the boss.

"Actually," said the salesman, "he came in for a bottle of aspirin for his wife's migraine. I told him, 'Your weekend's shot. Might as well go fishing.'"

Our nephew was getting married to a doctor's daughter. At the wedding reception, the father of the bride stood to read his toast, which he had scribbled on a piece of scrap paper. Several times during his speech, he halted, overcome with what I assumed was a moment of deep emotion. But after a particularly long pause, he explained, "I'm sorry. I can't seem to make out what I've written down." Looking out into the audience, he asked, "Is there a pharmacist in the house?"

— TONY BELMONTE

As my husband, the county highway commissioner, was driving to the hospital for treatment of his painful leg, he decided to use the valet parking service so he wouldn't have to walk far. Staring at his official-looking vehicle, one of the valets asked my husband if he was driving a government car. "Why, yes," my husband replied, surprised by the question. "In fact it's an unmarked police car."

"Wow!" the young man said, sliding behind the wheel. "This will be the first time I've been in the front seat."

— PATTY ANN HEINEMANN

I thought I wanted a tattoo, so I had a friend come with me to the tattoo parlor. As I nervously paused outside the door, I noticed the T had slipped off their sign. Now it read "Creative ouch."

— KAREN BLOUNT

Doctors are used to getting calls at any hour. One night a man phoned, waking me up. "I'm sorry to bother you so late," he said, "but I think my wife has appendicitis."

Still half asleep, I reminded him that I had taken his wife's inflamed appendix out a couple of years before. "Whoever heard of a second appendix?" I asked.

"You may not have heard of a second appendix," he replied, "but surely you've heard of a second wife."

— JAMES KARURI MUCHIRI

Finishing up our work at a trade show in San Diego, my co-worker Maureen and I decided to go sightseeing across the border in Tijuana, Mexico. While there, we went shopping and bought a few pieces of clay kitchenware. As we crossed back into the United States, a customs official asked if we had anything of value to report. "Not really," Maureen replied, digging in her bag for the bean crock she had purchased. Everyone around us froze as she continued, "I only bought a little pot."

— RUSS TOMPKINS

My wife and I run a small restaurant where we often name our specials after our employees—dishes like "Chicken Mickey," after our dishwasher who gave us the recipe, and "Rod's Ribs," after a waiter who had his personal style of barbecue. One evening after rereading the menu, I broke with this tradition and changed the description of the special we had named after our chef.

Despite her skills and excellent reputation, somehow I didn't think an entrée named "Salmon Ella" would go over big with our customers.

— BRETT LEHIGH

Timeless Humor from the 50's

An acquaintance of mine was hired as a research assistant by the physics department of a West Coast university to investigate the thermodynamic properties of wood. Two weeks after starting work he was approached by an encyclopedia salesman who explained that purchase of the encyclopedia entitled the buyer to have any three special questions answered completely. To save himself a great deal of work, the researcher bought the encyclopedia, stipulating for his first free question a full dissertation on the thermodynamic properties of wood.

Three weeks later the head of the physics department called the research assistant into his office and said, "We have a request from an encyclopedia company. One of their customers has asked for a report on the thermodynamic properties of wood. Please prepare the report for them."

— JOHN F. MELLOR

APPOINTMENTS

DISAPPOINTMENTS

CALDWELL.

49

"Do you want a **salary** or benefits?"

Walking through the hallways at the middle school where I work, I saw a new substitute teacher standing outside his classroom with his forehead against a locker. I heard him mutter, "How did you get yourself into this?"

Knowing he was assigned to a difficult class, I tried to offer moral support. "Are you okay?" I asked. "Can I help?"

He lifted his head and replied, "I'll be fine as soon as I get this kid out of his locker."

— HELEN BUTTON

Because I was processing my first accident report at the transport company where I worked, I was being particularly attentive. The driver had hit a deer on the highway, and the result was a severely damaged hood and fender. My serious mood was broken, however, when I reached the section of the report that asked, "Speed of other vehicle?"

The driver had put "Full gallop."

— DOUGLAS WAKEHAM

On the afternoon of Administrative Professionals Day, my co-worker and I finally found the time to get gifts for our secretaries. While at the store, my colleague noticed my disappointment when I discovered the shop didn't provide gift wrapping.

After being on the phone forever with a customer who had been having difficulties with a computer program, a support technician at my mother's company turned in his report: "The problem resides between the keyboard and the chair."

Nicole Milligan

"What's wrong?" he asked.

"They won't wrap the gifts for us," I answered.

"No problem," he said quickly. "I'll ask my secretary to do it."

— WENYAN MA

The college football player knew his way around the locker room better than he did the library. So when my husband's co-worker saw the gridiron star roaming the stacks looking confused, she asked how she could help. "I have to read a play by Shakespeare," he said.

"Which one?" she asked.

He scanned the shelves and answered, "William."

— SANDRA J. YARBROUGH

As a high-school football coach, I'm aware that student athletes tend to focus too much on sports. A fellow coach, Bob, was talking about one such player, who called him at home one night. When his wife informed the kid that Bob wasn't home, he became frantic and said he had to speak to the coach right away.

"Just calm down, and I'll have him call you as soon as he gets home," the coach's wife told him. "What's your number?"

The flustered kid replied, "Three."

— ALLAN FLOYD

"I'll need the saw again, sir."

I'm a life-and-career coach and one morning, when a prospective client called for an appointment, I asked him what he wanted to get out of our sessions. "Clarity," he said very firmly.

"And on what issues are you looking for clarity?" I probed.

"Well," he said in a less confident tone, "I really don't know."

— SHANA SPOONER

Four students walked in halfway through the American history test my father was giving at the local community college. "Sorry," they said, "we had a flat tire."

An understanding man, Dad said that if they could all answer just one question correctly, he would give them each an "A" for the exam. The students agreed. So my father handed each one a piece of paper, placed them in four separate corners and said, "Write down which tire was flat."

— KURT SMITH

My husband and I arrived at the auto dealership to pick up our new car, only to be told that the keys had been locked inside. We went to the service department, where a mechanic was working to unlock the driver's side door. Instinctively, I reached for the passenger door and—voilà!—it was unlocked. "Hey," I shouted to him. "It's open!"

"I know," yelled the mechanic. "I already got that side. Now I'm working on this door."

— BETTY M. PHILLIPS

Hal's handyman wasn't the swiftest guy on earth. But he was cheap, and so was Hal, which is why he hired the guy to paint his porch for $50. "You tightwad," scolded Hal's wife. "Our porch covers half of the house! He'll be there for days." Hal simply smirked.

An hour later, there was a knock at the door. The handyman had finished. "How did you get done so quickly?" Hal asked.

"It was a piece of cake," the handyman replied. "Oh, and it's a Ferrari, not a Porsche."

My buddy applied for a job as an insurance salesperson. Where the form requested "prior experience," he wrote "lifeguard." That was it. Nothing else.

"We're looking for someone who can not only sell insurance, but who can sell himself," said the hiring manager. "How does working as a lifeguard pertain to salesmanship?"

"I couldn't swim," my pal replied. He got the job.

— TEDD C. HUSTON

sign language

On the door of the post office in rural Esperance, N.Y.:

PULL. If that doesn't work, PUSH. If that doesn't work, we're closed. Come again.

— VERA KASSON

A first-grader came to the ophthalmology office where I work to have his vision checked. He sat down and I turned off the lights. Then I switched on a projector that flashed the letters F, Z and B on a screen. I asked the boy what he saw.

Without hesitation he replied, "Consonants."

— STEPHEN DOWNING

Hard to believe, but many of our customers at the bank still don't know how to swipe their card through the ATM card reader. Because of this, my fellow tellers and I often find ourselves having to explain how it's done. One teller complained that she kept getting odd looks every time she explained it. I found out why when I overheard her tell one man, "Strip down facing me."

— VICKI STONE

While editing announcements for a newspaper, I came across an item promoting a camp for children with asthma. Aside from all the wonderful activities the kids could enjoy, such as canoeing, swimming, crafts and more, it promised that its lakefront property offered something the kids probably did not expect: "breathtaking views."

— CHRISTY NICHOLS

A neighbor had invited some friends, including our minister, over for dinner. On the menu were mashed potatoes, stuffing, butter peas and baked chicken. As we prepared to eat, we were serenaded by a crowing rooster. "Listen to that rooster," said one of the guests.

Glancing at our pastor digging into his chicken, the host said, "You'd crow too if your child was going into the clergy."

— E. LENORE MILLER

Unfortunately, we humans don't come equipped with delete buttons for our mouths. My friend and his rock band were playing a concert at the psychiatric hospital where he worked as a musical therapist. The audience was a little too quiet for his taste, so the guitarist decided to do something about it. He grabbed the microphone, pointed to the group and yelled, "Are you ready to get a little crazy?"

— STEPHAN DERVAN

A guy shows up late for work. The boss yells, "You should've been here at 8:30!"

The guy replies, "Why? What happened at 8:30?"

"Good news, Mr. Hawkins. Companies have laid off too much deadwood, and now there's a shortage."

53

Caddy Hack

► BY RICK REILLY

I know I'll never play golf like the great golfers, pro or celeb. I'll never play it like those guys' gardeners. But in golf, more than in any other sport, I can get close to great athletes without actually being one: I can be a caddy.

I persuaded Jack Nicklaus, the greatest golfer in history, to let me carry his bag for him at the grand opening of The Summit at Cordillera, a course he designed near Vail. I felt stupid caddying for Jack Nicklaus, really. I mean, the man had two U.S. Amateur titles, 71 Tour wins, six Masters, four U.S. Opens, was eight times the leading money winner and now, at age 63, builds some of the finest golf courses around. What is the point of telling Jack Nicklaus, "Okay, this is a little 389-yard dogleg with a pond guarding the green left," when the guy designed and built the freaking thing?

It rained most of the day. And that, combined with trying to caddy and interview him, plus the ridiculous distances between green and tee, plus the altitude, plus the bottles of wine the night before—well, these things started to chip away at my skills. And that's about when it happened.

On the 15th hole, the rain was coming in sideways and the wind was serious. Nicklaus's umbrella had been a pill. It kept trying to poke me in the eye or fake a "click," making me think it was locked open and then nearly collapsing. This time, it went too far.

Jack was giving some folks in the gallery a chipping lesson and I was standing on a hill trying to write, not realizing I had the bag a little upside down, and perhaps I forced the umbrella too hard, because suddenly it folded up the wrong way. And as I looked on in horror, the bag toppled over backward, sending some of the clubs flying and, unfortunately, some of the balls out of the unzipped pouch—oops—just as Nicklaus asked me for another ball to chip. Busted. Jack looked at me, waited for the laughter to die down and then said, "Don't quit your regular job."

On the day I'm caddying for

What is the point of telling Jack Nicklaus, "Okay, this is a little 389-yard dogleg with a pond guarding the green left," when the guy designed and built the freaking thing?

Hauling bags for the stars

Donald Trump at his preposterously wonderful Trump National Golf Club in Briarcliff Manor, N.Y., there's a problem. Trump wants me to play instead of caddy. He's already got his usual caddy, Billy, ready to go—"Best caddy in the world!" he declares—and he won't play by himself under any circumstances. You don't get the feeling Trump is a guy who requires a lot of personal quiet time. I ask him, "Any chance maybe you'd have a game tomorrow I could caddy for?"

Trump looks at me. "Believe me," he says, "one day of me is enough."

Just a word on Trump's hair. There are those who do not like it. And I admit, when I asked Trump if I could caddy for him, I was wondering if we would need a separate caddy for the hair. Up close, though, it is much less threatening and possibly real. It resembles red cotton candy. It seems to have been spun off a wheel and fired. Maybe the hair is fiberglass. I cannot imagine the teams of artists it must take to do Trump's hair each day, but I know they must arrive by the busload. And somehow they've managed to make his hair look like the moment when you open a bottle of aspirin and you can't quite get the cotton ball out and it comes partially out, all teased. That's Trump's hair.

Trump plays golf fast, and well. Mostly he hits the ball low, far and straight. He owns the joint, so he parks the cart where he wants the rest of the world not to—edges of greens, backs of tee boxes. We will end up going 18 holes in three hours and 15 minutes and that includes stopping often to harangue the stonemason and the greenskeeper to re-do the bricks or re-trim a tree that is not absolutely, immaculately Trumpalicious. Before long, the bricks have been ripped out and the stonemason is starting over.

When Trump sees work that is Trumpalicious, he is practically moist. Just now he saw five workers doing a job he liked on a cart path. "Beautiful!" he says. So we gotta go over and tell them. They're from Chile, and they don't speak a syllable of English. He whips out three $100 bills and gives them out. The workers smile melon slices, shocked at their good fortune. Trump climbs back in the cart, pleased mightily. "Now those guys are the Donald Trumps of Chile!" he says.

Before caddying for Bob Newhart—the former accountant turned genius stand-up comic, TV psychologist and Vermont

I admit, when I asked Trump if I could caddy for him, I was wondering if we would need a separate caddy for the hair.

inn owner—I had lunch with him in the grill overlooking the first tee at Bel-Air, L.A.'s club of the stars. Soon enough, people were wondering why a caddy was having lunch with Bob in the grill, so we set out. Bob said we'd start on the back nine and then play the front nine. But somebody was playing the 10th and 11th, so we started on 12. I asked Bob what his handicap was. "Nine," he said. "I say I'm a nine no matter what I am. I like being a nine."

Right off, Bob proved he wasn't a nine. He was more like a four. He hit a perfect drive and then a perfect five-wood toward the Mae West green at 12. It's called that because it used to have two huge humps guarding it. The humps are gone now, but then so is Mae West. Bob was on in two strokes but three-putted. "Does golf drive stars crazy too?" I asked.

"Oh, yeah," he said. "Like, I'll come home after a bad round, swearing. And my wife will say, 'I thought you played golf to relax!' and I'll snap, 'Dammit, honey, you don't know the first thing about the game!' "

Bob lives among the mansions in the Bel Air hills. "We live next to the house Dean Martin owned," he said. "Dean sold it to Tom Jones, who sold it to Nicolas Cage. Next to that is the house that Clark Gable and Carole Lombard lived in. It sounds glamorous, I guess. But sometimes I'll be doing some menial task and I'll say to my wife, 'Hon, do you think Carole Lombard ever asked Clark Gable to take out the recycling?' "

By the round's end, Bob hit 7 out of 13 fairways, 6 out of 16 greens, and shot what probably would've been an 88 if we'd counted everything and played

18 holes. On the second ball he hit, though, Bob was probably more like an 81. But then, aren't we all?

Oh, one last thing. You're thinking, "How come you didn't ask Tiger Woods if you could caddy for him?" I did. I asked him 100 ways. And he always said no. "Why not?" I wondered.

"Because," Tiger explained, "I suck. I need good help." ▲

---

sign language

Sign above the scale in a Mission Hills, Calif., doctor's office:

"Pretend it's your I.Q."

— LYNN MICLEA

QUOTABLE QUOTES

Responsible, who wants to be responsible? Whenever something bad happens, it's always, Who's responsible for this?

— JERRY SEINFELD

You're never allowed to step on people to get ahead, but you can step over them if they're in your way.

— STAR JONES on "The View"

If an idea's worth having once, it's worth having twice.

— TOM STOPPARD, Indian Ink

The key to success? Work hard, stay focused and marry a Kennedy.

— ARNOLD SCHWARZENEGGER

If men can run the world, why can't they stop wearing neckties? How intelligent is it to start the day by tying a little noose around your neck?

— LINDA ELLERBEE in The Seattle Post-Intelligencer

Money doesn't talk, it swears.

— BOB DYLAN, "It's Alright Ma (I'm Only Bleeding)"

Many an optimist has become rich by buying out a pessimist.

— ROBERT G. ALLEN, Multiple Streams of Income (John Wiley & Sons)

When I hear about people making vast fortunes without doing any productive work or contributing anything to society, my reaction is, How do I get in on that?

— DAVE BARRY in The Miami Herald

While reviewing math symbols with my second-grade pupils, I drew a greater-than (>) and a less-than (<) sign on the chalkboard and asked, "Does anyone remember what these mean?" A few moments passed, and then a boy confidently raised his hand. "One means fast-forward," he exclaimed, "and the other means rewind."

— TERESA DON

Desperate for registered nurses, my colleagues and I in hospital administration often share ideas to recruit employees. Out of exasperation, I made a joking plea to two of my colleagues, asking them to send me six nurses from each of their hospitals. That request prompted one of them to suggest a unique solution: "Send six nurses to the top three names on the list of hospital administrators, and then send your request to five other colleagues. In 14 days you will have received 1,567 nurses."

— DAVID PARKS

My musical director wasn't happy with the performance of one of our percussionists. Repeated attempts to get the drummer to improve failed. Finally, in front of the orchestra, the director said in frustration, "When a musician just can't handle his instrument, they take it away, give him two sticks and make him a drummer!"

A stage whisper was heard from the percussion section: "And if he can't handle that, they take away one of his sticks and make him a conductor."

— QUINCY WONG

A New York retail clerk was suffering from aching feet. "It's all those years of standing," his doctor declared. "You need a vacation. Go to Miami, soak your feet in the ocean and you'll feel better."

When the man got to Florida, he went into a hardware store, bought two large buckets and headed for the beach.

"How much for two buckets of that seawater?" he asked the lifeguard.

"A dollar a bucket," the fellow replied with a straight face.

The clerk paid him, filled his buckets, went to his hotel room and soaked his feet. They felt so much better he decided to repeat the treatment that afternoon. Again he handed the lifeguard two dollars. The young man took the money and said, "Help yourself."

The clerk started for the water, then stopped in amazement. The tide was out. "Wow," he said, turning to the lifeguard. "Some business you got here!"

— CARL D. KIRBY

sign language

Seen on the door of a repair shop:

WE CAN FIX ANYTHING. (Please knock on the door—the bell doesn't work.)

— VICTORIA GOLDEN

58

On the job as a dental receptionist, I answered the phone and noticed on the caller-ID screen that the incoming call was from an auto-repair shop. The man on the line begged to see the dentist because of a painful tooth. "Which side of your mouth hurts?" I asked the patient.

He sighed and answered, "The passenger side."

— CHERYL PACE SATTERWHITE

I am a deputy sheriff assigned to courthouse security. As part of my job, I explain court procedures to visitors. One day I was showing a group of ninth-graders around. Court was in recess and only the clerk and a young man in custody wearing handcuffs were in the courtroom. "This is where the judge sits," I began, pointing to the bench. "The lawyers sit at these tables. The court clerk sits over there. The court recorder, or stenographer, sits over here. Near the judge is the witness stand and over there is where the jury sits. As you can see," I finished, "there are a lot of people involved in making this system work."

At that point, the prisoner raised his cuffed hands and said, "Yeah, but I'm the one who makes it all happen."

— MICHAEL MCPHERSON

A livestock truck overturned in my town, and the accident made the local news. The young reporter who covered the story declared on camera, "Two cows, Black and Gus, escaped into nearby woods."

At the studio there was muffled laughter as they cut to a commercial. After the break, the reporter sheepishly added, "About that overturned truck—make those Black Angus cattle."

— JULIANA KEMP

The boss placed a sign directly over the sink in the men's room at work. It had a single word on it: Think!

The next day when the boss went to the men's room, he saw another sign had been placed immediately above the soap dispenser.

It read: Thoap!

— MURIEL NAYLOR

"Technically, we're not firing you. We're just moving you into an exit-level position."

A client recently brought her two cats to my husband's veterinary clinic for their annual checkup. One was a small-framed, round tiger-striped tabby, while the other was a long, sleek black cat. She watched closely as I put each on the scale. "They weigh about the same," I told her.

"That proves it!" she exclaimed. "Black does make you look slimmer. And stripes make you look fat."

— SUSAN DANIEL

I was inspecting communications facilities in Alaska. Since I had little experience flying in small planes, I was nervous when we approached a landing strip in a snow-covered area. The pilot descended to just a couple hundred feet, then gunned both engines, climbed and circled back. While my heart pounded, the passenger next to me seemed calm. "I wonder why the pilot didn't land," I said.

"He was checking to see if the landing strip was plowed," the man replied.

As we made a second approach, I glanced out the window. "It looks plowed to me," I commented.

"No," my neighbor replied. "It hasn't been cleared for some time."

"How can you tell?" I asked.

"Because," the man informed me, "I'm the guy who drives the plow."

— LAWRENCE D. WEISS

"How much do you charge?" a man asked a lawyer.

"I get $50 for three questions," the lawyer answers.

"That's awfully steep, isn't it?" says the man.

"Yes, it is," replies the lawyer. "Now, what's your final question?"

At the busy dental office where I work, one patient was always late. Once when I called to confirm an appointment, he said, "I'll be about 15 minutes late. That won't be a problem, will it?"

"No," I told him. "We just won't have time to give you an anesthetic."

He arrived early.

— TERRI SPACCAROTELLI

Corporate managers are always a good source of memorable quotes. Here are some examples of mediocrity rising to the top.

- "As of tomorrow, employees will only be able to access the building using individual security cards. Pictures will be taken next Wednesday, and employees will receive their cards in two weeks."
- "What I need is a list of specific unknown problems we will encounter."
- "E-mail is not to be used to pass on information or data. It should be used only for company business."
- "This project is so important, we can't let things that are more important interfere with it."
- "We know that communication is a problem, but the company is not going to discuss it with the employees."

— E. T. THOMPSON

The customer ordering a floral arrangement from my shop was giving me very specific guidelines. "Nothing fragrant," she instructed. "Nothing too tall or too wild. And no bright colors, please. My house is decorated in beige and cream. Here is a wallpaper sample." She handed me a plain square of tan-colored paper.

"Your name?" I asked.

"Mrs. Bland," the woman replied.

— STEPHEN STANLEY

A teller at the bank where I work noticed that a drive-in customer was writing something on one of the documents he was going to place in the transaction basket. As she looked at the contents of the basket, she saw "This is robbery!" printed on one of his bills to be paid.

She panicked, looked up at the man in the car and asked in a shaky voice, "What do you want?" The customer, realizing the teller's apprehension, began apologizing. "I'm so sorry! That wasn't for you—it's a message for the electric company."

— JIM CHOMA

M y brother Jim was hired by a government agency and assigned to a small office cubicle in a large area. At the end of his first day, he realized he couldn't see over the panels to find his way out, so he waited until he saw someone else leaving and followed him. He did the same the next day. On the third day he had to work late, long after his colleagues had left. He wandered around lost in the maze of cubicles and corridors, but then, just as panic began to set in, he came upon another employee in a cubicle.

"How do you get out of here?" Jim asked.

The fellow looked up from his desk, smiled and said, "No cheese for you."

— CHRISTINE PROBASCO

G iving a sermon one Sunday, I heard two teenage girls in the back giggling and disturbing people. I interrupted my sermon and announced sternly, "There are two of you here who have not heard a word I've said." That quieted them down.

When the service was over, I went to greet people at the front door. Three adults apologized for going to sleep in church, promising it would never happen again.

— WILLIAM C. RUSS

Timeless Humor from the **70's**

My brother-in-law, head chef in a New Orleans restaurant, underwent major surgery. His wife, who spent anxious hours awaiting news, supposed that the atmosphere in the operating room was comparable to what she was experiencing. Things obviously were less tense there than she had pictured.

When they wheeled my brother-in-law out, this memo was pinned to his hospital gown: "Don't forget to give operating-room nurse recipe for remoulade sauce."

— MRS. E. G. LEBLANC

"There's an important job I'd like you to tackle, Haffner—yours."

Me and My Big Mouth

▶ BY TERRY BRADSHAW WITH DAVID FISHER

When my football-playing career ended, I had no idea how I wanted to spend the rest of my life. Fortunately for me, there is a fine tradition in this country that if you are a successful athlete or performer, people supposedly want to eat the same peanut butter that you do, drink the same beer, wear the same pants, etc. That's how I got involved in the worst product endorsement I ever did. I am bald and I agreed to be the spokesman for a toupee company. The basic concept of the campaign was that if a he-man football player like Terry Bradshaw was not embarrassed to wear a toupee, no one else should be. To show potential customers how good I looked with hair, the company made and distributed to salons all over the country a plastic model of my head. These salons then stuck a toupee on the model and put it on the counter or in the front window. They made the mold for my head at a Holiday Inn near the Shreveport Regional Airport. I lay down on a bed while people stuck straws up my nose so I could breathe, and then covered my entire head with plaster.

The plaster began drying too quickly, and they had trouble getting it off my head. In the meantime I was having difficulty breathing. There are lots of bad ways to die, but being suffocated by plaster while getting your head duplicated for a toupee display is high on the list. Eventually, they mass-produced my head, and it did look just like me. The toupee people were so proud of the plastic bust, they mailed one to my dad. The problem was I didn't tell him it was coming. This big box arrived at my parents' house, and my father opened it up. He was shocked to see me looking right back at him. "Novis," he yelled to my mother, "you better get in here. They sent us Terry's head in a box." It bothered my mother so much that they put it back in the box and stored it in the attic. As another part of the deal, I filmed several toupee commercials. In one, I swam with a hairpiece on as an announcer said, "You, too, can have a full robust life with our toupee. Look

How Terry Bradshaw fumbled his way to success

how natural it looks." Then I surfaced with what looked like roadkill stuck to my head.

Maybe the worst part of the deal was that I agreed to wear a toupee whenever I appeared in public. One day I was playing in a pro-am golf tournament on a hot afternoon. Sweat was pouring out from under the dense synthetic wig. Finally I just couldn't take it anymore; I went behind a tree, ripped off the hairpiece and shoved it into my back pocket. What I didn't realize was that I had cut my head when I took it off, so my scalp was bleeding. I spent the rest of the tournament walking around with blood running down my face and the hairpiece hanging out of my back pocket like a squirrel's tail. After that, for some reason, the company decided I was not a proper spokesman for their toupee and fired me. I had to hand in my hair.

Once again I needed to find a way to make a living. Talking is what I do best, and I like to make people smile. When I was playing, reporters liked to interview me because I gave them good sound bites.

Luckily this had attracted the attention of TV network executives. One day my phone rang. A CBS executive asked, "Want $5,000 just for talking?" And that is how I got into the broadcasting business long term.

When I signed with CBS, Terry O'Neil, the executive producer of CBS Sports, teamed me with veteran play-by-play announcer Verne Lundquist. Verne was facing a big challenge; he had to teach me how to do my job before I destroyed his career. My first broadcast was a preseason game in San Diego between the Chargers and some other team. As a quarterback, the big picture

had been the only thing that mattered to me, but as a broadcaster I soon learned it was the small frames that make up the big picture. I didn't know the players and their assignments; I didn't know when to talk and when to keep quiet. I didn't know what to look at, how to describe what I was seeing. There was so much I didn't know, I didn't even know it. I would not describe my first game as a disaster, mostly because that would be understating how truly bad I was. For example, in about the middle of the first quarter it became obvious to me that in addition to a lack of knowledge and preparation, I had a serious problem. "Verne," I said, "I can't see a thing down there." I had never watched a football game from that distance in my life. All I could see was a bunch of people with numbers I couldn't read running around.

The first few games I was probably more nervous than at any time during my entire playing career. I would always bring two clean shirts with me, because I knew I was going to sweat through one of them.

"Really," said Verne, amazingly calm, considering that the broadcasting partner he was depending on for insightful commentary had just announced he was basically useless. "We've got to get you binoculars for the next game." Gradually I got better. Very, very gradually. The first few games I was probably more nervous than at any time during my entire playing career. I would always bring two clean shirts with me, because I knew I was going to sweat through one of them. Maybe I was so nervous because I really cared. I worked hard. I wanted to be good, to please the viewers. And I needed that job. With a lot of help from Verne, I guess I did okay because CBS eventually offered me another job as co-host of "The NFL Today" with Greg Gumbel. I'd be the analyst.

Before the first show I was extremely nervous. Then, minutes before we went on the air, a heavy boom microphone smacked me upside the head so hard it nearly knocked me out. I felt dizzy, sick to my stomach, and my ears rang. In a strange way, that hit in the head relaxed me. Being in the studio was brand-new to me, but I could relate to a pain in my head. During my playing career, there had been many games when I had to play hurt, but as one reporter wrote, this was the first time I had to talk hurt.

Fortunately all went well. Since then I've gone from CBS to Fox, and have made the transition from football player to football entertainer. My role on TV is not to be serious. People do not want to hear me speak football, things like "That's the old sixty-six inside release." They expect to hear me say things like "The Giants are having a bad offensive day, and they've got to make some changes. It's like when I went fishing with my dad last week and we were catching a lot of fish and all of a sudden we couldn't catch mud. Then my daddy said to me, 'Son, either these fish got real bright all of a sudden or they're not interested in these lures. We got to change lures.' When the defensive isn't biting, you've got to change your offensive at halftime. You got to change lures." For a man who thought his best talent was throwing an inflated ellipsoid a long way, I've been fortunate in my career. In the end I discovered my real talent—just being myself. ▲

"Wouldn't it be easier if you just took my salary out of the taxes?"

Being the office supervisor, I had to have a word with a new employee who never arrived at work on time. I explained that her tardiness was unacceptable and that other employees had noticed that she was walking in late every day. After listening to my complaints, she agreed that this was a problem and even offered a solution. "Is there another door I could use?"

— BARBARA DAVIES

In my job as an electronics salesman, I've seen the rise in popularity of sport-utility vehicles and minivans, which has created a market for rear-seat entertainment. Monitors that keep passengers occupied with movies and television have been selling like crazy. One day as I was showing a young couple how a monitor could play videos, DVDs, and even pick up local TV stations, the husband asked matter-of-factly, "Does it get cable?"

— JOSEPH WADE

"Sanders, I just sold your soul. You weren't using it, were you?"

During a shopping trip to a department store, I was looking around for a salesperson so I could pay for my purchase. Finally I ran into a woman wearing the store's ID tag. "Excuse me," I said. "I'm trying to locate a cashier."

"I can't help you," she briskly replied, barely slowing down. "I work in customer service." And she walked away.

— SERENA HEARTZ

After harvesting the usual bumper crop of squash last year, I took a half-dozen to the office. I piled them on the table in the break room, and posted a sign advertising them as free. The next day I noticed an addition to my sign. Below "Free Zucchini," someone had written, "Save the Whales."

— DAN ARCHEY

I'm an attendant in a Laundromat. A woman came in, sat near my counter and chain-smoked cigarette after cigarette. The smoke was bothering me, so I turned on a fan. "Could you please point that thing in another direction?" she asked. "I'm just getting over pneumonia and the last thing I need is a breeze blowing on me."

— HOLLY SNAPP

A young man asked for a job with the circus, any job at all. The manager decided to give him a chance to become an assistant lion tamer and took him to the practice cage.

The head lion tamer, a beautiful young woman, was just starting her rehearsal. Entering the cage, she removed her cape with a flourish and, standing in a gorgeous costume, motioned to a lion. Obediently the lion crept towards her and then rolled over twice.

"Well," said the manager to the young man, "do you think you can learn to do that?"

"I'm sure I could," he replied, "but first you'll have to get that lion out of there."

— SCOTT M. RIVA

As an obstetrician, I sometimes see unusual tattoos when working in labor and delivery. One patient had some type of fish tattoo on her abdomen. "That sure is a pretty whale," I commented.

With a smile she replied, "It used to be a dolphin."

— RON NORRIS

Late one night I stopped at one of those 24-hour gas station mini-marts to get myself a fresh brewed cup of coffee. When I picked up the pot, I could not help noticing that the brew was as black as asphalt and just about as thick. "How old is the coffee you have here?" I asked the woman who was standing behind the store counter.

She shrugged. "I don't know. I've only been working here two weeks."

— PETER CULVER

When employees of the restaurant where I work attended a fire-safety seminar, we watched a fire official demonstrate the proper way to operate an extinguisher. "Pull the pin like a hand grenade," he explained, "then depress the trigger to release the foam."

Later, an employee was selected to extinguish a controlled fire in the parking lot. In her nervousness, she forgot to pull the pin.

Our instructor hinted, "Like a hand grenade, remember?"

In a burst of confidence, she pulled the pin—and hurled the extinguisher at the blaze.

— BECKI HARRIS

Timeless Humor from the 70's

My friend John and I, determined to see the world, signed on a Norwegian freighter as deckhands. We were being trained as helmsmen, and John's first lesson was given by the mate, a seasoned but gentle white-haired seafarer. John was holding the heading he had been given, when the mate ordered, "Come starboard."

Pleased at knowing immediately which way starboard was, John left the helm and walked over to his instructor.

The mate had an incredulous look on his face as the helm swung freely, but he merely asked politely, "Could you bring the ship with you?"

— BRUCE INGRAHAM

I got stuck in a traffic jam while commuting into Los Angeles one day. The woman in the SUV in front of me took full advantage of the slowdown. She whipped out her eyebrow pencil, lip gloss and a mirror, applying the finishing touches on her face in the ten minutes it took us to creep through the Cahuenga Pass.

Finally, the traffic broke up and as she zoomed away, I caught a glimpse of her vehicle's license plate: NTRL BTY.

— CHRIS DURMICK

Students in the adult French class I teach include quite a few health-care professionals. During one class, I was coughing so badly a doctor in the class raised her hand. "If you like, I could give you a prescription for that," she offered. Another hand shot up. "I could fill it for you," said a pharmacist's assistant. Not to be outdone, a paramedic added, "And I can take you there to pick it up!"

— JOANNE DUGUAY

When my daughter was preparing for her school's "career week," a time when career options are discussed and often led by representatives of different professions, we talked about my job as an airline customer-services representative. I mentioned that one of my responsibilities was to load passengers' luggage at the check-in counter. I later found out to my dismay that my daughter had listed my occupation as "Bag Lady."

— VICKI FREEMAN

A man rushed to the jewelry counter in the store where I work soon after the doors opened one morning and said he needed a pair of diamond earrings. I showed him a wide selection, and quickly he picked out a pair.

When I asked him if he wanted the earrings gift-wrapped, he said, "That'd be great. But can you make it quick? I forgot today was my anniversary, and my wife thinks I'm taking out the trash."

— ANDRE F. PAYSON II

A Kid's World

They're innocent, earnest, and accidentally hilarious. The priceless things kids say, the unlikely things they do, and the brain-squashing challenges they pose to us unsuspecting adults.

"Can you hear me now?"

My perspective on my mother has changed immensely. She was a lot taller when I was younger.

— HOWIE MANDEL in I Love You, Mom! by Kelly Ripa and Others (Hyperion)

A perfect parent is a person with excellent child-rearing theories and no actual children.

— DAVE BARRY

All mothers have intuition. The great ones have radar.

— CATHY GUISEWITE, quoted in The Joys of Motherhood by Jane Hughes Paulson (Andrews McMeel)

Having a family is like having a bowling alley installed in your head.

— MARTIN MULL

Nowadays they say you need a special chip to put in the TV so kids can't watch this and that. In my day, we didn't need a chip. My mom was the chip. End of story.

— RAY CHARLES in Esquire

There's no such thing as fun for the whole family.

— JERRY SEINFELD

Raising kids is part joy and part guerrilla warfare.

ED ASNER

Just be good and kind to your children. Not only are they the future of the world, they're the ones who can sign you into the home.

— DENNIS MILLER

How Did That Get There?

▶ BY LINDA M. SCHMITZ

My son, Adam, has always been an industrious child. One time, when he was four years old, he set out to invent a paper airplane with egg-carton wings. But he didn't just make one prototype—he mass-produced an entire fleet. Don't get me wrong. I loved those airplanes …for several days. With two creative kids in the house, however, Adam's crafts had plenty of company—Popsicle-stick sculptures, rubber-band contraptions and polystyrene peanut people, to name just a few. So in an effort to declutter our home, I decided it was time for the last of the jumbo jets to be stored in its final hangar, if you know what I mean. After all, I told myself, we really can't keep everything.

After making sure the kitchen was child-free, I discreetly squashed the airplane deep into the trash can. As a precaution, I camouflaged it with a cereal box and a few carrot peelings.

Why did I think I could get away with it? I should know that no matter how sly I am, my kids always know when I'm trashing their treasures. And sure enough, just when I'd slid the garbage can back into place, in walked Adam. Right away he noticed something was amiss. Must be some kind of preschool radar, I figured.

He headed to the trash can, tossed in a tissue and trotted off to play. Whew, I thought, I'm in the clear. But suddenly he turned around and went back for a closer inspection.

Imagine my horror as I peered over his shoulder to see that the silly aircraft had wriggled its way out from under the cereal box, waving its feeble egg-carton wings in a last-ditch effort to be saved. Carrot peelings dangled accusingly from the tail.

"Mommmm! My airplane!" Adam howled. I quickly realized I had two choices: 1) feign disbelief—"How did that land there?"—and resurrect the aircraft, or 2) explain the impracticality of

keeping everything he ever made.

I went for No. 1 this time. Gingerly I gathered up the smelly, broken jet in my arms as if it were museum-worthy and placed it on top of the refrigerator. I'll get you next time, I said under my breath.

The other person who knows instinctively when I'm trashing something "valuable" is my daughter, Emily, who is three years older than Adam. Emily has saved everything from the moment she could wrap her fingers around it. A while ago, a survey of her "treasure boxes" revealed a foil candy wrapper dating back to Christmas '96, a napkin from a friend's birthday party, and a vast assortment of plastic pinkie rings.

But the real problem is her photographic memory of the loot.

She once asked me, "Mom, do you know where my plastic pinkie ring is that Aunt Laura gave me on my second birthday?"

Gulp. "Hmm…" I muttered thoughtfully, stalling for time.

There's no sneaking a kid's "treasure" into the trash.

"You know, it was in my heart-shaped box next to the friendship bracelet Suzanne gave me last May."

Of course. How could I forget? "Umm…I think the dog ate it."

"Mom, we don't have a dog!"

"Yes, but did I mention that Daddy and I are thinking of getting one?"

Even recycling isn't simple anymore. Adam once brought home a Styrofoam turtle he'd made at Bible school. We oohed and aahed appropriately. A few days later I encouraged the turtle to take a little swim in the recycle bin marked Styrofoam. Then I forgot all about it.

Three weeks later, off we went to the recycling center to do our part as responsible citizens. My kids love to help dump the containers, something that turtle was apparently counting on. It waited until just the right moment to tattle on me as it tumbled out of our bin. "She threw me away-ay! She threw me away-ay," it seemed to chant.

My children stared at me in disbelief. There goes that Mother of the Year Award, I thought as I escorted the turtle back to the car.

After that incident I decided on a new plan: 1) wait till the kids are at school, 2) use a trash bag separate from the kitchen one, and 3) fill 'er up!

With twisted glee, I set about my task. Into the bag marched toilet-paper-tube soldiers, soggy party-favor blowers and a pink plastic alligator. I strangled the bulging bag with a knot even Houdini couldn't untie and tossed it into the garage. As I patted myself on the back that Tuesday morning, I failed to recognize the flaw in my plan: trash pickup wasn't for three more days.

By the time Friday rolled around, that annoying pink alligator from Chuck E. Cheese's had worked a hole in the bag with its pointy snout. Of course, I wasn't the only one to notice this, but you already guessed that. It was that preschool radar again.

My mom has been warning me for years that this, too, shall pass. All too soon I'll have a showroom-worthy refrigerator that won't double as an art gallery.

The dust bunnies under my kids' beds will long for the company of a rolled-up sock or half a crayon. Worst of all, this mom's trash will be painfully ordinary—banana peels, milk jugs, soup cans.

So with a tear in my eye—born partially of defeat, but mostly of sentiment—I rescued the struggling alligator from the garbage bag. For more than a year it sat proudly on a kitchen shelf.

But I didn't see it as just another piece of clutter. It served as a reminder to enjoy my children and their treasures today. Because the day will come when I'll throw something away, and it will actually stay there. ▲

I am an oral surgeon, and once I was scheduled to extract four wisdom teeth from Jim, a high-school football player, who had opted to be sedated for the procedure. As the intravenous anesthesia was being administered, I asked Jim how he was feeling.

"Man," he replied, struggling to keep his eyes open, "I feel like I'm in English class."

— THOMAS F. KELLY, D.D.S.

During our computer class, the teacher chastised one boy for talking to the girl sitting next to him.

"I was just asking her a question," the boy said.

"If you have a question, ask me," the teacher tersely replied.

"Okay," he answered. "Do you want to go out with me Friday night?"

— TRACY MAXWELL

On a demographics survey given at our high school, students were asked, "What disadvantages do you see in having children?" Usual answers included "It's expensive to raise kids" and "They take up a lot of your time."

But one boy was not worried about money or responsibility. He wrote, "If I have children, I might have to drive a minivan."

— CHERITH DIEMERT

On vacation my nine-year-old son, Ryan, and I were at the pool, where two attractive young women wearing thong bikinis were sunning themselves. I noticed that Ryan kept staring at them, but he would occasionally glance back at me.

When they got up to leave, Ryan watched them particularly closely. I was bracing myself for questions he might have when he turned to me and whispered, "Dad, can I take that candy bar those girls left behind?"

— PAUL DELUCA

It began as an innocent game with my toddler son, Robert. I'd get in the fighter's stance and start shadowboxing. Jabbing with both fists, I'd say, "One-two, one-two," and he would imitate me over and over.

I never thought about the consequences of this little exercise until my wife took our son to a birthday party. When the boy's mother was handing out noise-makers she leaned over to Robert and asked, "Would you like one too?"

It took my wife a while to explain her way out of what happened next.

— ALFRED ISNARDI

My two-year-old cousin scared us one summer by disappearing during our lakeside vacation. More than a dozen relatives searched the forest and shoreline, and everyone was relieved when we found Matthew playing calmly in the woods.

"Listen to me, Matthew," his mother said sharply. "From now on when you want to go some-place, you tell Mommy first, okay?"

Matthew thought about that for a moment and said, "Okay. Disney World."

— LEAH HALLENBECK

Timeless Humor from the 60's

I was reading to my wife a newspaper report of the speech in which FCC chairman Newton N. Minow called television "a vast wasteland."

If you watch your TV set constantly, Minow had said, "you will see a procession of game shows, audience-participation shows, formula comedies about totally unbelievable families, blood and thunder, mayhem, violence, sadism . . ."

My 12-year-old son, hearing part of the quotation, interrupted excitedly, "What time does that show go on, Dad?"

— ALLYN W. OWEN

Rushing to get to the movies, my husband and I told the kids we had to leave "right now"—at which point our teenage daughter headed for the bathroom to apply makeup. Her dad yelled for her to get in the car immediately, and headed for the garage grumbling.

On the way to the multiplex my husband glanced in the rearview mirror and caught our teen applying lipstick and blush, which produced the predictable lecture. "Look at your mom," he said. "She didn't put on any makeup just to go sit in a dark movie theater."

From the back I heard, "Yeah, but Mom doesn't need makeup."

My heart swelling with the compliment, I turned back to thank this sweet, wonderful daughter of mine just as she continued, "Nobody looks at her."

— DELORES BREWINGTON

Our family was dazzled by the sights and the bustling crowds during a visit to Manhattan. "This is the city that never sleeps," I told my eleven-year-old daughter.

"That's probably because there's a Starbucks on every corner," she observed.

— LINDA FOLEY

THE KIDS ARE ASLEEP. LET'S GO TO EUROPE.

MUELLER

While I sat in the reception area of my doctor's office, a woman rolled an elderly man in a wheelchair into the room. As she went to the receptionist's desk, the man sat there, alone and silent. Just as I was thinking I should make small talk with him, a little boy slipped off his mother's lap and walked over to the wheelchair.

Placing his hand on the man's, he said, "I know how you feel. My mom makes me ride in the stroller too."

— STEVE ANDERSON

When my neighbor's grand-daughter introduced me to her young son, Brian, I said to him, "My grandchildren call me Mimi. Why don't you call me that too?"

"I don't think so," he retorted, and ran off after his mother.

Later I was asked to baby-sit for Brian, and we hit it off wonderfully. As he snuggled up to me, he said, "I don't care what your grandchildren say. I love you, Meanie."

— MARILYN HAYDEN

Our teenage son, Marc, never misses an opportunity to remind us that he needs his own car. One morning as I drove him to school, it was apparent that we would be late. I asked him to write a note, which I would sign when we arrived.

At school, he handed me a pen and the note, which read: "Marc is late this morning due to car trouble. The trouble is, Marc doesn't have his own car, and his mom drives too slowly."

— LAURA Z. SOWERS

Since I am a busy mom of four, I rely on my children to help me out with everyday chores around the house. One morning I was running around trying to get the children and myself ready, when I suddenly realized it was trash pick-up day. So I handed a bag of garbage to my sleepy seven-year-old son and told him to toss it in the trash bin on his way out the door.

Glancing out my window moments later, I saw him wearily boarding the bus. He was carrying his backpack, his lunchbox and a big white bag of garbage.

— LYNN PAREJKO

After years of using the same perfumes, I decided to try something different and settled on a light, citrusy fragrance. The next day I was surprised when it was my little boy, not my husband, who first noticed the change. As he put his arms around me, he declared, "Wow, Mom, you smell just like Froot Loops!"

— TRINA MULDOON

My older son loves school, but his younger brother absolutely hates it. One weekend he cried and fretted and tried every excuse not to go back on Monday. Sunday morning on the way home from church, the crying and whining built to a crescendo. At the end of my rope, I finally stopped the car and explained, "Honey, it's a law. If you don't go to school, they'll put Mommy in jail."

He looked at me, thought a moment, then asked, "How long would you have to stay?"

— TRINA REES

One night about 10 p.m., I answered the phone and heard, "Dad, we want to stay out late. Is that okay?"

"Sure," I answered, "as long as you called."

When I hung up, my wife asked who was on the phone.

"One of the boys," I replied. "I gave them permission to stay out late."

"Not our boys," she said. "They're both downstairs in the basement."

— LAWRENCE M. WEISBERG

"It's a painting. There is no sound."

The Cat Years

▶ BY ADAIR LARA

I just realized that while children are dogs—loyal and affectionate—teenagers are cats. It's so easy to be a dog owner. You feed it, train it, boss it around. It puts its head on your knee and gazes at you as if you were a Rembrandt painting. It bounds indoors with enthusiasm when you call it.

Then, around age 13, your adoring little puppy turns into a big old cat. When you tell it to come inside, it looks amazed, as if wondering who died and made you emperor. Instead of dogging your footsteps, it disappears. You won't see it again until it gets hungry—then it pauses on its sprint through the kitchen long enough to turn its nose up at whatever you're serving. When you reach out to ruffle its head, in that old affectionate gesture, it twists away from you, then gives you a blank stare, as if trying to remember where it has seen you before.

You, not realizing that the dog is now a cat, think something must be desperately wrong with it. It seems so antisocial, so distant, sort of depressed. It won't go on family outings.

Since you're the one who raised it, taught it to fetch and stay and sit on command, you assume that you did something wrong. Flooded with guilt and fear, you redouble your efforts to make your pet behave.

Only now you're dealing with a cat, so everything that worked before now produces the opposite of the desired result. Call it, and it runs away. Tell it to sit, and it jumps on the counter. The more you go toward it, wringing your hands, the more it moves away.

Instead of continuing to act like a dog owner, you can learn to behave like a cat owner. Put a dish of food near the door, and let it come to you. But remember that a cat needs your help and your affection too. Sit still, and it will come, seeking that warm, comforting lap it has not entirely forgotten. Be there to open the door for it.

One day, your grown-up child will walk into the kitchen, give you a big kiss and say, "You've been on your feet all day. Let me get those dishes for you." Then you'll realize your cat is a dog again. ▲

Adair Lara is the author of Hold Me Close, Let Me Go, *a memoir about raising a teenager (Broadway Books)*

"What? I thought I *was* wearing it backwards."

I overheard my nine-year-old son on the phone with a friend discussing a computer simulation game. The game involved creating a family, a house for them to live in, and so on. My son, an old hand at the game, gave this warning: "Whatever you do, don't get kids. They don't bring in any money, and all they do is eat."

— NICOLE KAULING

When I bought my new Lexus Sport Coupe, my two sons asked me who would inherit it if I met my demise. I pondered the question, then told them if I passed away on an even day, the son born on an even day would get it. If it happened on an odd day, the one born on the odd day would get it.

A few weekends later, while river rafting with one of my sons, I was tossed out of the boat. As I floated in the rapids, I heard my son yelling, "It's the wrong day!"

— GREG ZARET

Nothing seems to dim my 13-year-old son's sense of humor. And he's certainly not above being the butt of his own joke. Shortly after he was diagnosed with attention deficit disorder (ADD), he threw this at me: "Hey Dad—how many ADD children does it take to change a lightbulb?"

"I give up," I said.

"Let's go ride our bikes."

— RICHARD HURD

Don't ever pay a surprise visit to a child in college. You might be the one getting the surprise. I learned this the hard way when I swung by my son's campus during a business trip. Locating what I thought was his fraternity house, I rang the doorbell. "Yeah?" a voice called from inside.

"Does Dylan Houseman live here?"

"Yup," the voice answered. "Leave him on the front porch. We'll drag him in later."

— JERICHO HOUSEMAN

My doctor friend moved his family to a small town in Montana. An Italian American raised in Philadelphia, he wanted his kids to enjoy the benefits of clean air and the outdoors. The locals were thrilled to have a doctor of their own, and were always inviting him and his family over for dinner.

During one visit, one of his daughters told a rancher's daughter, "We're Italian."

Somewhat confused, the little girl replied, "We're Ranch."

— DOUGLAS STANGE

Recently I was grading history tests for my fourth-graders. I'd included an extra-credit question: "List up to five good facts about Abraham Lincoln."

One of my D students surprised me with this one: "After the war ended, Lincoln took his wife to a show."

— SHARON CLANTON

A teacher friend of my wife was discussing compound nouns with her class. "They're made up of two or more words," she explained. "For example, townhouse or boxcar. Can anyone think of another one?"

One boy raised his hand and offered, "Asphalt."

— JOSEPH R. VER BERG

Timeless Humor from the 70's

After his first day back at school in the fall, I asked my son if the high-school students were wearing anything new. "Well," he replied, "a lot of the fellows are showing up in see-through mustaches."

— BEATRICE W. COLVIN

We live less than a quarter-mile from the high school, but my son proudly drove there in a car he bought with his own money. A typical first car, it had lots of little problems and was sometimes slow to start.

One morning I was surprised to see it still in front of the house, so after school I asked him about it. "I had to get to school early," he said, "so I just ran."

— DENNIS DIGGES

My sister was busy getting ready to host our entire family for Easter. On her to-do list was a hair appointment for her daughter. "So, Katie," said the stylist as the little girl got up in the chair, "who's coming to your house this weekend with big ears and floppy feet?"

Katie replied, "I think it's my uncle Brian."

— MARSHA ECKERMAN

At the beginning of my junior year at Russellville High School in Arkansas, our homeroom teacher had us fill out a form stating our future goals. Out of curiosity, I leaned over to see what my friend put down for her aspirations.

Where it read "Vocational Plans," she had written, "Florida."

— CRYSTAL BRUCE

The day before my graduation from Soldan High School in St. Louis, the principal called an assembly. He wanted to say farewell informally, he explained, as he reviewed our years together. There was hardly a dry eye among us as he concluded, "We will remember you, and hope you will remember us; more importantly, we want you to remember each other. I want all of you to meet in this very auditorium 25 years from today."

There was a moment of silence; then a thin voice piped up, "What time?"

— MARVIN J. FRIEDE

A friend of mine has an adopted son who, at six-foot-one, loves to play basketball. The boy was applying to basketball camp, and a section of the application called for him to write a brief essay about himself. My friend got a lump in his throat as he read his son's words: "Most of all I am thankful that I am adopted…"

Then my friend got a cold dose of reality as he continued: "because my dad is so short."

— RALPH G. LOCKERBIE

"I'd like to work overtime till the kids are back in school."

What Do Kids Know
and why won't they tell us?

▶ BY JERRY ZEZIMA

In my children's eyes, I'm an out-of-touch old fogy, pathetically ill-informed about today's youth. I would feel tremendous guilt about this except for one thing: Today's teenagers know even less about what's going on in their lives than I do.

I base this belief on the following conversation, which takes place in thousands of American homes every day:

Parent: How was school today?
Child: Fine.
Parent: What did you do?
Child: Nothing.
Parent: Do you have any homework?
Child: I don't know.

Ask your child about any subject directly involving him or her and you'll get one of three responses: (a) "Fine," (b) "Nothing," (c) "I don't know."

If your child is in a particularly talkative mood, and by some miracle is not on the phone, you'll get all three. Otherwise, your mere existence will be deemed too annoying to acknowledge, in which case your child will pretend not to hear you.

Besides, kids are always listening to mind-numbing music played at decibel levels high enough to blow out windows, so your child may not be ignoring you. He or she may simply be deaf.

Still, it's alarming to know that even though everything is "fine," absolutely "nothing" happens in school. If this pattern continues for 20 or 30 years, when our kids are the leaders of this country, we may hear this:

Reporter: Mr. President, how did the summit go today?
President: Fine.
Reporter: What did you discuss?
President: Nothing.
Reporter: Does this mean that the world is on the brink of nuclear disaster?
President: I don't know.

How can our kids have absolutely no idea what's going on in their lives? In recent weeks I've asked my daughters the following simple questions: What time does your field hockey game start? How are you getting home from school? How are you? Who are you?

Each time, the response has been: "I don't know."

When I was a kid, things were different. If my parents asked me how school was, I would always say: "Great!" When they asked what I did in school, I would respond: "Stuff." When they asked if I had any homework, I answered: "No."

I lied, of course, but at least I lied creatively. And I always made it sound as if I were actually doing something, worthless though it often was. I never said: "I don't know."

Another irritating response today's parents get is: "Nobody." For example, if the phone rings and your teenager answers it and stays on the line for 45 minutes and eventually, perhaps because of a house fire, has to hang up, and you ask who called, the response you will almost always get is: "Nobody."

And the really scary part is that your child's friend will say the same thing to his or her parents when they ask the same question. Maybe that's why some people grow up to be nobodies.

All I can say, parents, is that if you want to find out what's going on in your children's lives and you expect to get more than three words out of them, call them on the telephone. ▲

Setting a good example for your children does nothing but increase their embarrassment.

— DOUG LARSON, United Feature Syndicate

No matter how old a mother is, she watches her middle-aged children for signs of improvement.

— FLORIDA SCOTT-MAXWELL, The Measure of My Days (Knopf)

If pregnancy were a book, they would cut the last two chapters.

— NORA EPHRON, Heartburn (Knopf)

Without enough sleep, we all become tall two-year-olds.

— JOJO JENSON, Dirt Farmer Wisdom (Red Wheel)

Like all parents, my husband and I just do the best we can, and hold our breath and hope we've set aside enough money for our kids' therapy.

— MICHELLE PFEIFFER

You know your kids are growing up when they stop asking you where they came from and refuse to tell you where they're going.

— P. J. O'ROURKE in First for Women

When it comes to raising children, I believe in give and take. I give orders and they take 'em.

— BERNIE MAC in People

There's an upside to grandparenthood. You play, you give, you love, then you hand them back and go to an early movie.

— BILLY CRYSTAL in Good Housekeeping

"It's hard to believe that in just a few weeks, I'll be refusing to eat it."

Being a teenager and getting a tattoo seem to go hand and hand these days. I wasn't surprised when one of my daughter's friends showed me a delicate little Japanese symbol on her hip. "Please don't tell my parents," she begged.

"I won't," I promised. "By the way, what does that stand for?"

"Honesty," she said.

— LINDA SINGER

Blood may be thicker than water, but baseball beats them both. I learned this after explaining to my two boys that they were half-Lithuanian on their father's side, and half-Yankee, meaning their other set of parents came from an old New England family.

My younger son looked worried. "But we're still a hundred percent Red Sox, right, Mom?"

— GAYLA BIEKSHA

Visiting his parents' retirement village in Florida, my middle-aged friend, Tim, went for a swim in the community pool while his elderly father took a walk. Tim struck up a conversation with the only other person in the pool, a five-year-old boy. After a while, Tim's father returned from his walk and called out, "I'm ready to leave."

Tim then turned to his new friend and announced that he had to leave because his father was calling. Astonished, the wide-eyed little boy cried, "You're a kid?"

— JANICE PALKO

One night our local newscaster was reading about an allegation that two Sesame Street characters, Bert and Ernie, were gay. The show's producer refuted this, pointing out that they were only puppets, not humans. They argued a lot and then made up to show children how to resolve conflicts and stay friends.

While watching this report, my wife, Donna, noticed that our seven-year-old daughter was also listening. As Donna struggled to come up with an explanation for the term "gay," our crestfallen daughter said in dismay, "They're puppets?"

— BILL DOERING

As she slid behind the wheel for her first driving lesson, my daughter couldn't contain her excitement. "You need to make adjustments so the car is comfortable for you, the driver," I began. "Now, what's the first thing you should do?"

"Change the radio station," she said.

— RHONDA BUCALO

While doing renovations in our house, one of the workmen paused to look at a flattering photo of me wearing makeup and a fancy gown. I heard him let out a low whistle and ask my son, Joshua, "Who's that?"

"That's my mom," Joshua answered.

"Wow," the man said, "my mother doesn't look like that."

"Yeah," my son said, "well, neither does mine."

— TAMMY L. VITULANO

88

My sister had been ill, so I called to see how she was doing. My ten-year-old niece answered the phone. "Hello," she whispered.

"Hi, honey. How's your mother?" I asked.

"She's sleeping," she answered, again in a whisper.

"Did she go to the doctor?"

"Yes. She got some medicine," my niece said softly.

"Well, don't wake her up. Just tell her I called. What are you doing, by the way?"

Again in a soft whisper, she answered, "Practicing my trumpet."

— SHARRON DISBRO

As my five-year-old son and I were heading to McDonald's one day, we passed a car accident. Usually when we see something terrible like that, we say a prayer for whoever might be hurt, so I pointed and said to my son, "We should pray."

From the back seat I heard his earnest voice: "Dear God, please don't let those cars block the entrance to McDonald's."

— SHERRI LEARD

Preparing my son for his first day of kindergarten, we were reviewing numbers and counting. Suddenly he asked, "What is the biggest number in the world?"

As briefly as possible, I tried to explain the concept of infinity. I thought I had done pretty well, but then he said, "Dad, what number comes just before infinity?"

— SHAWN FOSTER

For years I had been telling my friend Pete that he ate too much fast food, but he always denied it. One day he admitted I was right.

"What changed your mind?"

"My grandson. When my daughter told him I was coming to visit, he asked, 'Grandpa from Florida, or Grandpa from Pizza Hut?' "

— STEVE FRANK

I am a first-grade teacher and a new empty nester. One night I was trying out an art project: making a person with simple materials. I took a coat hanger, attached a paper-plate face, put a shirt on the hanger and stuffed it. Then I sat it on the couch to see how it looked.

Later that evening my son walked in the door, home for a surprise visit. Taking one look at my coat-hanger friend sitting on the couch, he said, "Mom, it's not that bad, is it?"

— LINDA ADAMS

"Go ask your mother."

I was teaching a life-skills class to my high school students one day, and we were discussing the various terms one might encounter in a restaurant. I asked,

"What does the phrase 'à la carte' mean?"
"It means," a student said, "you're in the wrong restaurant."

— ALBERT T. GRANDE

Time for "The Talk"

▶ BY BRET LOTT

"Boys pupate at around age 15," my older son, Zeb, said matter-of-factly one day after school.

"They what?" I asked.

"Pupate," he said. "Your voice changes. You get hair." He paused. "A lady from the medical school talked to our class today."

It was then I remembered that the month before, he'd come home and told us about metamorphosis in butterflies, the whole business of worms turning into miraculous flying creatures.

Holding back laughter, I said, "You mean puberty."

"Yeah," he replied, shrugging, "that's it."

"Pupate," I said. "That's good."

"Actually," my wife, Melanie, added, "that's a pretty good idea of what happens."

Zeb, at ten, knows more about sex than I did at his age. I am certain of this because Melanie and I took it upon ourselves to have The Talk with Zeb the summer before he started fourth grade.

Our decision to tell him the truth about where babies come from was a direct result of the mutant facts that Melanie and I had been given as kids.

We told our younger son, Jake, seven, he could watch TV in our bedroom, a treat that would assure our privacy in the kitchen. Then we got out our copy of *ABC's of the Human Body* and had Zeb sit with us at the kitchen table.

"There are some things we want you to know about before you start school this fall," Melanie said.

Zeb crossed his arms and looked at us with the level stare he employs when he suspects trouble: eyes half-closed, lower jaw jutting forward.

"Do you know where babies come from?" Melanie went on.

"Yes," he said too quickly. "I know." He held his arms tighter.

"Where?" I asked. I smiled, trying hard to soften what sounded like a cross-examination.

He shrugged.

"We want to explain it to you," Melanie said, "so that if kids try to tell you something crazy at school, you'll know the truth." Then, slowly, she turned to me. "Bret?"

I took a breath, swallowed and turned to Zeb.

He put his hands up to his ears and covered them.

I remember looking at my mom one night during dinner and asking flat out, "Where do babies come from?" This must have been in fourth grade, right about the time I picked up the facts of life "on the street." I'll never forget my dad's reaction.

"Hey!" he shouted, leaning toward me, a fork in one hand, a knife in the other. "Don't talk like that!"

I am not kidding. That's what he said.

Mom defended me, saying, "He just asked."

Dad sat straight in his chair. We four children were looking at him, waiting. Then he put his fork and

A defining moment of parenthood had arrived.

knife to the pork chop on his plate. "Well, this isn't the time or the place. It's rude."

I wouldn't get The Talk for another four years. By that time some friends and I had built a fort where we huddled and joked about creased pages torn out of *Playboy*.

Then one day Mom suddenly said, "You and your father need to have a talk." Dad looked at her, swallowed and said to me, "All right, let's go," then headed down the hall toward their bedroom.

He sat down on the bed. His eyes hadn't yet met mine. He put his hands on his thighs, lifted them, let them drop. "Well," he said. "Okay."

I had him in a way I'd never known before: powerless, stunned. So, to make matters worse, I said, "Go ahead. I'm listening."

He looked at me. "Well, what do you want to know?"

I shrugged, then let the question hang in the air a few moments before saying, "I already know."

"Okay," he said, and breathed out. "Good. That's good." Then he laughed. It was a nice, solid laugh, a kind of laugh I hadn't heard before.

That was The Talk for me, the one everyone either gets or doesn't get. I got one, but it gave me nothing, only a glimpse of my dad without armor, defenseless.

Zeb surrendered his hands from his ears once we brought out the diagrams and photos, his eyes wide open, taking in the images. I don't remember what we said, but the words lined up in a semblance of factual order.

Zeb finally started laughing. It was laughter like what my dad had shared with me: laughter of relief about this whole huge mystery—sex.

We finished off this astonishing set of facts by revealing to Zeb the greater truth behind it all: that this is all a result of love and respect. We told him this is part of what it means to be a husband and wife. Sex is a sacred act, a gift from God, carried out after love has been secured through marriage.

Now Zeb knows the truth. At least—and at best—both his mom and dad have had a hand in how he came to find out.

The mystery of it all is still revealing itself to me, here in my own marriage. One evening we were in the van, backing down the driveway.

"Wait," Melanie said, "my sunglasses." I stopped; she climbed out and headed toward the front door. There was something about the way her hair fell, something about the back of her neck, that made me say, "She's beautiful, isn't she?"

The boys were quiet behind me. Finally Zeb said, "Yeah."

Then came Jake's voice: "Hubba-hubba," he said. I turned around and looked at him. He was grinning. "Ooh, baby," he said.

"Where'd you hear that?" I asked, trying not to laugh.

"My friend Garrett," Jake said, still grinning. "He says that all the time about Sarah and Elizabeth."

I shook my head. One down, one to go. ▲

Football players at the high school where I worked were stealing the practice jerseys, so the coach ordered a set with "Property of Central High School" emblazoned on them. When the thefts continued, he ordered a new batch that had the imprint "Stolen From Central High School." But the jerseys still kept disappearing.

The larceny finally stopped after he changed the wording to "Central High School 4th String."

— HAL OLSEN

When my daughter was little, we took a vacation to Florida. Seated on the airplane near the wing, I pointed out to Rhonda that we were above the ocean. "Can you see the water?" I asked her.

"No," she said, peering out the window at the wing, "but I can see the diving board."

— REBECCA RICCI

My husband, a big-time sports fan, was watching a football game with our grandchildren. He had just turned 75 and was feeling a little wistful. "You know," he said to our grandson, Nick, "it's not easy getting old. I guess I'm in the fourth quarter now."

"Don't worry, Grandpa," Nick said cheerily. "Maybe you'll go into overtime."

— EVELYN BREDLEAU

Thinking his son would enjoy seeing the reenactment of a Civil War battle, my niece's husband took the boy, Will, to the event. But the poor child was terrified by the booming cannons. During a lull, Will's dad finally got him calmed down.

That's when the Confederate general hollered,

"Fire at Will!"

Betty Ammar

While driving on the highway, my daughter noticed a child in the window of a car in the next lane, holding up a handwritten sign that read "Help."

A few minutes later, the car passed her and she again glanced at it. The little boy held up the same sign and this time followed it with another, which read "My mother is singing!"

— LIL GIBSON

The board of education in a nearby town sold off a building that had been a one-room schoolhouse. The buyer converted it to a tavern. One day an elderly man was walking by the place with his grandson and pointed to the building.

"That's where I went to school when I was your age."

"Really," said the boy. "Who was your bartender back then?"

— DUANE SMITH

It was the first day of basketball practice at Wingate high school in Brooklyn, N.Y. Coach Jack Kaminer handed a ball to each player. "Fellas," he said, "I want you to practice shooting from the spots you might expect to be in during the game."

The No. 12 sub immediately sat down on the bench and began arcing the ball toward the basket.

— HERMAN L. MASIN

On our way to my parents' house for dinner one evening, I glanced over at my 15-year-old daughter. "Isn't that skirt a bit short?" I asked. She rolled her eyes at my comment and gave me one of those "Oh, Mom" looks.

When we arrived at my folks' place, my mother greeted us at the door, hugged my daughter, then turned to me and said, "Elizabeth! Don't you think that blouse is awfully low-cut?"

— ELIZABETH SCOTT

After registering for his high school classes, my son burst into the house, filled with excitement. "Dad," he announced in one breath, "I got all the classes I wanted. But I have to have my school supplies by tomorrow. I need a protractor and a compass for geometry, a dictionary for English, a dissecting kit for biology—and a car for driver's ed."

— JIM TIMMONS

My cooking has always been the target of family jokes. One evening, as I prepared dinner a bit too quickly, the kitchen filled with smoke and the smoke detector went off. Although both of my children had received fire-safety training at school, they did not respond to the alarm. Annoyed, I stormed through the house in search of them. I found them in the bathroom, washing their hands.

Over the loud buzzing of the smoke alarm, I asked them to identify the sound.

"It's the smoke detector," they replied in unison.

"Do you know what that sound means?" I demanded.

"Sure," my oldest replied. "Dinner's ready."

— DEBI CHRISTENSEN

Timeless Humor from the 70's

Toward the end of the school year, the sixth-grade teachers decide which of their students should be accelerated in certain subjects in the seventh grade. When a child is chosen, his parents are notified. When one boy was accelerated in science and math, his mother wrote to the teacher: "I think this is quite an honor for someone who just tried to make two quarts of lemonade in a one-quart pitcher!"

— MRS. MARVIN PADNICK

"Do you win every time?"

I had finished my Christmas shopping early and had wrapped all the presents. Having two curious children, I had to find a suitable hiding place. I chose an ideal spot—the furnace room. I stacked the presents and covered them with a blanket, positive they'd remain undiscovered.

When I went to get the gifts to put them under the tree, I lifted the blanket and there, stacked neatly on top of my gifts, were presents addressed to "Mom and Dad, From the Kids."

— LORALIE LONG

As I was nursing my baby, my cousin's six-year-old daughter, Krissy, came into the room. Never having seen anyone breastfeed before, she was intrigued and full of all kinds of questions about what I was doing.

After mulling over my answers, she remarked, "My mom has some of those, but I don't think she knows how to use them."

— LOIS SINGER

My husband and I both work, so our family eats out a lot. Recently, when we were having a rare home-cooked meal, I handed a glass to my three-year-old and told her to drink her milk.

She looked at me bewildered and replied, "But I didn't order milk."

— JANET A. NUSSBAUM

One of my fourth graders asked my teacher's assistant, "How old are you, Mrs. Glass?"

"You should never ask an adult's age," I broke in.

"That's okay," Harriett said smiling. "I'm fifty."

"Wow, you don't look that old," the boy said. I was breathing a sigh of relief when another child chimed in, "Parts of her do."

— KATHERINE NORGARD

I was having lunch with my daughter Rachel, who's three, at our local mall and was feeling particularly macho for a 46-year-old. All morning, women had been smiling at me and giving me the eye.

Getting up to leave the table, I ran my fingers through my hair—and discovered two yellow-ducky barrettes that had been lovingly placed there hours before.

— PAUL J. MEYER

My mother was away all weekend at a business conference. During a break, she decided to call home collect. My six-year-old brother picked up the phone and heard a stranger's voice say, "We have a Marcia on the line. Will you accept the charges?"

Frantic, he dropped the receiver and came charging outside screaming, "Dad! They've got Mom! And they want money!"

— RODNEY HOWELL

"I remind you that my client is nice until proven naughty."

Dumb and Dumber

People do dumb things—the dumber, the funnier.
Here are the verbal flubs, social gaffes, and fix-it fiascos
we love to laugh at—as long as they're not ours.

My wife received a credit-card application in the mail that she had not requested. She didn't want it, but I did. So I crossed off my wife's name on the form, entered my own and returned the application. I soon got a phone call from a woman saying my application had been rejected.

I asked her why, and she told me the card could only be issued to the person originally solicited by the offer. However, she invited me to reapply, which I did during the same telephone call.

A few days later I got another call to tell me my second application had been rejected.

Why? The woman told me their files showed that I had previously applied for a card and had been denied.

— SANFORD P. BLANK

When the skipper of an Icelandic trawler accidentally rammed Englishman Jim Hughes's yacht, he caused $30,000 worth of damage. Exactly a year and a day before, reported the London *Times*, the skipper, Eriker Olafsson, had hit the same boat, causing $40,000 in damage.

What are the odds of this happening twice? Pretty good, since Olafsson purposely steered toward Hughes to apologize for the previous year's collision.

— KIRSTY SCOTT

During our church service one Sunday, a parishioner was speaking about an emotionally charged topic and had trouble controlling her tears. Finishing her remarks, she told the congregation, "I apologize for crying so much. I'm usually not such a big boob."

The bishop rose to close the session and remarked, "That's okay. We like big boobs."

— L.S.

My family was in a celebrating mood, so we decided to go out to a fancy steakhouse. As our waiter stood there ready to take our orders, I was caught up listening to the background music that was piped into the restaurant. "What CD is this?" I asked him.

Apparently my East Texas accent confused him, because he leaned over and answered, "Fort Worth."

— JULIE A. FOLGER

On vacation in Hawaii, my step-mom, Sandy, called a café to make reservations for 7 p.m. Checking her book, the cheery young hostess said, "I'm sorry, all we have is 6:45. Would you like that?"

"That's fine," Sandy said.

"Okay," the woman confirmed. Then she added, "Just be advised you may have to wait 15 minutes for your table."

— KELLY FINNEGAN

Calling for information about one of my credit cards, I got the following recorded prompt: "Please enter your account number as it appears on your card or statement."

I did as instructed, and the system said, "Please enter your five-digit ZIP code."

After I put that in, I got a third message: "If you would like your information in English, press one."

— MICHELLE GOLF

Timeless Humor from the 60's

As a salesman, I was searching for a certain company in unfamiliar territory. I came to a likely-looking road marked with a small red sign reading: Industrial Center. I was not certain that this was the right road, so I drove back to a gas station to inquire.

The attendant took my arm and pointed to the sign that I had just read, now barely discernible in the distance. "See that little sign about three blocks away?" he asked.

"You mean the red one that says industrial center?" I asked.

"Man!" he exclaimed. "You've got eyes like an eagle!"

— EDWARD M. LONGAN

97

My husband decided life would be easier if he wired a new light switch in the master bedroom to save us from fumbling in the dark for the lamp. He cut through the drywall and found a stash of bottles and small boxes inside the wall. "Honey!" he called excitedly. "Come see what I found!" I ran in and quickly realized that his next task would be to fix the hole that now led into the back of our medicine cabinet.

—NOLA PIRART

It was the standard series of check-in questions that every traveler gets at the airlines counter, including, "Has anyone put anything in your baggage without your knowledge?"

"If it was put there without my knowledge," I asked, "how would I know?"

The agent behind the counter smiled smugly. "That's why we ask."

— KATE VETTER

"It says, 'Separate two eggs.' Is that far enough?"

When I moved to California, I was a nervous wreck about earthquakes. My friend Linda, who was born and raised there, was completely blasé. I remember once when we pulled up to a light, her Honda began to shake.

She looked worried until I stammered, "I think that we're having an earthquake."

"Thank goodness," Linda said. "I thought something was wrong with my car."

— DYAN ARNOLD

My mother, a meticulous housekeeper, often lectured my father about tracking dirt into the house. One day he came in to find her furiously scrubbing away at a spot on the floor and launching into a lecture. "I don't know what you've brought in," she said, "but I can't seem to get this out."

He studied the situation for a moment and, without a word, moved a figurine on the window-sill where the sun was streaming in. The spot immediately disappeared.

— MICHELE DONNELLY

During weekly visits to my allergist, I've noticed a lot of inattentive parents with ill-behaved children in the waiting room. So I was impressed one day to see a mother with her little boy, helping him sound out the words on a sign.

Finally he mastered it and his mother cheered, "That's great! Now sit there. I'll be back in 15 minutes."

What did the sign say? "Children must not be left unattended."

— DARLENE HOVEL

On my way to a picnic, I stopped at a fast food place to order a quart of potato salad. "We don't sell it by the quart," the clerk snapped.

"Okay, then give me two pints, please," I replied.

I'm proud to say I held my tongue when she asked, "Do you want it in one container?"

— JULIE GUITERREZ

An aching back sent me stumbling to the drugstore for relief. After a search I found what I was looking for: a selection of heating pads specifically for people with back pain—all on the bottom shelf.

— KATHERINE JOHNSON

While rummaging through her attic, my friend Kathryn found an old shotgun. Unsure about how to dispose of it, she called her parents. "Take it to the police station," her mother suggested.

My friend was about to hang up when her mother added, "And Kathryn?"

"Yes, Mom?"

"Call first."

— KAREN WHEDON

An unintentional double entendre, from the *Piedmont Shopper,* in Danville, Virginia: "Mixing bowl set designed to please a cook with round bottom for efficient beating."

— C.P. LEWIS

"Reservations? No, we definitely want to eat here."

One day while at the doctor's office, the receptionist called me to the desk to update my personal file. Before I had a chance to tell her that all the information she had was still correct, she asked, "Has your birth date changed?"

— MARGARET FREESE

Dining out one evening, I noticed some teenagers celebrating at a nearby table. When one girl pulled out a camera, I offered to take a picture of the group. After one photo, I suggested taking another just in case the first one didn't come out.

"Oh, no, that's okay," she said, as she took back her camera. "I always get double prints."

— DEANNA GUY

A Lineup of Fumbling Felons,
Clumsy Crooks
and Bumbling Bad Guys

▶ BY DANIEL BUTLER, ALAN RAY
AND LELAND GREGORY

Police work, like any other stressful profession, is full of moments when situations take a turn toward the absurd. Here are a few criminals who, through selfishness, ignorance or greed, proved themselves not just dumb, but dumber:

Positive ID. "We got a call that a woman's purse had been stolen," recalls Det. Chris Stewart of Brunswick, Ga. "A short time later we saw a man who fit the description the victim gave us. So we picked him up and took him back to the scene of the crime."

Stewart explained to the suspect that when they arrived he was to exit the vehicle and face the victim for a positive ID. The suspect did exactly as he had been told. He stepped from the car, looked at the victim and blurted out, "Yeah, that's her! That's the woman I robbed."

Run of Bad Luck. When the robber from Pensacola, Fla., entered a liquor store to hold it up, he found too many people around. So he switched to Plan B. Fishing in his pocket for a piece of paper, he scrawled a note demanding money.

The cashier quickly handed over all the money in the drawer, and the man was out the door in a flash. He seemed to have pulled off the robbery with flawless precision.

Except for one thing. He had written the note on the back of a letter from his probation officer—complete with his own name and address.

Right on His Heels. Outside Lawrence, Kan., an all-night market had just been robbed. Police units in the area responded quickly to the alarm, but the fleeing thief wasn't worried. It was dark, he was a fast runner, and he knew the neighborhood like the back of his hand.

It didn't take long for the thief to leave the first pair of officers behind. But more officers joined in the chase. Each time the frustrated suspect would elude one pursuer, he would be spotted by another, until he was finally captured.

He really hadn't been hard to find. Pursuing officers had simply followed the red lights on his heels—the ones that blinked on and off every time his high-tech running shoes hit the ground.

Clothes Make the Man. One day an apartment-complex maintenance man in Virginia Beach, Va., decided to supplement his income by robbing a 7-Eleven store. He wore a ski mask and made his voice deep as he ordered, "Give me all the money." Staring, the clerk handed it over.

When the police arrived, they asked the 7-Eleven employee to describe the robber. "He was wearing a ski mask," said the clerk, "and a blue maintenance uniform." On the front of the uniform were the name of an apartment house and the man's name.

The two officers looked at each other. Surely not. But when they appeared at the maintenance man's apartment, he hadn't even changed clothes. The ski mask? In his back pocket. The money? In his front pocket.

Winner Loses. When the woman hit the California state lottery for thousands, she was thrilled. It seemed things were really looking up. Her picture appeared in the local newspaper, and people on the street recognized her. Unfortunately for her, so did the police. A local cop remembered her as the woman wanted by authorities on an eight-month-old shoplifting warrant.

Some of the money she had just won went toward paying her fine. ▲

"But I have a witness. Here, talk to her yourself."

My wife and I were having lunch at a fashionable eatery in Annapolis when we noticed what looked like a familiar face at the next table. Screwing up my courage, I asked, "Excuse me. Aren't you Marlin Fitzwater, the former White House press secretary?"

"Yes, I am," he acknowledged, and graciously interrupted his lunch to talk to us.

As we were leaving the restaurant, I remarked to the hostess, "Do you know you have Marlin Fitzwater on the terrace?"

"I'm not sure about that," she replied, "but we have Perrier and Evian at the bar."

— BRUCE F. HENDERSON

Sometime around two in the morning our phone rang, waking us out of a sound sleep. "Wrong number," my husband growled and slammed down the receiver.

A few minutes later it rang again. I heard him say, "One with pepperoni and extra cheese and one with sausage. Pick up in 20 minutes."

"What was that?" I asked.

"I took his order. Now we can sleep."

— JACKIE HUTH

I was getting into my car when I noticed a dent. On the windshield was a note and a phone number from the driver. "I feel terrible," the woman apologized when I called. "I hit your car as I was pulling into the next parking spot."

"Please, don't worry," I said to her. "I'm sure our insurance companies will take care of everything."

"Thank you for your understanding," she said. "You're so much nicer than the man I hit on the way out."

Laurie Payne

After I asked for a half-pound trout fillet at my supermarket's seafood counter, the clerk picked one out of a pile and set it on the scale. It weighed precisely eight ounces.

Impressed, I asked, "How did you know?"

Looking pleased with himself, he declared, "I'm psychotic."

— GLADYS HOCUTT

While on the freeway in Los Angeles, I was behind a pack of cars. The last driver was on the phone and drifting all over the road. This did not escape the attention of a California Highway Patrol officer, who snuck up behind her and said over his loudspeaker, "If you can't stay in your lane while on the phone, pull over until the call is completed."

Immediately eight cars pulled over.

— GREG ASH

I was preparing to teach a college course on the history of movie censorship and went to the library to take out films that had been censored. "Do you have any banned movies in your collection?" I asked the librarian.

"Oh yes," she answered. "We have some really good ones. What would you like: Tomy Dorsey? Glenn Miller?"

— PAUL H. STACY

The first day at my new health club I asked the girl at the front desk, "I like to exercise after work. What are your hours?" **"Our club is open 24/7," she told me excitedly, "Monday through Saturday."**

— APRYL CAVENDER

Stormy weather diverted our Dallas-bound flight to another airport. As we approached the runway, the pilot came on the intercom: "For those of you who are not familiar with the area, this is Lubbock, Texas."

Then he paused. "And for those of you who are familiar with this area, I *think* this is Lubbock, Texas."

— DARRELL BURTON

No one is more cautious than a first-time parent. After our daughter was big enough to ride on the back of my bicycle, I bought a special carrier with a seat belt and got her a little helmet. The day of the first ride I put her in the seat, double-checked all the equipment, wheeled the bike to the end of the driveway, carefully looked both ways and, swinging my leg up over the crossbar, accidentally kicked her in the chin.

— ZACHARY GIBBS

Living in a dry county was the bane of my friend Robert's existence. He was complaining to me one day about having to make a 60-mile round trip to get his favorite brand of bourbon. "I buy it by the case," he said.

"Are you addicted to that stuff?" I asked.

Robert thought for a second. "I don't know. I've never run out."

— RICK WORKMAN

For my grandmother's 80th birthday, we had a huge family celebration and even managed to get a photo announcement printed in the local paper. "That was a nice shot," I commented.

"It's my passport picture," she revealed.

"Really?" I stared in amazement at my homebody grandma. "Where did you go?"

"Walgreens," she replied.

— KAREN THOMPSON

My mother is always trying to understand what motivates people, especially those in her family. One day she and my sister were talking about one relative's bad luck. "Why do you suppose she changed jobs?" Mother asked my sister. "Maybe she has a subconscious desire not to succeed."

"Or maybe it just happened," said my sister, exasperated. "Do you know you analyze everything to death?"

Mother was silent for a moment. "That's true," she said. "Why do you think I do that?"

— BOBBIE S. CYPHERS

Famous faux pas recounted by a best-selling author who knows how it feels to…

Open Mouth, Insert Foot

"**G**ood to see you again," I greeted the gentleman, a family friend, one of America's premier entrepreneurs. It had been a while. "How's your wife?" He kept the friendly grin, but I caught a quick shadow. "She died three years ago," he said.

Where do you go from there? The weather? I made my way to the men's room and banged my head against the tiles.

Faux pas, the phrase for these embarrassments, is from the French for "false step." It's not a phrase that one hears much anymore, and more's the pity. The moment *homo* became *erectus*, he started stepping in it, and he has been at it ever since.

Faux pas remind us that however much the human race may dress itself up, you still cannot take it out. But what could be more satisfying than the high and mighty brought low by a real stinker of a faux pas? Such was the balm I sought after my own disaster, as I set out to collect faux pas.

Two Pickets to Where?

Pundit Michael Kinsley's definition of a gaffe is "when a politician accidentally speaks the truth." At the 1980 Democratic Convention, Jimmy Carter extolled the windy former Vice President Hubert Horatio Humphrey as "Hubert Horatio Hornblower."

Another slip of the tongue is the Unfortunate Mispronunciation. Consider the story of the wealthy socialite Mrs. Stuyvesant Fish, who once attended a fancy-dress ball in Newport, R.I. At the door, it is said, she whispered to the butler the theme of her costume: "A Norman peasant." The major-domo thundered aloud to the assembled crowd in the hall: "An enormous pheasant."

Then there's Dr. Freud's eponymous slip of the tongue—that awkward moment when the id crawls up your esophagus and bellows your secret across the room.

My favorite Freudian slip story is the man who went to the train station to buy tickets to Pittsburgh. "The ticket agent," he said, "had an amazing figure, and when I got to the counter, I asked her for 'two pickcts to Tittsburgh.'"

▶ BY CHRISTOPHER BUCKLEY

Royal Oops

One of Queen Elizabeth's subjects recently made tabloid headlines by not curtsying to her. The offender was the scantily clad Geri Halliwell, at the time Ginger of the Spice Girls. But Americans and royalty do not necessarily agree on what constitutes a faux pas. In 1981 U.S. Chief of Protocol Leonore Annenberg created a sensation by curtsying to Prince Charles when she welcomed him officially to the United States. Mrs. Annenberg, a gracious woman, was only trying to be courteous. The problem was that America had fought a war two centuries earlier precisely to win the privilege of not bowing or scraping before royalty.

"Madame, May We Dance?"

Then there is the Department of Unfortunate Misunderstandings. Author and wit Robert Benchley, bibulously leaving a smart restaurant one night, saw a uniformed man, assumed he was the doorman and instructed him to call a cab. The man starchily replied, "I happen to be a rear admiral in the U.S. Navy."

"In that case," said Benchley, "get me a battleship."

Costumes can lead to confusion. At a diplomatic reception he attended in the 1960s—some say in Vienna, others say in Brazil—British Foreign Minister George Brown had apparently enjoyed his wine. When he heard the orchestra strike up a tune, he turned to an exquisite creature in scarlet beside him and asked, "Madame, may we dance?"

The exquisite creature in scarlet is said to have replied in perfect English, "No, Mr. Brown, for three reasons. First, this is a reception, not a ball. Second, even were this a ball, this would still be a state anthem and not a waltz. And third, were this a ball and not a reception and were that a waltz and not a state anthem, I would still be the Cardinal Archbishop."

How appearances deceive.

The only thing more satisfying than a faux pas is a good recovery. Actor David Niven was once at a fancy ball, standing at the bottom of a grand staircase, talking to a man he had just met. Two women at the top of the stairs began to descend.

Niven said to the man, "That's the ugliest woman I've ever seen."

The man stiffened. "That's my wife."

"I meant the other one."

"That's my daughter."

Niven looked the man calmly in the eye and said, "I didn't say it!"

Maybe I'll try that next time. ▲

Our pastor was winding down. In the back of the church the fellowship committee stood to go to the church hall and prepare snacks for the congregation. Seeing them get up, Pastor Michel singled them out for praise.

"Before they all slip out," he urged, "let's give these ladies a big hand in the rear."

— GORDON MOORE

Recently my wife was behind a car with three bumper stickers: "Don't be fooled by genetically engineered food—demand labels and safety testing for food"; "Eat for the health of it"; and "Support organic farmers."

The car was in front of her at a McDonald's drive-through.

— BROOKS MONK

"Frankly, I'm quite disappointed with the technology."

Low on gas while on a vacation trip to Las Vegas, I pulled my van into a service station. As I was turning in, I spied lying on the ground a gas cap that looked like it might replace my missing one. I hurriedly parked by the pump, jumped out of the van, ran over and picked up the cap. I was pleasantly surprised to find that it screwed easily onto my tank.

A perfect fit, I thought. And then I noticed the keyhole in the top of the cap.

— BOB SJOSTRAND

New to the United States, I was eager to meet people. So one day I struck up a conversation with the only other woman in the gym. Pointing to two men playing racquetball in a nearby court, I said to her, "There's my husband." Then I added, "The thin one—not the fat one."

After a slightly uncomfortable silence she replied, "And that's my husband—the fat one."

— NITYA RAMAKRISHNAN

My new credit card arrived in the mail with a large sticker on it, giving the phone number to activate the card. I called the number and got one option: "Press One" to activate the credit card. That led me to a live person, who answered with her first name and the title "Credit Card Activator."

As I got ready to give her the necessary information, she interrupted me, asking, "How can I help you?"

— ANGELA NOLAN

sign language

On a Pittsburgh plumbing contractor's truck:

"You Don't Have to Sleep With That Drip Tonight."

— CARL C. WURST

I am full-figured, and when I dine in restaurants, I often find the chairs too small and uncomfortable. The last time I ate out, I filled in a comment card, saying that while the food and service were wonderful, the chairs did not accommodate anyone over a size 14.

Several weeks later I received a note of apology—and a coupon for a free dessert.

— PAT BALLARD

The road by my house was in bad condition after a rough winter. Every day I dodged potholes on the way to work. So I was relieved to see a construction crew working on the road one morning.

Later, on my way home, I noticed no improvement. But where the construction crew had been working stood a new, bright-yellow sign with the words "Rough Road."

— SARAH KRAYBILL LIND

A couple of hours into a visit with my mother she noticed I hadn't lit up a cigarette once. "Are you trying to kick the habit?"

"No," I replied, "I've got a cold and I don't smoke when I'm not feeling well."

"You know," she observed, "you'd probably live longer if you were sick more often."

— IAN A. HAMMEL

For our honeymoon my fiancée and I chose a fashionable hotel known for its luxurious suites. When I called to make reservations, the desk clerk inquired, "Is this for a special occasion?"

"Yes," I replied." It's our honeymoon."

"And how many adults will there be?" she asked.

— LARRY REEVES

My father and I belong to the religion of Sikhism. We both wear the traditional turban and often encounter strange comments and questions. Once, in a restaurant, a child stared with amazement at my father. She finally got the courage to ask, "Are you a genie?"

Her mother, caught off guard, turned red in the face and apologized for the remark. But my dad took no offense and decided to humor the child.

He replied, "Why, yes I am. I can grant you three wishes."

The child's mother blurted out, "Really?"

— MANVIR KALSI

Over the years, my husband and I have usually managed to decode the cute but confusing gender signs they sometimes put on restroom doors in restaurants (Buoys & Gulls, Laddies & Lassies, etc.), but every so often we get stumped. Recently my husband, Dave, wandered off in search of the men's room and found himself confronted by two marked doors. One was labeled "Bronco" and the other was designated "Cactus."

Completely baffled, he stopped a restaurant employee passing by. "Excuse me, I need to use the restroom," Dave said. Gesturing toward the doors, he asked, "Which one should I use?"

"Actually, we would prefer you to go there," the employee said, pointing to a door down the hall marked "Men." "Bronco and Cactus are private dining rooms."

— SHERRIE LEE

An author was coming to my local bookstore to discuss her novel set in Appalachia. The main character was "a strong-willed heroine fighting to survive the hardships of the times."

When I went to the reading, I was disappointed to learn the writer had cancelled her appearance. The reason? She didn't want to drive in the rain.

— DIANE MARSHALL

Our first day at a resort my wife and I decided to hit the beach. When I went back to our room to get something to drink, one of the hotel maids was making our bed. I grabbed my cooler and was on my way out when I paused and asked, "Can we drink beer on the beach?"

"Sure," she said, "but I have to finish the rest of the rooms first."

— LOUIS ALLARD

A friend of ours was puzzled with the odd messages left on his answering machine. Day after day friends and family would talk and then say, "Beep." He discovered the reason for the joke when he decided to listen to his greeting.

"Hi," it said. "I'm not in right now, so please leave a beep after the message."

— SHEEBA MATHEW

After a recent move, I made up a list of companies, agencies and services that needed to know my new address and phoned each to ask them to make the change. Everything went smoothly until I made a call to one of my frequent-flier accounts. After I explained to her what I wanted to do, the woman I reached in customer service told me, "I'm sorry; we can't do that over the phone. You will have to fill out our change-of-address form."

"How do I get one of those?" I asked.

"We'd be happy to provide you with one," she said pleasantly. "Can I have your new address so I can mail it to you?"

Bad weather had backed up all flights, and as a result our plane sat on the runway for three hours. All attempts to placate the passengers weren't working. Then the pilot came on the intercom to announce his umpteenth update: "Folks, we'll be getting permission to take off, but I have to tell you that we're 26th in line for departure."

As a collective groan filled the aircraft, a flight attendant took the mike and added, "Ladies and gentlemen, please close your window shades. We'll soon be showing our almost-inflight hit movie, *Anger Management*."

— STEVE NORTH

After booking my 90-year-old mother on a flight from Florida to Nevada, I called the airline to go over her needs. The woman representative listened patiently as I requested a wheelchair and an attendant for my mother because of her arthritis and impaired vision. I also asked for a special meal and assistance in changing planes.

My apprehension lightened a bit when the woman assured me everything would be taken care of. I thanked her profusely.

"Why, you're welcome," she replied. I was about to hang up when she cheerfully asked, "And will your mother be needing a rental car?"

— THOMAS A. CORBETT

During a beautiful spring afternoon, I was attending the Cheat River Festival in West Virginia. Just as I stopped to listen to a folk singer, a group of exhibitors, dragging out tools and sawhorses, began setting up their display booth nearby. All their shouting and hammering made it difficult to enjoy the music. The noise they made got louder and even more obnoxious and intrusive as time went on.

Finally, to everyone's relief, they completed the construction. As a finishing touch, they hung a sign on their booth. It read "Silent Auction."

— JIM TRUMAN

Timeless Humor from the 70's

One October my wife and I spent a vacation on Washington's Olympic Peninsula. We were eager to visit the rain forests near the coast, but we heard that snowslides had made some of the roads impassable. Although apprehensive about the conditions we might run into, we drove on.

Sure enough, we had gone only a short way up the Hoh Rain Forest road when we saw a sign: "Ice 10 miles."

Five miles farther on there was another: "Ice 5 miles."

The next one was: "Ice 1/2 mile." We practically crept that half mile.

Then we came to the last sign. It was outside a small grocery, and it read: "Ice 50¢."

— GIFFORD S. WALKER

There's a scar on my face from a car accident. A customer came into the gas station where I work, glanced at me and exclaimed, "My God, what happened to you?" I told him and hoped that would be the end of it. But he kept pressing me for more information.

Finally, he made his purchase and, just before walking away, said, "Hey, don't worry about it. It's not that noticeable."

— ROBERT GOEBEL

At 82 years old, my husband applied for his first passport. He was told he would need a birth certificate, but his birth had never been officially registered. When he explained his dilemma to the passport agent, the response was less than helpful.

"In lieu of a birth certificate," the agent said, "you can bring a notarized affidavit from the doctor who delivered you."

— ELGARDA ASHLIMAN

One day my wife and I came home to find a message from a friend of hers on our phone machine. She said she had applied for a job and needed a character reference—basically someone to verify she was honest and trust-

"Of course, it's nothing serious, honey... just a flooded engine."

worthy—and had given the interviewer my wife's name. Also, she said, there was a form for my wife to sign.

"But I couldn't find you," the friend concluded, "so I forged your signature."

— WILL PETERS

When I walked up to the ATM at my bank, I noticed someone had left his card in the slot. Since it was a Friday evening, I thought the Good Samaritan thing to do was try to find the card's owner so he wouldn't go the weekend without it. I looked up the

person's name in the phone book and gave him a call.

"I found your ATM card," I told the man who answered.

He then asked hopefully, "You didn't happen to find my sunglasses too?"

— G. DAVID PETERSON

My friend Ann and I were eating at a Chinese restaurant. When an elderly waiter set chopsticks at our places, Ann made a point of reaching into her purse and pulling out her own pair. "As an environmentalist," she declared, "I do not approve of destroying bamboo forests for throwaway utensils."

The waiter inspected her chopsticks. "Very beautiful," he said politely. "Ivory."

— ERICA CHRISTENSEN

I played for a semipro baseball team. At every game we sold raffle tickets. Half the money paid the team's expenses and the other half went to the winning ticket holder. One day they held the drawing just as I was stepping up to bat.

The home plate umpire pulled the winning ticket, and then turned to me. "Could you read me the number?" he asked. "My vision's not too good."

— EDWARD NANDOR

A co-worker of mine was admiring a pair of delicate white earrings that Sue, another co-worker, was wearing. "Those are lovely," the woman said. "Are they ivory?"

Appalled at the suggestion, Sue replied, "I would never consider wearing anything made by killing innocent elephants. These are bone."

— HEATHER WILLIAMS

Thanks to my daughter, I have become thoroughly sensitized to environmental issues. Recently I purchased a greeting card, and when the cashier started to place it in a plastic bag, I remembered my daughter's repeated warnings and immediately declined its use.

"I'll be mailing that quickly," I told the clerk. "You can take the bag back."

"Okay. Have a good day," she said with a smile. Then I watched as she scrunched the bag into a ball and tossed it into the garbage.

— ARLENE KUSHER

My three sisters and I have weight problems and are always sharing diet tips. One day my oldest sister was showing us a low-fat cookbook and pointed out a chicken dish she had tried the night before. Reading the ingredients, I commented, "It looks like it would taste really bland."

"It did," she replied, "until I added cheese and sour cream."

— PATRICIA LAANSMA

While away on business, a colleague and I decided to catch a movie. As we approached the theater, we read the marquee. It bore the name of the feature film followed by the numbers "7," "5," and "9." Assuming these were the show times, we were somewhat perplexed by their order.

I went inside to ask about it. "Our next show is at eight o'clock," the woman in the box office announced.

"Eight o'clock?" I said, surprised. "But the marquee says seven, five and nine."

"Right," she agreed. "That's 7:59. We lost our number eight."

—DIANE CLANCY

After shopping for weeks, I finally found the car of my dreams. It was only two years old and in beautiful condition. The salesman asked if I would like to take it for a test drive. We had traveled no more than two miles when the car broke down. The salesman called for a tow truck.

When it arrived, we climbed into the front seat. While the driver was hooking up the car, the salesman turned to me with a smile and said, "Well, now, what is it going to take to put you behind the wheel of that beauty today?"

— JAN BAIRD

Dad is from the old school, where you keep your money under the mattress—only he kept his in the underwear drawer. One day I bought my dad an unusual personal safe—a can of spray paint with a false bottom—so he could keep his money in the workshop. Later I asked Mom if he was using it.

"Oh, yes," she replied, "he put his money in it the same day."

"No burglar would think to look on the work shelf!" I gloated.

"They won't have to," my mom replied. "He keeps the paint can in his underwear drawer."

— JUDEE MULVEY

My very pregnant sister-in-law had just returned from another disappointingly uneventful trip to the hospital when she went into true labor. With no time to make it back to the hospital, my brother called 911. In shock, he followed the telephone instructions of the operator to deliver the baby. He even tied the umbilical cord with a string.

The Emergency Medical Service team arrived shortly thereafter, only to see an exhausted mother holding her beautiful daughter—with a tennis shoe dangling on the cord between them!

— SABRINA FORD

There was a notice that appeared in my mailbox. It told me I was required to go to court as a witness against someone whose name I did not recognize. Calling for more information, I found out my notice was for reporting a driver who had illegally passed my stopped school bus—ten years ago when I had been driving a bus part time.

The appearance date was the same time as my night class, so I called to see if my court appearance could be rescheduled. Two days later someone returned my call.

"We cannot push the date back," they said. The reason? "The accused is entitled to a speedy trial."

— JANIS SMITH

When my wife and I showed up at a very popular restaurant, it was crowded. She went up to the hostess and asked, "Will it be long?"

The hostess, ignoring her, kept writing in her book. My wife again asked, "How much of a wait?"

The woman looked up. "About ten minutes."

A short time later we heard an announcement over the loudspeaker: "Willette B. Long, your table is ready."

— HERBERT R. KARP

"He just sits there all day, waiting to chase the e-mail man."

Hoping to learn more about financial matters, I visited a bookstore and grabbed a copy of *Personal Finance for Dummies*. A glance at the book's price sticker, however, revealed just how little credit the store's management gave people like me. It read:

"Publisher's list price: $16.95; our discount price: $17.99."

— NAOMI WELSH

Although I am of Chinese descent, I never really learned to speak Chinese. One evening, I came home boasting about a wonderful meal I'd had in Chinatown. Unfortunately, I couldn't remember the name of the restaurant, but was able to write the Chinese character that was on the door and show it to my mother.

"Do you know what it says?" Mom asked with a smile. "It says 'Pull.'"

— BARBARA MAO

Early one Saturday morning, the flashing lights of a police car appeared in my rearview mirror. After checking my license and registration, the officer asked, "Do you know why I pulled you over?"

"No," I responded.

"One of your taillights is out," he said. "I'm going to have to issue a warning."

"Whew," I said, without thinking. "I thought it was because my inspection had expired."

— ANDREA SHIPPER

Driving through New Jersey on Interstate 80 en route from Pennsylvania to New York, I came upon a group of cars that were abnormally traveling exactly at the 55 m.p.h. speed limit. In the middle of the group was a state police cruiser that everyone was reluctant to pass.

After several minutes the officer's voice rang out over his roof-mounted loudspeaker. "For heaven's sake, move!" he commanded. "I am a *Pennsylvania* state trooper."

— AMITABH V. W. MITTAL

I was sitting behind an enthusiastic mom at my son's Little League game. Her boy was pitching for the opposing team and she cheered as he threw wild pitch after wild pitch. The poor kid walked every batter. It was only the first inning and the score was 14–0. Then one batter finally smacked the ball.

"Oh no," the mom wailed. "There goes his no-hitter."

— NORMALU COOPER

I called my local utility for help with a minor malfunction in my outdoor gas grill. Their automated phone system put me on hold for over 20 minutes.

As I waited, I was grateful my problem wasn't worse—especially when I heard a pre-recorded message repeatedly advise, "If you smell gas, stay on the line."

— HERB GITLIN

While sitting in the emergency room of our local hospital, I watched as a panicked father-to-be rushed in and told a nurse that his wife had called him at work about 15 minutes earlier. She was going into labor prematurely, he said, and would be arriving at the hospital any minute now.

"How far along is your wife?" the nurse asked calmly.

Glancing down nervously at his watch, the man replied, "Right about now, she should be on Washington Street."

— KAREN MORRIS

When I was in the sixth grade, I lost the sight in my right eye during a playground mishap. Fortunately, the accident had little effect on my life. When I reached my 40s, however, I needed to get glasses.

At the optometrist's office, the doctor's young assistant pointed to an eye chart. "Cover your right eye and read line three," she said.

"I'm blind in my right eye," I told her. "It's a glass eye."

"Okay," she responded. "In that case, cover your left eye."

— BILL SLACK

My flight was delayed in Houston. Since the gate was needed for another flight, our aircraft was backed away from the terminal, and we were directed to a new gate. We all found the new gate, only to discover a third gate had been designated for our plane.

Finally, everyone got on board the right plane, and the flight attendant announced: "We apologize for the gate change. This flight is going to Washington, D.C. If your destination is not Washington, D.C., you should deplane at this time."

A moment later a red-faced pilot emerged from the cockpit, carrying his bags. "Sorry," he said, "wrong plane."

— ROY SCHMIDT

While walking through a parking lot, I tripped and fell flat on my face. As I was lying there, a woman stopped and called out,

"Are you hurt?"

"No. I'm fine,"

I said, touched by her concern.

"Oh, good,"

she continued.

"So will you be vacating your parking spot?"

HARIETT WELLING

Frustrated at always being corrected by her husband, my aunt decided the next time it happened she would have a comeback. That moment finally arrived, and she was ready. "You know," she challenged, "even a broken clock is right once a day."

My uncle looked at her and replied, "Twice."

— CINDY COOKSEY

One evening my former boss was getting out of the shower when his wife called, asking him to turn off an iron she had mistakenly left on in the basement before she left for the weekend. Thinking no one would see him, he ran down the stairs into the dark basement without even a towel on.

As he flipped on the light switch, though, he was shocked to hear dozens of people yell "Surprise!" His wife had orchestrated the secret party to celebrate his 40th birthday.

— JENNIFER JASEK

I began viola lessons as an adult. When I started, I called my mother to share my excitement. "Wonderful!" she exclaimed. "But I've never heard a viola. What does it sound like?"

Unable to give an apt description, I phoned my mother a few days later, after buying a CD of viola music. "Listen to this," I said as I placed the telephone receiver next to the stereo speaker, and turned the music on for about 30 seconds of a Schubert sonata. Then I picked up the receiver. "Well, Mom, what do you think?"

A moment of silence followed, then a question: "I'm speechless, Debbie. How many lessons have you had?"

— DEBORAH HAYS

My husband and I stopped at a sporting-goods store famous for its huge once-a-year sale. Seven months pregnant at the time, I caught the attention of a reporter covering the event. When he asked me what we were looking for, I patted my stomach and said we needed a new tent for our growing family.

Then the reporter turned to my distracted husband: "Is this your first?"

"Uh, no," he replied. "We have another tent at home."

— MARY ANN HAEFNER

I frequently receive calls from pollsters asking me to participate in telephone surveys. One woman began with a barrage of questions.

"Wait a moment," I interrupted. "Who are you and whom do you represent?"

She told me and immediately continued asking questions.

"What's the purpose of this survey?" I asked.

"Sir," she replied irritably, "I don't have time to answer your questions." Then she hung up.

— HENRY SHEPPARD

A steak fanatic, my father always picks out cuts that include a bone because he loves to nibble on it. One night Father and I were finishing our dinners at a steakhouse, and I could tell he wanted to start gnawing on the bone. But he couldn't bear to do so in public.

"Excuse me," he said, calling the waitress over, "would you please wrap this bone up for my dog?" Father has never owned a dog in his life, but the white lie seemed a tactful solution to his dilemma.

A few minutes later the waitress returned to our table. "Here's your bone, sir," she said, handing over a large package. "And while I was in the kitchen, I grabbed a few more out of the scrap bucket."

— KAREN FREEMAN

"There's nothing wrong with your eyesight. You're wearing your seat belt too high!"

One afternoon, while touring the Canyonlands of southern Utah, my husband and I pulled into the only hotel in a small town. While signing the register, we asked the young woman behind the desk if our room was air-conditioned.

When she shook her head no, we hesitated, wondering if we should push on to the next town. Sensing our doubt, she brightened as she came up with a solution. "Just turn on the heater," she suggested. "Our customers tell us all that comes out is cold air anyway."

— MARY J. PAYERLE

Flying above northern Arizona in an airliner, I listened as the captain described points of interest over the loudspeaker. He indicated a giant crater on the ground that was formed by a meteorite thousands of years ago.

A young woman in the row ahead of me looked out the window. She then turned to her companion and exclaimed, "Gee, if it had landed a little farther to the right, it would have hit the highway!"

— WALLY COX

The Know-It-All

▶ BY A. J. JACOBS

I had toyed with the notion of reading the Encyclopaedia Britannica for a few years. I figured it would be a crash course in everything—something I desperately needed. At age 35, about the only thing I could remember from four years of college was that a burrito left on the dorm-room floor is still edible after eight days, as long as you chew really hard. If I read the whole encyclopedia, from A to Z, I might very well become the smartest man in America. My father, a New York lawyer, had actually tried reading the Britannica years ago. He made it to the mid-B's—I think it was right around Borneo—before he bailed out, blaming his busy schedule.

I called him with the good news. "I'm going to finish what you started," I told him. "I'm going to read the Encyclopaedia Britannica."

There was a pause. "I hear the P's are excellent," he said.

I could tell my wife, Julie, was just as skeptical. "I don't know, honey," she said. "What about eating dinner at every restaurant in New York? You could start with the restaurants with A names and work your way to the Z's." Valiant try. But I was dead serious about Operation Encyclopedia.

I did some research. The Britannica is still the gold standard, the Tiffany's of encyclopedias. Founded in 1768, it's the longest continuously published reference book in history. Over the years contributors have included Einstein, Freud and Harry Houdini. Its current roster includes dozens of academics with Nobels, Pulitzers and other awards with ceremonies that don't feature commentary from Melissa Rivers. During the dot-com craze the Britannica passed through hard times, and it has

phased out its door-to-door salesmen. But it keeps chugging.

Yes, there's the Internet. I suppose I could try reading Google from A to Z. But the Internet's hardly what you would call trustworthy, and besides, I prefer books. I don't even want the newfangled CD-ROM for $49.95 or the Britannica's monthly online service. I'll take the leatherette volumes for $1,400—not cheap, but certainly less expensive than grad school.

A couple of days after placing my order, three giant boxes arrive. I rip them open and find a handsome set of books—sleek and black, with gold embossing on the spine. Seeing them in three dimensions not only causes Julie to panic that they'll eat up all our apartment's shelf space, it also drives home the magnitude of my quest. I am looking at 33,000 pages, 65,000 articles, 24,000 illustrations. I have 32 volumes,

116

44 million words. 33,000 pages.
One obsessed guy.

each weighing 4 pounds. Total word count: 44 million.

I pile all the volumes on the floor in one big stack. It measures four-foot-six—practically a Danny DeVito of knowledge. I look at it again. Is this really the best use of my time? Maybe I should try something that's a little easier, like buying a new bathing suit.

I plunk the first volume on my lap. It feels weighty. It feels good. I crack it open. And then I start to read.

A-ak. That's the very first word, followed by this write-up: "Ancient East Asian music. See gagaku."

What a tease this crafty old Britannica is! Now I have a dilemma. Should I flip ahead to Volume 5 and find out what's up with gagaku, or should I stick with the plan and move on to the second word? I decide to stay. Why ruin the suspense? If anyone brings up a-ak in conversation, I'll just bluff. "I love gagaku!" I'll say. Or, "Did you hear that Madonna's recording an a-ak track on her next CD?"

A cappella. A lovely surprise. I know this one. An ex-girlfriend of mine belonged to an a cappella group in college. They sang songs from Def Leppard and called it Rockapella. One for two. Not bad.

Aachen. The next few entries destroy my average. I don't recognize the name of a famous Chinese general or a Buddhist compendium. And I've never heard of Aachen, the German city that's home to Schwertbad-Quelle, the hottest sulfur spring in the country. Oh, well. I try to memorize the information. There can be no discriminating here, not even against obscure Teutonic landmarks.

Aaron. Ah, the brother of Moses. Seems Mom didn't talk about him too much. "Oh, Aaron? He's okay. Still finding his way. But back to Moses: Did you hear about the Red Sea?" This is good

stuff. I'm Jewish, but I never got any religious training, though I do have a light lunch on Yom Kippur. So the Britannica will be my savior.

Abbott, Bud, and Costello, Lou. After a bunch of Persian rulers named Abbas, I get to these familiar faces. But any sense of relief fades when I read about their sketchy past. Their partnership began when Costello's regular straight man fell ill during a gig at the Empire Theater in New York. So Abbott—working in the box office—substituted. It went so well, he became Costello's permanent partner.

This is not a heart-warming story; it's a cautionary tale. I'm never calling in sick again. I don't want to come back after the 24-hour flu and find out that Robbie from the mail room is now a senior editor. It's a tough world.

Addled Brain Syndrome. Okay, I made this one up. But I'm definitely suffering from something. As I vacuum up facts, I find I'm so overwhelmed I have to take breaks. Walk it off, as my gym teachers used to say. You only sprained that brain; it's not a fracture. Walk it off, son.

Still, the encyclopedia is perfect for someone like me who has the attention span of a gnat on amphetamines. Bored with Abilene, Texas? Here comes abolitionism. Tired of that? The Abominable Snowman's lurking right around the corner (by the way, the mythical Snowman's footprints are probably produced by running bears).

The changes are so abrupt and relentless, you can't help but get mental whiplash. You go from tiny to cosmic, from ancient to modern. There's no segue. Just a little white space and boom! Another fact. But I forge on.

Alcott, Bronson. The father of novelist Louisa May Alcott was famous in his own right. A radical reformer, he opened several schools that had a particularly unusual discipline system: Teachers received punishment from the offending pupils. It was supposed to instill shame in the kids' minds. This is brilliant. I have a long list of teachers I wish I could have disciplined, among them my fourth-grade instructor, who forced us to have a sugar-free bake sale, which earned a humiliating $1.53.

Alger, Horatio. I knew he was the 19th-century author of famous rags-to-riches novels. I didn't know he began writing after being kicked out of a Massachusetts church for allegations of sexual misconduct with boys. The Britannica can be a gossip rag.

Antarctica. One night, when Julie and I go to her friends' house for dinner, I'm prepared to dazzle with all of my newfound knowledge. We arrive at Shannon and David's, exchange kisses and "Great to see you's." Then Julie mentions she's feeling cold.

"Not quite as cold as Antarctica's Vostok Station, which reached a record 128 below zero," I reply.

We sit down and Shannon tells us about an upcoming vacation to St. Barth's. "I can't wait to get some sun," she says. "Look how white I am."

"Albinism affects one in 20,000 Americans," I say.

Shannon doesn't know quite how to respond. So Julie rescues me by spilling my secret. "A. J.'s decided to read the encyclopedia," she says.

"Wow. That's some light reading," replies David. Pause. So much for social success.

I am constantly being told how absurd this all is. My aunt Marti from Berkeley confronted me in a phone call the other day. "Why are you reading the encyclopedia?" she asked.

"I'm trying to become the smartest man in the world," I replied.

"How are you defining intelligence? The amount of information you have?"

"Yup."

"That's not very intelligent."

"Well," I replied, "I haven't gotten to the letter I." ▲

A. J. Jacobs, a senior editor at Esquire, *did get to the letter "I"—and every other letter. He finished reading the Encyclopaedia Britannica one year and 55 days after he started. He was accepted by Mensa and appeared on "Who Wants to Be a Millionaire," winning $1,000 after narrowly missing $32,000 when he couldn't define erythrocyte, which means red blood cell ("I'll never forget that word for as long as I live," he says).*

It's easy to get a reputation for wisdom. It's only necessary to live long, speak little and do less.

— P.D. JAMES, A Certain Justice (Knopf)

You can't have everything. Where would you put it?

— STEVEN WRIGHT

The one thing that unites all human beings, regardless of age, gender, religion or ethnic background, is that we all believe we are above-average drivers.

— DAVE BARRY, Dave Barry Turns 50 (Crown)

I've come to learn that the best time to debate family members is when they have food in their mouths.

— KENNETH COLE, Footnotes (Simon & Schuster)

When you don't know what you're talking about, it's hard to know when you're finished.

— TOMMY SMOTHERS

Graduation speeches were invented largely in the belief that college students should never be released into the world until they have been properly sedated.

— GARRY TRUDEAU

They say you only go around once, but with a muscle car you can go around two or three times.

— TIM ALLEN on "Home Improvement"

Before you criticize someone, you should walk a mile in their shoes. That way, when you criticize them, you're a mile away and you have their shoes.

— Quoted in The Sisterhood of the Traveling Pants by Ann Brashares (Delacorte Press)

After his wife died, the uncle of one of my friends decided to plan ahead and order a gravesite marker for himself. A week or so later he came home to find a message on his answering machine. It was from a young woman at the company where he'd placed his order.

"I don't know if it's good news or bad," she said, "but your headstone is ready."

— OLIVIA VAZ

On a recent vacation at a resort with my in-laws, we planned to spend an afternoon at the pool with our kids. We wanted to bring our own drinks, but were unsure of the hotel's policy.

My brother-in-law called the front desk, and assuming everyone was familiar with the brand of ice chest he had, asked if it was all right if he brought a Playmate to the pool.

After a pause the clerk asked, "Does she have her own towel?"

— TINA M. DIGIOVANNA

My wife asked me to help one of our neighbors, a young mother whose sailor husband was at sea. Her car had to have something called a freeze plug replaced—a job that took two days. Then I discovered the battery was dead and the starter was shot, so I fixed those too.

Days later I proudly handed the woman her keys saying, "Now your car is good for many more miles."

"Thanks," she said. "All I care is that it runs long enough to make it to the dealer. I'm trading it in tomorrow."

— GEORGE T. MARSHALL

We purchased an old home in northern New York State from two elderly sisters. Winter was fast approaching, and I was concerned about the house's lack of insulation. "If they could live here all those years, so can we!" my husband confidently declared.

One November night the temperature plunged to below zero, and we woke up to find interior walls covered with frost. My husband called the sisters to ask how they had kept the house warm. After a brief conversation, he hung up. "For the past 30 years," he muttered, "they've gone to Florida for the winter."

— LINDA DOBSON

When I was a high school senior, I saw an inspirational ad on TV about becoming a teacher. I called the number shown: 800-45TEACH. After a woman answered, I babbled on about how I thought I had found my life's calling and could she send me information. She asked what number I was calling.

After I told her, there was a long pause. Then she said, "You misspelled teach."

— AMY PORTER

I was in line at the souvenir booth of a Renaissance fair when a man asked the clerk, "Do you sell sunglasses?" "Alas, yeoman," she answered in her best fake old English, "colored bits of glass suspended before the eyes were not invented until after the Renaissance, so those are not goods we purvey."

As he began to turn away, ye olde Renaissance clerk added, "But we do carry baseball caps with our logo on them."

— KATHY SHEEHAN

sign language

At a coffee bar in Lansing, Mich., a sign on the staff's tip container said **"Thanks a Latte."**

My sister Susan and her husband, Frank, were entertaining for the first time since the birth of their baby. Everything ran smoothly until one of Frank's buddies arrived with his new girlfriend—a woman Susan did not particularly care for. Susan beckoned her husband upstairs with the excuse that they had to check on the baby. In the privacy of the nursery, she spoke freely of her disdain for the new guest.

When they went downstairs to rejoin the party, they were greeted with an awkward silence — except for the occasional murmurings of the sleeping baby that came from the infant monitor sitting on the table.

— JANE HAWORTH

Before our daughter went off to college, our family vacationed in Colorado, flying to Denver and renting a car. We visited the Royal Gorge Bridge, which is more than 1,000 feet above the Arkansas River.

Walking out onto the bridge, I noticed it swayed in the wind. Then a car went past us, and the wood-plank roadway moved beneath my feet. "I don't think I want to drive the car across this bridge," I finally said.

"What are you worried about?" our college-bound daughter replied. "It's a rental."

— ROBERT COOLEY

I was having a drink at a local restaurant with my friend Justin when he spotted an attractive woman sitting at the bar. After an hour of gathering his courage, he approached her and asked, "Would you mind if I chatted with you for a while?"

She responded by yelling at the top of her lungs, "No, I won't come over to your place tonight!"

With everyone in the restaurant staring, Justin crept back to our table, puzzled and humiliated.

A few minutes later, the woman walked over to us and apologized.

"I'm sorry if I embarrassed you," she said, "but I'm a graduate student in psychology and I'm studying human reaction to embarrassing situations."

At the top of his lungs Justin responded, "What do you mean, two hundred dollars?"

— J. SMODISH

There was a fire in my neighborhood, and I arrived just in time to see firefighters carry one of their men out of the burning house and lower him to a sitting position on the lawn. Visibly shaken, he took out a cigarette, lit it and sat there puffing on it to calm his nerves.

"What happened to that poor guy?" I asked a bystander.

"Smoke inhalation," he replied.

— TIM TUINSTRA

121

My husband and I were touring our friends' new home. Mr. and Mrs. Henry Curtis had put special touches everywhere. In the bathroom my husband leaned over to me and whispered, "They even have monogrammed faucets."

— PAT GNAU

One day I noticed that my sister wasn't wearing a watch. When I asked her about it, she replied, "I don't need a watch. At home there's a clock in every room, and in the car there's a clock on the dashboard."

Knowing my sister's an avid shopper, I inquired, "Well, how do you tell time when you're shopping?"

"That's easy," she replied. "I buy something else, and look at the time printed on the sales receipt."

— MARTITA MCGOWAN

I was in line at a restaurant. In front of me was a mother with her college-age son and his girlfriend. It was the middle of the dinner rush, and many customers were restless at the long wait, but the young couple, holding hands and kissing, were oblivious to everything around them. Although clearly not approving, the mother was silent, until one

"'On Dasher, on Dancer, on Prancer and Vixen. On Comet, on Cupid, on Donner and Blitzen...' Wait—this can't be right."

prolonged kiss when the young man had his face and hands buried in his girlfriend's long, curly locks.

"Do you have to do that here?" the embarrassed mother asked.

"I'm not doing anything, Mom," came her son's muffled voice. "My earring's caught in her hair."

— KATHY GASTON

When our dryer broke, my husband set to work. He found the problem quickly and, since he needed to replace the belt, decided to repair a cracked knob and broken hinge too. Upon arrival at the Sears parts counter,

he said he needed a belt, knob, hinge and a crescent-shaped wire he'd found inside the dryer. He didn't know where it belonged, but he confidently assured the clerk that he could figure it out once he got into the job.

"I have the other parts," the clerk said, "but for the wire you have to go to Lingerie. This is an underwire from your wife's bra."

— BARBARA A. YEAGER

When I arrived at school for my daughter's parent-teacher conference, the teacher seemed a bit flustered, especially when she started telling me that my little girl didn't always pay attention in class and was sometimes a little flighty.

"For example, she'll do the wrong page in the workbook," the teacher explained, "and I've even found her sitting at the wrong desk."

"I don't understand," I replied defensively. "Where could she have gotten that?"

The teacher went on to reassure me that my daughter was still doing fine in school and was sweet and likable. Finally, after a pause, she added, "By the way, Mrs. Gulbrandsen, our appointment was tomorrow."

— J. GULBRANDSEN

Fresh from a visit to the dentist, I decided to stop at my bank. Barely able to enunciate, I told the teller, "I'm sorry about not speaking more clearly. I've just had novocaine."

"You should have used the drive-through," she said.

"Why?"

"Everyone who goes through sounds like that," she explained.

— SUSAN ANDERSON

Dispatching her ten-year-old son to pick up a pizza, my sister handed him money and a two-dollar coupon. Later he came home with the pizza, and the coupon.

When asked to explain, he replied, "Mom, I had enough money. I didn't need the coupon."

— MARGARET E. METZ

I have a cousin who was on a plane that had taken off and was approaching cruising altitude, when one of the flight attendants came on the public-address system. She announced that she was sorry, but the plane's restroom was out of order. The flight attendant went on to apologize to the passengers for any inconvenience.

But then she finished cheerily with: "So, as compensation, free drinks will be served."

— MANJIRI V. OAK

Early in our romance, my fiancé and I were strolling on a beach. He stopped, drew a heart in the sand and inscribed our initials inside the heart. I was thoroughly charmed, and took a photo of his artwork. Later we used that same picture on our wedding invitations.

Seeing the photo, Emily, the preteen daughter of a friend, exclaimed, "Wow! How did you ever find one with your initials on it?"

— CHRISTY G. SMITH

For a late snack, my sisters and I stopped at a diner. Walking in, we smelled cooking gas. When the waitress came to seat us, we urged her to tell someone so they could find the leak. She thanked us, saying she'd look into it right away.

Then she asked us in her most pleasant waitress voice, "Will that be smoking or nonsmoking?"

— SHARON SWEENEY

My mother had just finished taking a CPR class at a local college when she and I were in the mall and saw a big crowd gathered around a still body. Suddenly my mother took off running at a speed I didn't know she could muster. "Everyone back," she yelled. "I know CPR!"

Just as she threw herself next to the body and was about to begin the procedure, a pair of strong hands pulled her to her feet.

"Ma'am," barked a police officer standing beside her, "we are trying to arrest this man."

— TALEA TORRES

After an unusually heated argument with what he considered his overbearing parents, my brother announced that the minute he graduated from high school he intended to join the Navy. No more was said until a few days later, when he walked proudly into the house and declared that he was to report for duty the following morning.

"Why?" my mother asked tearfully.

"Because," he stormed, "I am sick and tired of taking orders!"

— MRS. A. V. HEIGHES

Because our new refrigerator was taller than our old one, I told my wife I'd have to cut away part of an overhanging cabinet to make it fit. Not wanting to mess it up, I called a local radio home-fix-it program for advice. I was in the middle of getting the instructions when my wife burst into the room. "You won't believe this," she said, "but there's a guy on the radio with the same problem!"

— GARY BRINGHURST

I sold an item through eBay but it got lost in the mail. So I stopped by my local post office and asked them to track it down.

"It's not that simple," the clerk scolded. "You have to fill out a mail-loss form before we can initiate a search."

"Okay," I said. "I'll take one."

He rummaged under his counter, then went to some other clerks who did the same—only to return and confess, "You'll have to come back later. We can't find the forms."

— DOREEN L. ROGERS

As a professor at the Air Force Institute of Technology, I taught a series of popular courses on software engineering. The program was highly competitive and difficult to get into, but one prospective student made our decision whether to accept him quite simple.

When asked to fax over his college transcript, the student told me, "Well, I would, but it's the only copy that I've got."

— JIM SKINNER

My husband, who is an auto mechanic, received a repair order that read: "Check for clunking noise when going around corners." Taking the car out for a test drive, he made a right turn, and a moment later heard a clunk. He then made a left turn and again heard a clunk. Back at the shop, he opened the trunk and soon discovered the problem.

Promptly he returned the repair order to the service manager with this notation: "Remove bowling ball from trunk."

— KOREY A. TUTTLE

Which windshield wiper blade always quits first? That's right—the driver's side. This happened to me one day while driving home in the middle of a blinding storm.

Unable to see, I pulled over and tried to figure out a quick fix. I found it in a yellow cotton work glove that was lying on the floor. I wedged the cloth hand under the wiper arm.

It did a great job keeping my windshield clear. Not only that— you'd be surprised at how many people waved back.

— TOM BISCHEL

Aging

Gracelessly

▶———————————————

Face it—you're not getting better, you're getting older,
and the sooner you come to terms with that, or incorporate
Botox injections into your budget, the better.

"That's strange. This suit wasn't a thong last year."

Our dear friend Trudy attended my husband's birthday party. Though she's been through a lot—including a double mastectomy and reconstructive surgery—Trudy was the life of the party as usual. Hugging her goodbye, I couldn't help noticing she had nothing on under her blouse.

"Trudy, you're not wearing a bra!" I whispered.

With a twinkle in her eye she replied, "I may be 70, honey, but they're only 15."

— JUDITH L. KROL

The plane was only half-full. When an attractive young woman asked if the seat next to mine was free, my male ego soared. Soon we were chatting pleasantly, and she told me it was her first flight.

"Mom said to sit next to someone I thought I could trust," she confessed nervously, "and you look just like my dad."

— ROY RAGSDALE

My brother and his wife started their family in their early 40s. One day my sister-in-law and I were commiserating about the effects of time marching on.

"I just got my first pair of glasses," she said, and paused as her two preschool boys thundered past her. "Now, if only my hearing would go."

— IRENE PALM

Rock concerts are a little different now than when I was younger. Recently, I went to a concert with some friends. As the band started to play a ballad, we instinctively raised our cigarette lighters, like all good rock fans I grew up with. But looking around me, I noticed that times had indeed changed.

The mostly under-25 crowd was swaying to the upraised glow of their cell phones.

— ANGELA STIMA

As my 40th birthday approached, my husband, who is a year younger, was doing his best to rub it in. Trying to figure out what all the teasing was about, our young daughter asked me, "How old is Daddy?"

"Thirty-nine," I told her.

"And how old will you be?"

"Forty," I said sadly.

"But Mommy," she exclaimed, "you're winning!"

— KELLEY MARTINEZ

I was hospitalized with an awful sinus infection that caused the entire left side of my face to swell. On the third day, the nurse led me to believe that I was finally recovering when she announced excitedly, "Look, your wrinkles are coming back!"

— FRANCES M. KRUEGER

"Keep making that face and it's going to freeze that way," was what my mother used to say to us as kids. I knew times had changed after she noticed my sister scowling recently and warned, "Keep making that face and you're going to need Botox."

— MARY BOUCK

After working for months to get in shape, my 42-year-old husband and I hiked to the bottom of the Grand Canyon. At the end of two grueling days, we made it back to the canyon's rim. To celebrate, we each bought an "I hiked the canyon" T-shirt.

About a month later, while my husband was wearing his shirt, a young man approached him. "Did you really hike the canyon?" he asked.

My husband beamed with pride and answered, "Sure did!"

"No kidding!" the fellow said. "What year?"

— CAROL LATKIEWICZ

127

I was having trouble with the idea of turning thirty and was oversensitive to any signs of advancing age. When I found a prominent gray hair in my bangs, I pointed to my forehead.

"Have you seen this?" I indignantly asked my husband.

"What?" he asked. "The wrinkles?"

— WENDY LILLIE

My 20th high-school class reunion was held at a hotel on the same night that another school's tenth-year reunion was taking place. While my friends and I were in the rest room talking, some unfamiliar women entered.

After their stares became uncomfortable, we turned toward them. One of the women said, "Don't mind us. We just wanted to see how we'd look in another ten years."

— SONDRA OLIVIERI

The summer after college graduation, I was living at home, fishing in the daytime, spending nights with my friends—generally just hanging out. One afternoon my grandfather, who never went to college, stopped by.

Concerned with how I was spending my time, he asked about my future plans. I told him I was in no hurry to tie myself down to a career.

"Well," he replied, "you better start thinking about it. You'll be thirty before you know it."

"But I'm closer to twenty than to thirty," I protested. "I won't be thirty for eight more years."

"I see," he said, smiling. "And when will you be twenty again?"

— MARSHALL K. ESSIG

"We all do a lot of stupid things when we're young. So, what'll it take to remove that 'Butterball' tattoo?"

My sister, Sharon, and I are close, and that allows us to be honest with each other. As I fidgeted in front of the mirror one evening before a date, I remarked, "I'm fat."

"No, you're not," she scolded.

"My hair is awful."

"It's lovely."

"I've never looked worse," I whined.

"Yes, you have," she replied.

— PATRICIA L. SOUZA

On my birthday I got a really funny card from a friend. It joked about how our bodies might be getting older, but our minds were still "tarp as shacks."

I wanted to thank the friend who sent the card, but I couldn't. She forgot to sign it.

— MERIS M. MACK

When a woman I know turned 99 years old, I went to her birthday party and took some photos. A few days later, I brought the whole batch of prints to her so she could choose her favorite.

"Good Lord," she said as she was flipping through them, "I look like I'm a hundred."

— HELEN B. MARROW

Out bicycling one day with my eight-year-old granddaughter, Carolyn, I got a little wistful. "In ten years," I said, "you'll want to be with your friends and you won't go walking, biking, and swimming with me like you do now."

Carolyn shrugged. "In ten years you'll be too old to do all those things anyway."

— JAMES F. AHEARN

My senior citizens' refresher driving course was almost finished, and the teacher began to drill us. "What do you do when you want to exit from a freeway?" he asked.

"Pull into the exit lane before you slow down," the class chorused.

"Good," replied the instructor. "And what do you do when you want to get off the freeway but miss your exit?"

There was a pause before a woman volunteered, "Ask the post office to forward your mail."

— KATHRYN E. MASON

I had been thinking about coloring my hair. One day while going through a magazine, I came across an ad for a hair-coloring product featuring a beautiful young model with hair a shade that I liked. Wanting a second opinion, I asked my husband,

"I do stay in shape. This is the shape I stay in."

"How do you think this color would look on a face with a few wrinkles?"

He looked at the picture, crumpled it up, straightened it out and studied it again. "Just great, hon."

— JOAN KEYSER

My grandfather has a knack for looking on the bright side of life. Even after receiving the terrible diagnosis that he had Alzheimer's, he was philosophical.

"There's one good thing that'll come from this," he told my father.

"What's that?" asked Dad.

"Now I can hide my own Easter eggs."

— CHRIS KERN

Both my fiancé and I are in our 40s. I thought it was both amusing and touching when he assumed the classic position to propose to me—down on one bended knee.

"Are you serious?" I asked, laughing.

"Of course I'm serious," he said. "I'm on my bad knee."

— DEBORAH MASSEY

My friend and I were celebrating our 40th birthday the same year. As a gag gift, I gave her a CD by the band UB40.

For my birthday, she retaliated with a CD as well. The group? U2.

— MONA TURRELL

I'm always relieved when someone delivers a eulogy and I realize I'm listening to it.

— GEORGE CARLIN

The last birthday that's any good is 23.

— ANDY ROONEY,
Years of Minutes (PublicAffairs)

Learn to enjoy your own company. You are the one person you can count on living with for the rest of your life.

— ANN RICHARDS in O: The Oprah Magazine

Age is nothing at all...unless you are a cheese.

— ACTRESS BILLIE BURKE ("Glinda, the Good Witch")

Summer is a drag because even normal people become obsessed with their bodies. A bad bathing suit can humiliate you more than anything else in life.

— CONAN O'BRIEN in Details

It's all right letting yourself go, as long as you can let yourself back.

— MICK JAGGER

Retirement is like a long vacation in Vegas. The goal is to enjoy it to the fullest, but not so fully that you run out of money.

— JONATHAN CLEMENTS in The Wall Street Journal

Wrinkles only go where the smiles have been.

— JIMMY BUFFETT,
Barefoot Children in the Rain

My mother always used to say, "The older you get, the better you get. Unless you're a banana."

— BETTY WHITE on "The Golden Girls"
— LIZZY PHAN

During the last days of my mother's life, we discussed many things. One day I raised the topic of her funeral and memorial service.

"Oh, honey," she responded, "I really don't care about the details."

Later she woke from a nap and grasped my hand, clearly wanting to share something with me. As I leaned forward, she said urgently, "Just don't bury me in plaid."

— DIANE WILSON

I was just settling into a barber's chair when I overheard the elderly man next to me say, "I'm not much for pills, but I am taking Ginkgo-Viagra. I want to remember what sex was like."

— BILL WRIGHT

Because they had no reservations at a busy restaurant, my elderly neighbor and his wife were told there would be a 45-minute wait for a table.

"Young man, we're both 90 years old," he told the maitre d'. "We may not have 45 minutes."

They were seated immediately.

— RITA KALISH

I had just moved to an address between Sunset Avenue and Sunrise Boulevard, one of Sacramento's major streets, and was explaining to a clerk where my home was located for billing purposes.

"I live between Sunrise and Sunset," I told her.

"Oh, honey," she knowingly replied, "we all do."

— LINDA MCLEAN

For over 40 years my grandfather put in long hours at his job, so I was more than a little curious about the way he filled his days since his retirement.

"How has life changed?" I asked.

A man of few words, he replied, "Well I get up in the morning with nothing to do, and I go to bed at night with it half-done."

— DENNIS LUNDBERG

I was having some chest pains, but my cardiologist assured me nothing was wrong. Then I told him I was planning a cruise to Alaska and asked if he had any suggestions for avoiding the discomfort.

"Have fun," he said with a straight face, "but don't go overboard."

— LES WANDEL

When I was a 20-something college student, I became quite friendly with my study partner, a 64-year-old man, who had returned to school to finish his degree. He confessed he had once thought more than friendship might be a possibility.

"So what changed your mind?" I asked him.

"I went to my doctor and asked if he thought a 40-year age difference between a man and woman was insurmountable. He looked at my chart and said, 'You're interested in someone who's 104?'"

— KELLY MOORE

"I wouldn't raise my hopes too high if I were you."

131

The Way I Can't See It

▶ BY MARY ROACH

This is a story of loss and denial. It begins in Colorado, on the freeway. I am looking for an exit called Drake Way. I notice I am hunched forward, squinting, barely going 40. All around me, drivers beam hate rays into my car. At precisely the moment at which it is too late to veer out of the exit lane, I note that the sign above me does not say Drake Way; it says Homer P. Gravenstein Memorial Highway. This is not good.

I go to my optometrist, who hesitates to up my prescription. She says that with a stronger distance correction, I'm going to start having trouble with what she calls "close work." Apparently she has mistaken me for one of her patients who assemble microchips or tat antimacassars by firelight. I tell her she should go ahead and change the prescription because I don't do close work.

"Do you look things up in phone books?" she asks. "Use maps?" She means, Do I read small print? She means I'm going to have trouble with small print. That I'm suddenly, without warning, old and enfeebled. Nonsense, I insist.

She shrugs and gives me a pair of stronger lenses to try. Then she hands me a bottle of lens drops, points to the label and asks me to read it. This puzzles me, for any fool can see there's nothing written on that label, just tiny lines of decorative filigree. I study it harder. It is writing. "Do not use while operating heavy machinery?" I am guessing. "Now with more real fruit? Homer P. Gravenstein Memorial Highway?" I hang my head. It's time to read the hand-

writing on the wall, which I can most assuredly do—provided it is neatly spaced and billboard-sized. I am old and my eyesight is going. She says to cheer up, that I don't have to get bifocals, "just a pair of reading glasses." In my book, reading glasses are not cause for cheer. They are cause for depression, or regression, or diphtheria, I don't know exactly, because I can no longer read what's in my book.

There was a time when I wanted to wear half-glasses, the way young children want to have crutches or braces until the day they actually need them. Today I do not want to wear reading glasses, not at all. Reluctantly, I wander over to the local drugstore.

The packaging on the reading glasses shows kindly white-haired people in business suits. The eye-

In my book, reading glasses are not cause for cheer. They are cause for depression, or regression, or diphtheria, I don't know exactly, because I can no longer read what's in my book.

glass company has gone out of their way to dress the models like functioning adults, as though people who need reading glasses can still contribute to society, when everyone knows they just sit at home tatting and reading telephone books. I can't go through with it. There has to be another way.

At home, I do an Internet search for "presbyopia." This is a mistake. The websites that turn up have names like SeniorJournal or Friendly4Seniors.com. One site informs me that "presbyopia" comes from the Greek for "elder eye." I don't appreciate this, not one bit. I'm not elderly. I'm 43. Besides, I know some Greek (spanakopita, Onassis, that word you say when the appetizer ignites), and "presbyopia" doesn't

sound like any of it. I believe someone made up this "elder eye" business, someone cruel and youthful, with four-point lettering on his business card. I look up the etymology of "presbyopia" in my dictionary, but alas, someone has replaced the words with lines of decorative filigree.

So here's what I'm going to do. I'm not getting bifocals or reading glasses. I'm going to leave my contacts under-corrected and get a pair of distance glasses to wear on top

of them, for driving. I figure I've got another five or six years before anyone calls me Elder Eyes. You could say I'm in denial. Or you could write it on a piece of paper, and by God, I'll be able to read it. ▲

I sat there waiting for my new doctor to make his way through the file that contained my very extensive medical history. After he finished all 17 pages, he looked up at me. "You look better in person than you do on paper."

— CAROLYN BLANKENSHIP

Someone recommended a new dentist to me. On my second visit the technician finished cleaning my teeth, and as I prepared to leave, I asked brightly, "And what is your name?"

"Patricia," she answered.

"I can remember that," I commented. "It's my sister's name."

Her reply: "That's what you said last time."

— IRIS CRADDOCK

I was turning 40 and decided to celebrate by fulfilling my long-time dream to go sky-diving. Before the jump, my mother and I spent the day at a festival, where we bumped into two of my cousins. They inquired about my upcoming birthday, and when I told them about my jump from 10,000 feet, I could tell they were a bit mystified.

Finally one of them remarked, "Why don't you just get your breasts done like everyone else?"

— BARBARA BIANCO

My husband was bending over to tie my three-year-old's shoes. That's when I noticed my son, Ben, staring at my husband's head.

He gently touched the slightly thinning spot of hair and said in a concerned voice, "Daddy, you have a hole in your head. Does it hurt?"

After a pause, I heard my husband's murmured reply: "Not physically."

— LAURIE GERHARDSTEIN

Just as she was celebrating her 80th birthday, our friend received a jury-duty notice. She called to remind the people at the clerk's office that she was exempt because of her age.

"You need to come in and fill out the exemption forms," they said.

"I've already done that," replied my friend. "I did it last year."

"You have to do it every year," she was told.

"Why?" came the response. "Do you think I'm going to get younger?"

— JONNIE SIVLEY

"You mean the older I get, the older *you* get?"

Checking out of the grocery store, I noticed the bag boy eyeing my two adopted children. They often draw scrutiny, since my son's a blond Russian, while my daughter has shiny black Haitian skin.

The boy continued staring as he carried our groceries to the car. Finally he asked, "Those your kids?"

"They sure are," I said with pride.

"They adopted?"

"Yes," I replied.

"I thought so," he concluded. "I figured you're too old to have kids that small."

— CYNTHIA S. MEYER

I was middle-aged when I went back to college, which meant some of my classmates were 20 years younger. Still, many became my friends.

I ran into one of them recently in a restaurant he manages, and he, my husband and I all had a pleasant chat at the cashier's counter. As we said good-bye, my young friend explained to the couple behind us, "She and I were college classmates." I noticed the confused look on their faces.

Later, I asked my husband, "What do you suppose they were thinking?"

"Either that he's had a very easy life," he replied, "or you've had a very hard one."

— BARBARA OUTLAW LEE

Fans of '60s music, my 14-year-old daughter and her best friend got front-row tickets to a Peter, Paul and Mary concert. When they returned home, my daughter said, "During the show, we looked back and saw hundreds of little lights swaying to the music. At first we thought the people were holding up cigarette lighters. Then we realized that the lights were the reflections off all the eyeglasses in the audience."

— TRACY FLACHSBARTH

Back at my high school for the tenth reunion, I met my old coach. Walking through the gym, we came upon a plaque on which I was still listed as the record holder for the longest softball throw.

Noticing my surprise, the coach said, "That record will stand forever."

I was about to make some modest disclaimer that records exist to be broken, when he added, "We stopped holding that event years ago."

— GENE HEAD

"Higher."

Recently visiting my hometown, I ran into Bev, a classmate I had not seen in years. We updated each other on careers, marriages, children, and found common ground discussing the joys and hardships of being the single parent of a teenager.

She admitted the decisions she made and advice she gave as a mother were based on hope and instinct rather than any certainty of what was best. I agreed, but said our parents probably felt the same way—and we hadn't turned out too badly.

"Yeah," she replied. "But we had real parents. Our kids just have us."

I understood exactly what she meant.

— JOHN R. GRIFFIN

As a professor at Texas A&M, I taught during the day and did research at night. I would usually take a break around nine, however, calling up the strategy game Warcraft on the Internet and playing with an online team.

One night I was paired with a veteran of the game who was a master strategist. With him at the helm, our troops crushed opponent after opponent, and after six games we were undefeated. Suddenly, my fearless leader informed me his mom wanted him to go to bed.

"How old are you?" I typed.

"Twelve," he replied. "How old are you?"

Feeling my face redden, I answered, "Eight."

— TODD SAYRE, PH.D.

My hearing had gotten worse, and ultimately I was faced with a decision: buy a pontoon boat, which I could enjoy all summer, or get a hearing aid. The choice was obvious—to me at least. However, my sisters did not approve of the boat.

One day during lunch with them, I was having trouble following the conversation. Finally I leaned over to one of my sisters and asked what had just been said.

"Giving up on the diet, Lenny?"

"You should have brought along your pontoon boat," she replied.

— BETTY JO HENDRICK

One of the English classes I taught at Deltona high school in Florida consisted of a particularly well-motivated group of juniors. Students felt free to ask questions on any subject that concerned them.

One afternoon a girl raised her hand and asked me to explain all the talk about a woman's "biological clock." After I'd finished, there was a moment of silence, and then another hand shot up.

"Mrs. Woodard," a student asked, "is your clock still ticking, or has the alarm gone off?"

— LINDA R. WOODARD

We had our ten-year-old daughter late in life, long after our two boys were born. She is the joy of my husband's life, but he is self-conscious about being an older father. He likes to jokingly tell people that by the time she graduates from high school, he'll be in a nursing home.

One day she asked, "Mom, you know how Dad always says he'll be in a home when I graduate?" I nodded, expecting some sad question about mortality.

"Can I have the car then?"

— TERRI GRAY

As an assistant high-school track coach, I recorded the results of each home meet and made copies for all the coaches. But because our track shed did not have electricity, I had to use carbon paper. A freshman team member offered to help, and I showed her how to place the carbon paper shiny side down so that the image would transfer to the sheet beneath it.

"What will they think of next?" she said in astonishment. "Pretty soon we won't need copy machines anymore."

— BARBARA LOOMIS

Korey, my granddaughter, came to spend a few weeks with me, and I decided to teach her how to sew. After I had gone through a lengthy demonstration of how to thread the machine, Korey stepped back and put her hands on her hips. "You mean you can do all that," she said in disbelief, "but you can't operate my Game Boy?"

— NELL BARON

While my friend Emily was visiting her mother, they went for a walk and bumped into an old family acquaintance. "Is this your daughter?" the woman asked. "Oh, I remember her when she was this high. How old is she now?"

Without pausing, Emily's mother said, "Twenty-four." Emily, 35, nearly fainted on the spot.

After everyone had said their good-byes, Emily asked her mother why she'd told such a whopper.

"Well," she replied, "I've been lying about my age for so long, it suddenly dawned on me that I'd have to start lying about yours too."

— ROBERT LEE WHITMIRE

I've been considering a face-lift, but it's very expensive, so I've seesawed back and forth. One day my husband and I discussed it yet again when I asked, "What if I drop dead three months later? Then what would you do?"

After a moment of reflection he offered, "I guess we'd have an open casket."

— CAROL FUGERE

During a visit with a friend at an assisted living center, I was invited to stay for lunch. As we entered the cafeteria, she leaned toward me and whispered, "They have two lines here. We call them cane and able."

— MARTHA LEONARD

At his 103rd birthday party, my grandfather was asked if he thought that he'd be around for his 104th.

"I certainly do," he replied. "Statistics show that very few people die between the ages of 103 and 104."

— HARRY P. COLEMAN

Most of my students at Choate Rosemary Hall, a boarding school in Wallingford, Conn., are more computer literate than I. So I was surprised to find one sophomore writing a term paper on an electric typewriter.

In a reminiscent mood I said, "When I was in school my type-writer wasn't even electric."

She looked at me in shock and asked, "Do you mean it was battery-operated?"

— AMY D. FOSTER

"Not those! At our age, we need all the preservatives we can get."

Facing My Midlife Crisis

▶ BY CATHERINE GILDINER

Not long ago I hit the high-water mark, the big 5-0. I was having breakfast with my rowing team at 6:30 a.m. after a tough workout on the lake. We were sprawled in our booth, in unflattering spandex uniforms that were designed for 18-year-olds, when an old friend sauntered by looking like Miss America on the runway. Naturally we grilled Nicole* about her spa, her masseuse, her skin cream. She dismissed all with a flick of her acrylic nails. "I had my eyes done," she whispered.

Impressed, I booked an appointment with Nicole's plastic surgeon. I had to wait three months for the appointment, but as Nicole said, I'd need it more by then, anyway.

On a summer's day when everything except me was in bloom, I trooped off to Toronto's tony Yorkville district, which should

have been my first financial tip-off, and there, appropriately located near an antique store, was a door that simply said Cosmetic Surgery.

I figured if I was at my worst, the good doctor might be more sympathetic and give me an extra stitch or two, so I arrived in my rowing uniform, a hideous hat and tube socks. Out of breath, I approached the desk at 9 a.m. to announce my wrinkled arrival and was told the doctor was already running an hour late. I had no idea you could be "done" at dawn.

I was greeted by four very thin assistants in taupe Armani outfits. One of them asked if I needed water, another brought Swiss water-washed decaf from a gold carafe, and one handed over a clipboard that asked my age and "how I wanted to see myself." The last one told me I had to pay $160 for the consultation before I saw the doctor.

The office was decorated entirely in taupe. In fact the taupe assistants were detectable only when they moved. As a woman next to me placed her pedicured feet upon a Ralph Lauren ottoman, she advised, "It's always best to elevate." Every one of the other clients looked about 35, yet somehow exhausted. All had deep tans, small black T-shirts and sandals with huge platform soles. Their hair was tousled, looking as though they had just stepped out of a Mercedes convertible, and highlighted with various shades of blonde. Most wore a size 4, and no one was larger than a 6. I felt like a sumo wrestler in my size 8.

Later when I told Nicole about these 30-something, fatigued and wasted women in the waiting room, she looked at me as though I was too stupid to be believed and said, "They looked strained because they're in their 50s and they've been done—stretched to

*Not her real name

138

the limit." I was facing an aesthetic dilemma. Was it better to look 35, tired and anorexic, or 50, happy and rested? To put this in some perspective: I could still look really young and spry at a seniors' yoga class.

I was soon called in to meet The Doctor. Deposited in one of a labyrinth of consulting rooms, I gazed around at walls covered in gold-filigreed mirrors.

The light was unflattering; I found wrinkles I'd never noticed, even in sunlight. Naturally I did what any woman my age would do: I pulled back my skin at the hairline to see how a face-lift would help.

Finally the doctor entered, jauntily. He was trim and wore a sports jacket in raw-silk pastel, the kind men wear to early-bird dinners in Miami. "I don't think I really need to be here—I just came for a consult," I said.

He glanced at my chart and looked intently at my face. He then uttered his first bit of insight in what turned out to be a seven-minute consult: "Mrs. Gildiner," he said, "let me assure you—you look every one of your 51 years." (For this I'm paying $23 a minute!) Trying to scrape my face off the floor, I replied with suitable understatement, "I thought I might just get my eyes done—very subtly of course."

"Look in the mirror." He held up a magnifying mirror, the kind they used on Snow White's stepmother, and asked, "What could be improved?" As I gazed, the mirror began announcing, actually screaming, all kinds of new imperfections.

I hesitated, mesmerized by the Medusa before me, and the doctor leaped into the pause.

"I'll tell you what I see. The eyes are a given. I won't even go there. What about the bags underneath, and the puffiness? Of course, the brow would have to be tightened." He tapped my chin and all along my jawbone. "What are we to do with this Elizabethan collar? This all needs tightening." Staring at my face dead-on, he said: "Then, of course, there are the jowls. I'd get a jump on it."

I managed to whimper, "Nicole only had her eyes done."

"Well," he said, "you're not Nicole." He pulled my cheeks out until they almost hit the opposite walls, and said, "Nicole doesn't have that kind of elasticity."

Concluding his seven-minute consultation, he announced, "Whatever you have done will have to be repeated in five years."

As he breezed out the door, he called: "I'm off! The girls will tell you all you need to know."

One of the taupe four came in and took me to a wood-paneled room, dimly lit by a green-shaded desk lamp. In this light, she showed me a scrapbook of miracle lifts.

A few of the women really looked a lot younger, but most looked like Zsa Zsa Gabor before and after.

No one had mentioned price. At the risk of sounding crass, I asked what the cost would be for eyes and the tiniest of tucks, say two or three stitches. She slid an envelope that said Personal and Confidential in tiny taupe letters across the table.

I opened it. In my head I heard the ka-ching! of a cash register. The tab was more than $20,000, payable by certified check.

"Gee, $20,000 seems like a lot of money," I squeaked. The assistant replied: "It beats the $37,500 you'd pay for the work that was suggested. Remember, it's an investment. Do you ever take your car in for a tune-up and an oil change?" I nodded my corrugated face in the affirmative. "Well, that's only a car."

Later that day I went for my annual dermatologist's appointment, to find out if any of my thousands of freckles had turned into melanomas. When I told the doctor about my morning sojourn, he asked one question: the price. When I told him, he chirped like a bird on speed:

Once you realize that the fear of death is the hub of the midlife crisis and deal with that, the rest is just details.

"Cheap, cheap, cheap. Go for it!" Looking closely at my forehead, he added: "But for God's sake, don't let them inject Botox into those worry lines in your forehead. Tell them to just cut that muscle or they'll grow back."

"What's Botox?"

"It's a poison from the same family as botulism toxin. The plastic surgeon injects Botox to paralyze your muscles so you can't pull your eyes together or furrow your brow and make those lines again."

I wondered aloud, "If you can't furrow your brow, does that mean you aren't worried anymore?"

The dermatologist rolled his eyes.

When I finally staggered home, walking up my street feeling like the Elephant Man, my neighbor Helen, who is over 70 and still looks beautiful and vibrant in every light, was out tending her nasturtiums. As I regaled her with the day's events, she furrowed her non-Botoxed brow and said, "I'll give you a free bibliographic consult." She went into the house and reappeared with a book— *The Denial of Death* by philosopher Ernest Becker. Handing it to me, she said, "I'll bet that doctor doesn't have this in his waiting room." Samuel Johnson was right when he suggested that the prospect of death wonderfully concentrates the mind. Once you realize that the fear of death is the hub of the midlife crisis and deal with that, the rest is just details.

I now tuck my Elizabethan collar into my turtleneck and fold my jowls under my balaclava in winter. I have begun to realize that I earned these lines. And on the odd day when I want to deny the inevitability of death, I simply wear a tight hair band. ▲

"No gel—I mixed Rogaine and Viagra."

Shortly after my father's death, my 90-year-old grandmother insisted that my mother have a complete physical. After some debate, my mother reluctantly made an appointment. The doctor not only gave her a clean bill of health, but remarked that she'd probably live to be 110.

To our surprise, my grandmother did not seem entirely pleased by the good report. She sat quietly for a few minutes, then said with a sigh, "And just what am I going to do with a 110-year-old daughter?"

— B.L.M.

When my husband worked at a prison, we only had one car, so I used to roll out of bed at 5 a.m., drive him to work, then come home and go back to sleep. One day while talking to some co-workers, my husband took out his wallet and showed them pictures of me and my daughter. One of the photos of me was a "glamour shot" that I had posed for at the mall.

"Wow," a colleague remarked. "Who's that?"

"My wife," my husband proudly replied.

"Oh," his friend responded, looking puzzled.

"Then who's that woman who drops you off in the mornings?"

— LISA J. PROCTOR

My grandfather's aunt passed away, and he went to pay his respects. At the funeral home, he overheard two women as they peered into the open casket.

"She looks wonderful," said one. "I've never seen her look so good. Why, she looks better than I do!"

"You're right," the other replied. "But remember, you have the flu."

— SARAH SHORT

A friend spent more than two hours in the salon getting her hair colored, cut and blow-dried. After all that, was it too much to ask to be treated like Cinderella entering the ball?

Yet when she went to the desk to pay, the receptionist said to her, "Hello, who is your appointment with today?"

— PETER CROMPTON

Heading off to college at the age of 40, I was a bit self-conscious about my advancing years. One morning I complained to my husband that I was the oldest student in my class.

"Even the teacher is younger than I am," I said.

"Yeah, but look at it from my point of view," he said optimistically. "I thought my days of fooling around with college girls were over."

— BRENDA MCMILLEN

"It's definitely hereditary. It's called aging."

A few years ago, I opened the invitation to my cousin's 100th birthday party. On the front—in bold letters—it screamed, "If he's heard it once, he's heard it a hundred times. Happy Birthday, Sam!"

— LOUIS GLICKMAN

My four-year-old nephew, Brett, had drawn a picture for his grandmother, and was anxious to show it to her. Finding the door to her bathroom unlocked, he burst inside just as she was stepping out of the shower, soaking wet and without a towel.

He looked her up and down for a moment, then stated quite matter-of-factly, "Grandma, you look better with your glasses on."

A student in my math course at Ohlone State College in Fremont, Calif., developed a severe case of tendinitis. Since she couldn't write, she brought a video camera to tape my lectures. After three or four classes, I asked her if she found the method satisfactory. She said it was working quite well, even better than note-taking.

"Actually," she confessed, "I have another reason for doing this. When I told my mother you were a widower, she wanted to see what you look like."

— GERSHON WHEELER

I had laryngitis and finally decided to go to the doctor. After the nurse called for me, she asked my age. "Forty-nine," I whispered.

"Don't worry," she whispered back. "I won't tell anyone."

Lola P. Bell

Turning 50 two years ago, I took a lot of good-natured ribbing from family and friends. So as my wife's 50th birthday approached, I decided to get in some needling of my own. I sat her down, looked deep into her eyes, then said I had never made love to anyone who was over 50 years old.

"Oh, well, I have," she deadpanned. "It's not that great."

— BOB MORELAND

Approaching 40, my frugal husband yearned for a boat. Frugality won out until the day he came across the obituary of an old high-school classmate, Ted. Certain this was a sign that life was too short, my husband purchased a boat that weekend.

Days later, a former classmate called. "Sure was a sad thing, wasn't it?" he said. "You know, Ted's boating accident and all."

— CHRISTINE CRAIG

I was having lunch with several thirty-something friends when talk turned to the dismal prospect of our growing older.

"Well, judging by my mother," I said, "at least my hearing will improve. My mother can hear my biological clock ticking from 200 miles away."

— SHERRY YATES

I had just had my 50th birthday and found the decade marker traumatic. When I went to get my driver's license renewed, a matter-of-fact woman typed out the information, tested my vision, snapped the camera and handed me a laminated card with my picture on it.

"You mean I have to look at this for the next four years?" I jokingly said to her.

"Don't worry about it," she replied. "In four years it'll look good to you."

— NANCY FIRESTONE

We invited some old friends to help celebrate my 40th birthday. My husband went out to buy a gift, and he saw some cute little music boxes. A blue one was playing "Happy Birthday to You." Thinking they were all the same, he picked up a red one and asked the clerk to have it gift-wrapped.

When we sat down to dinner, he gave it to me, asked me to open it and—surprise—out came the tune to "The old gray mare, she ain't what she used to be."

— MRS. EARL DAVENPORT

Now that I'm over 40, younger teammates have begun to tease me about my declining abilities as a softball player. During one game, I was playing third base when a batter ripped a shot over my head. I leapt as high as I could, but the ball tipped off the end of my glove and fell safely for a hit.

At the end of the inning, I was heading for the dugout when our left fielder caught up with me. "That much!" he called, holding his thumb and forefinger a couple of inches apart.

"I know," I replied. "I almost had it."

"No," he said. "I mean that's how far you got off the ground."

— RANDY HAWKINS

"Dad?!"

After a shopping expedition, my friend Gina and I stopped in a local bar for a drink. We hadn't been seated long when she leaned over and said that four young men at the next table were watching us. Since we're both 30-something, married with children, we found the situation flattering. We sat a little straighter and tried to look slimmer and younger.

In a few minutes, one of the men got up and came toward our table. "Excuse me," he said. Then he reached over our heads to turn up the volume on the televised ball game.

— SANDRA LYONS

While on maternity leave, a woman from our office brought in her new bundle of joy. She also had her seven-year-old son with her. Everyone gathered around the baby, and the little boy asked, "Mommy, can I have some money to buy a soda?"

"What do you say?" she said. Respectfully, the boy replied, "You're thin and beautiful."

The woman reached in her purse and gave her son the money.

— MERCURY NICKSE

144

You can get old pretty young if you don't take care of yourself.

— YOGI BERRA,
What Time Is It? You Mean Now? (Simon & Schuster)

I wear glasses so I can look for things I keep losing.

— BILL COSBY, *Time Flies* (Bantam Books)

Hair is the first thing. And teeth the second. A man's got those two things, he's got it all.

— JAMES BROWN

Wisdom comes with age, but keep it to yourself.

— MARY ROACH in Health

I'm at the age where my back goes out more than I do.

— PHYLLIS DILLER

One of the best parts of growing older? You can flirt all you like since you've become harmless.

— LIZ SMITH
in The Older the Fiddle, the Better the Tune by Willard Scott (Hyperion)

Let the wind blow through your hair while you still have some.

— DAVE WEINBAUM

What I've learned is that life is too short and movies are too long.

— DENIS LEARY in GQ

The key to successful aging is to pay as little attention to it as possible.

— JUDITH REGAN in More

The Naked Truth

▶ BY MARY ROACH

Once you hit 40, it is time to think twice about miniskirts. Also, string bikinis, midriff-baring tops, skintight or low-rise jeans that have been sanded white the length of the thighs, as though the wearer had been tied to a bumper and dragged face-down around the block a few times. These are clothes for young people.

Alas, this is what the stores are selling. Today's popular clothing chains appeal strictly to teen-agers, who can be counted upon to change their tastes every 30 days, as the latest *Cosmo Girl* or *Teen Vogue* arrives in the mail. Customers like me cannot possi-bly afford new clothing more than once a decade, owing to the finan-cial strain of paying for teenage children's rapidly shifting fashion needs. So no one bothers to make clothing for us.

This is a dangerous situation. Expose a middle-aged woman to nothing but miniskirts and abbre-viated tops for long enough, and she's bound to cave. One day, when her self-esteem is danger-ously high and the dressing room lights dangerously low, she'll try on something designed for her daughter and say to herself, "Oh, why not?" If she happens to be shopping with her children, the answer to this question will be provided for her. But middle-aged husbands offer no such reality

A bikini is not so much a garment as a cloth-based reminder that your parts have been migrating all these years.

check. They live in a candyland of denial and residual carnality. They still, bless them, like to see a little flesh.

My husband recently made me try on a bikini. A bikini is not so much a garment as a cloth-based reminder that your parts have been migrating all these years. My waist, I realized that day in the dressing room, has completely disappeared beneath my rib cage, which now rests directly on my hips. I'm exhibiting continental drift in reverse.

The buttocks, too, have overrun their boundaries, infringing on territory that rightly belongs to the thighs. I have encouraged my thighs to do something about this—restraining order, guard dog—but they have not. Your thighs are rarely there for you.

"Cute!" says Ed dementedly. "Turn around."

Ed does not understand what all women my age understand. The mature lady's buttock does not wish to come out and take a bow. Designers of mature ladies' swimwear know this. They've built little curtains into their designs, enabling the sagging buttock to keep hidden, and/or cast votes in privacy. God help me, I've entered the Age of Skirted Swimwear. This is the age right after Accessorizing with Reading Glasses and a few years before Can't Name Anyone on the Radio.

Even the knees are in on the betrayal. I recently saw a tabloid photograph of a 40-something Demi Moore with her knees circled in red, highlighting the fact that they were disappearing under the shifting shoals of her thighs. Ha-ha, I said to myself. Just deserts for having a face and breasts (and a boyfriend) that look 25. Then I looked at my own knees, which I plan never to do again.

God help me, I've entered the Age of Skirted Swimwear.

The foot is more or less the one body part that time leaves alone. Well into your 70s, you can wear whatever style shoes you feel like wearing. Positioned, as they are, at the bottom of the heap, gravity is not an issue. Or so I thought. Shortly after the swimsuit debacle, I tried on a pair of pointy-toed black pumps, the sort that actresses on "Sex and the City" were wearing for 30 days back in spring.

"How do those work for you?" the salesgirl asked. I told her they were pinching me, and not in an appreciative, you-look-just-like-that-gal-on-"Sex and the City" way.

"You know," she said brightly, "your feet flatten as you age."

I went to find Ed, and I told him about my flattening instep. He smiled and put his arm around me. That still fits, and for this I'm happy. ▲

Paul was in his mid-60s and had just retired. He was planning to landscape his yard and was trying to find some small shrubs or trees. Burleigh, a 90-year-old from across the street, offered Paul some white-ash saplings that were about two feet tall.

Paul asked, "How long will it take them to be full grown?"

"Twenty years or so," replied Burleigh.

"No good for me, then," said Paul. "I won't be around that long."

The 90-year-old shook his head and replied, "We'll miss ya!"

— CLYDENE SAVAGE

My friend Brad, whose youthful looks belied his actual age and experience, flew charter flights in Florida. One day he was assigned to take an elderly woman across the Everglades to Naples. She studied him carefully as he helped her with her seat belt.

Once airborne, with nothing but water and swamp below, she cleared her throat and said apprehensively, "You seem awfully young. How long have you been flying?"

Brad flashed his most charming grin. "You mean counting today?" he answered.

— BOB WHITE

One of the salesclerks at a local stationery store had to be a good sport to survive her 40th birthday. Not only did she have to put up with two large banners that announced: "Cathy is 40 today!" but she also had to spend the day with other saleswomen who wore tags saying: "I'm not Cathy."

— HELEN BECOUVARAKIS

Having fought the battle of the bulge most of my life, I found the battle getting even harder as I approached middle age. One evening, after trying on slacks that were too tight, I said to my husband, "I'll be so glad when we become grandparents. After all, who cares if grandmothers are fat?"

His prompt reply: "Grandfathers."

—IRIS CAVIN

Listening to the radio, I heard the disc jockey announce, "This next record is for Pete Malloy, who is 111 years old." There was a pause, and then, "My goodness, that is old, isn't it!"

Another pause. "Oh, I'm sorry. I got that wrong. This next record is for Pete Malloy, who is ill."

— VALERIE BALL

To celebrate his 40th birthday, my boss, who is battling middle-age spread, bought a new convertible sports car. As a finishing touch, he put on a vanity plate with the inscription "18 Again." The wind was let out of his sails, however, when a salesman entered our office the following week.

"Hey," he called out, "who owns the car with the plate 'I ate again'?"

— CINDY GILLIS

Jim, my 40-something husband, was playing basketball with friends his age. "Pretty soon," said one of his teammates, "we'll have to count it as a basket if the ball just hits the rim."

"Yeah," Jim agreed. "It's scary when you have to look through the bottom part of your bifocals to shoot layups and the top part on jump shots."

— PAMELA HELMER

149

My father, at age 93, had only the most basic needs and very few wants. Last fall, my sister-in-law, hoping to get a little help in choosing a suitable birthday gift for him, asked, "Pa, what would you like for your birthday this year?"

"Nothing," he replied.

"But, Pa," she kidded, "that's what we gave you last year."

"Well," he answered, "I'm still using it."

— L.M. COUILLARD

I was with my husband at a baseball game in Boston's Fenway Park when I decided to go get myself a hot dog. As I stood up my husband asked me to buy him a beer. The young clerk at the concession stand asked to see verification of age.

"You've got to be kidding," I said. "I'm almost 40 years old." He apologized, but said he had to insist. When I showed him my license, the clerk served me the beer. "That will be $4.25."

I gave him $5 and told him to keep the change. "The tip's for carding me," I said.

He put the change in the tip cup. "Thanks," he said. "Works every time."

— ANGIE DEWHURST

Venus and Mars

Speaking of war and laughter—put together, it's called marriage. Despite thousands of years of practice, men and women still don't connect well. But it's fun to watch 'em try.

"My son's into extreme sports, my daughter's into extreme makeover,
and my husband's into extreme denial."

Our Lamaze class included a tour of the pediatric wing at the hospital. When a new baby was brought into the nursery, all the women tried to guess its weight, but the guy standing next to me was the only male to venture a number. "Looks like 9 1/2 pounds," he offered confidently.

"This must not be your first," I said.

"Oh, yes, it's my first."

"Then how would you know the weight of a baby?"

He shrugged. "I'm a fisherman."

— TIM LOVERSKY

Heavy snow had buried my van in our driveway. My husband, Scott, dug around the wheels, rocked the van back and forth and finally pushed me free. I was on the road when I heard an odd noise. I got on my cell and called home.

"Thank God you answered," I said when Scott picked up. "There's this alarming sound coming from under the van. For a moment I thought I was dragging you down the highway."

"And you didn't stop?"

— PAIGE FAIRFIELD

My husband and I, married 13 years, were dressing for a party. I'd spent all day getting a haircut and permanent, then as we were leaving, we met in the hall and he said nothing. I complained that he had not even noticed my hair. "You used to pay attention to every little thing, and now you don't notice anything! You take me for granted!"

My husband stood there rubbing his face as he let me rant and rave. Then it hit me: He'd shaved off his six-month-old beard.

— MELONY ANDERSON

My sister's lack of sports knowledge recently became evident when we attended a pro-hockey game. After one of the home players scored, the crowd screamed and the monitors around the rink flashed: "G O A L."

After cheering wildly, my sister turned and asked, "Who's Al?"

— KAREN KELLY

As part of our regular service, members of the congregation are permitted to make announcements or requests for prayers. One man, Bob, mentioned his upcoming 37th wedding anniversary. At the obvious nudging of his wife, he quickly corrected that to 38.

As the chuckling died down, heard from the back of the church was, "I'd like to offer a prayer for Bob."

— JUDITH L. LENSINK

My sister went shopping for blue jeans with her husband, Steve. She chose a few pairs to try on and went into the fitting room, while Steve waited outside. A minute later he heard her crying softly. Concerned, Steve said through the door, "Honey, really, it doesn't matter if you've gone up a size or two."

Soon she came out, limping slightly and pretty upset. The problem wasn't the size of her pants; she had stubbed her toe in the dressing room.

— JULIE LAW

Timeless Humor from the 50's

A husband-and-wife photography team we know shoot their pictures together, do their developing and printing together—in fact, they're together 24 hours of the day. We wondered how they managed to keep up such good working relations.

"Well, frankly," the wife said, "it wouldn't work out if one of us didn't have a good disposition."

"Which one?" we asked.

"Oh," she laughed, "we take turns."

— ELIZABETH JETER

153

After my husband and I had a huge argument, we ended up not talking to each other for days. Finally, on the third day, he asked where one of his shirts was. "Oh," I said, "now you're speaking to me."

He looked confused. "What are you talking about?"

"Haven't you noticed I haven't spoken to you for three days?" I challenged.

"No," he said. "I just thought we were getting along."

— BETH DORIA

After the birth of my son, a woman from the records department stopped by my hospital room to get information for his birth certificate. "Father's date of birth?" she asked. When I told her, she said, "Do you realize that his birthday is exactly nine months before your son's birth?"

"No, I hadn't thought about it," I responded, "but now that you mention it, I have a daughter who turned two a couple days before the same date."

After she finished taking down all the data, she patted my hand and said, "Maybe you should start buying your husband a tie for his birthday."

— M. K. PIGOTT

"Romance has nothing to do with it. Dan and I are renewing our marriage vows because he has forgotten them."

When my parents run the dishwasher, they let each other know the dishes are clean by placing the box of detergent on the counter. When Mom got home from work one day, she was surprised to find the detergent on the counter, since she had emptied the dishwasher the night before. She couldn't understand why my dad would run the dishwasher again—until she opened it and found the top tray full of golf balls.

— MICHELE FERGUSON

My daughter had absentmindedly left her sneakers on our kitchen table. "That's disgusting," my husband grumbled. "Doesn't she realize we eat off that table?" Then he went out back to work on the car.

I cleaned the table and left to do my grocery shopping. When I came home I couldn't set my bags down anywhere. Sitting in the middle of the kitchen table was a car muffler.

— KATHERINE HORGAN

It seemed that all our appliances had broken in the same week, and repairs were straining our budget. So when I picked up the kids from school and our Jeep started making rattling sounds, I decided that rather than burden my husband, I'd deal with it. I hadn't reckoned on my little tattletales, however. They rushed into the house with the news: "Daddy, the Jeep was breaking down, but Mom made the noise stop!"

Impressed, my husband asked, "How did you fix it?"

"I turned up the volume on the radio," I confessed.

— RUTH TEN VEEN

154

Curious when I found two black-and-white negatives in a drawer, I had them made into prints. I was pleasantly surprised to see they were of a younger, slimmer me taken on one of my first dates with my husband.

When I showed him the photographs, his face lit up. "Wow! It's my old Plymouth."

— DONNA MARTIN

During my brother's wedding, my mother had managed to keep from crying—until she glanced at my grandparents. My grandmother had reached over to my grandfather's wheelchair and gently touched his hand. That was all it took to start my mother's tears flowing. After the wedding, Mom went over to my grandmother and told her how that tender gesture triggered her outburst.

"Well, I'm sorry to ruin your moment," Grandmother replied. "But I was just checking to see if he was awake."

— MARK SAMPLE

Every December it was the same excruciating tradition. Our family would get up at the crack of dawn, go to a Christmas tree farm and tromp across acres of snow in search of the perfect tree. Hours later our feet would be freezing, but Mom would press on, convinced the tree of her dreams was "just up ahead."

One year I snapped. "Mom, face it. The perfect tree doesn't exist. It's like looking for a man. Just be satisfied if you can find one that isn't dead, doesn't have too many bald spots and is straight."

— CHRISTY MARTIN

Standing in line at the clothing store's counter, I watched as the woman ahead of me handed the clerk her credit card. The customer waited for a long time while the saleswoman went to verify the account. When she finally returned, the clerk said, "I'm sorry, but this card is in your husband's name, and we can't accept it because the records show he is deceased."

With that, the woman turned to her spouse, who was standing next to her, and asked, "Does this mean I don't have to fix lunch for you today?"

— MARILYN ARNOPOL

"You realize, of course, there's a five-day cooling-off period on sports car loans."

While I was dining out with my children, a man came over to our table and we started talking. He asked where my kids go to school. I told him we home-school them. With a raised eyebrow he asked if my husband is the sole breadwinner for our family. I said no, I also work—out of our home. Then, noticing our two-month-old son, he mentioned that his daughter had just had a baby, and he wondered what hospital our son was born in.

"He was born at home," I answered.

The man looked at me, then said, "Wow, you don't get out much, do you?"

— LAURA HANSER

After his marriage broke up, my manager became very philosophical. "I guess it was in our stars," he sighed.

"What do you mean?" I asked.

"Her astrological sign is the one for earth. Mine is the one for water. Together we made mud."

— LORI PHILLIPS

The first time I met my wife, she was an intense aerobics instructor at my health club and I was an out-of-shape new member. After one grueling workout, I gasped, "This is really helping me get toned."

She looked me up and down. Feeling self-conscious, I added, "Big men run in my family."

She raised an eyebrow. "Apparently not enough."

— JOHN PARKER

My mom had always wanted to learn to play the piano, so Dad bought her one for her birthday. A few weeks later, I called and asked how she was doing. "We returned the piano," said Dad. "I persuaded her to switch to a clarinet."

"Why?" I asked.

"Because," he explained, "with a clarinet, she can't sing along."

— DON FOSTER

His aching back made it impossible for my friend's husband to get a decent night's rest on their lumpy mattress. "Until I feel better, I'm going to sleep on the couch," he announced.

Ordinarily, a spouse moving out of the bedroom isn't a good sign for the marriage. So his wife couldn't resist: "Okay, but as soon as we have an argument you're back in our bed."

— ANNA GUTHRIE

When my friend got a job, her husband agreed to share the housework. He was stunned by the amount of effort involved in keeping a house clean with small boys to pick up after, and insisted that he and his wife shop for a new vacuum cleaner.

The salesman gave them a demonstration of the latest model. "It comes equipped with all the newest features," he assured them.

The husband was not convinced. "Don't you have a riding one?" he asked.

— PAT MONTGOMERY

"God may have forgiven you, George, but I haven't."

Mobile phones are the only subject on which men boast about who's got the smallest.

— NEIL KINNOCK, British politician

The remarkable thing about my mother is that for 30 years she served us nothing but leftovers. The original meal has never been found.

— CALVIN TRILLIN

Weddings have less to do with being married than with the fact that it is best to begin the most arduous journeys surrounded by friends and wearing nice clothes.

— TONY EARLEY, Somehow Form a Family (Algonquin)

Behind every great man is a woman rolling her eyes.

— JIM CARREY in "Bruce Almighty"

Men want the same thing from their underwear that they want from women: a little bit of support, and a little bit of freedom.

— JERRY SEINFELD

When you're in love, it's the most glorious two-and-a-half minutes of your life.

— RICHARD LEWIS

Here's the secret to a happy marriage: Do what your wife tells you.

— DENZEL WASHINGTON

She's Got Game

▶ BY MARY ROACH

On any given night for the 14 or so months of the year corresponding to baseball season, our TV is likely to be tuned to a sports channel. In order to maintain some semblance of personal contact with my husband, Ed, during these months, I often sit beside him on the couch with a book. I don't mind the chatter of the sportscasters, for my brain processes sports talk in the same way it processes paid political announcements and the cellphone conversations of strangers.

A man in a navy blazer will say, "No atta-babies in that at-bat!" and his companion will chime in with, "It was right there, in the whack-me zone!" and it's as though they're not there.

Sometimes I find myself staring at the game anyway. I watch sports the way a dog will watch TV: I'm attracted by the motion and color, but no actual comprehension is taking place. Ed forgets that this is the case. He'll see me looking at the screen and assume I'm following the game and expect me to keep track of what happens while he goes to the kitchen for a refreshing beverage. Sometimes I'm able to bluff my way through it ("He had it right there in the whack-me zone, honey!"), but more often I am forced to confess that I have not grasped the significance of anything I have seen.

This is where it gets ugly. This is where Ed tries to turn his wife into—as the men in the blazers like to say—a serious student of the game. Plainly put, this cannot be done. You'd have more luck getting a pug to understand "Jeopardy." Take, for instance, the Infield Fly Rule, which begins, in the breezy parlance of the Official Baseball Rules, like this: "The batter is out when it is

declared, and the ball does not have to be caught. Because the batter is declared out, the runners are no longer forced to run, but they can run if they wish, at the risk of being put out…"

"What?" Ed will ask. "What don't you get?" Apparently this language speaks to him in a way that it does not speak to me. One night I decided to try putting it to work. It was seven o'clock and cutlets were growing cold. I cleared my throat. "The wife is declared put out when it is dinnertime and the game is still running. The husband's attention has to be caught and because the wife is put out, the husband may wish to run…"

Ed begged leniency on the grounds that it was "the top of the ninth." Here again, communication breaks down. For me, there can be no understanding of a sport where the "top" of an inning is the first half. "Think

Mary Roach does not see a Heisman Trophy in her future.

of ladders," I said, as Marvin Benard stepped up to the plate. "You start at the bottom and go to the top." But Ed wasn't listening.

Sometimes I'm able to bluff my way through it ("He had it right there in the whack-me zone, honey!").

Benard struck out, and Ed said hurtful things about him. This is my other qualm with pro sports. I feel bad for the players when they mess up. The ball Benard missed was going 90 m.p.h., and it went all crooked. If I were the umpire, I would have laid a hand on the man's shoulder and said, "Take your base, Marv. You were really close."

Last October my tolerance for Ed's devotion to sports, already threadbare, began to unravel. The baseball season was winding down, leading me to think that we could resume our normal adult activities, if only we had any. I came into the living room one Sunday to find Ed, a man who dismisses football as "a bore," engrossed in a Broncos game. He wore a guilty grin. "Third and long, sweetie!"

It was around that time that I came across a book about sports "addiction." It said that for many men, their relationship with their team fulfills a need for intimacy. This got me right there in the whack-me zone. Was J. T. Snow doing more for my husband than I was?

I confronted Ed. There was an NFL game on that day, but he wasn't watching. He was making banana bread. Though he denied the charges, he wouldn't rule out

the possibility that J. T. Snow could make him happy. Then he asked if I wanted to go for a bike ride. I decided to drop the sports addiction thing, because truly, Ed doesn't deserve the hassle. He's the winningest guy I know, and I mean that from the bottom of my heart, which is the part that comes before the top. ▲

In the frozen-foods department of our local grocery store, I noticed a man grocery shopping with his son. As I walked by, he checked something off his list, and I heard him whisper conspiratorially to the child, "You know, if we really mess this up, we'll never have to do it again."

— JANET CAMPBELL

During the hectic time after our son was born, my husband and I went weeks without being romantic, and it was taking its toll. As he helped me fold the laundry one day, I pointed to a pile of socks. "Those haven't been mated," I said.

"I know the feeling," my husband muttered under his breath.

— ROBBIN CEDERBLOM

After I completed a frantic afternoon of chores, I walked into the living room to find my husband reclining in his chair. He was looking bemusedly at our new puppy, who was napping. "If I wanted to look at something lying around sleeping all day," he complained, "I would have bought a cat."

"Or you could have just bought a mirror," I said.

— TRACEY SMITH

My husband is a big Atlanta Braves fan. When I saw an ad on television for a baseball autographed by one of his favorite players that cost $42, I rushed out and bought it for him as a gift.

That evening as we were watching television, the same commercial came on. Slyly I glanced over at my husband just as he commented, "What kind of idiot would pay $42 for a baseball?"

— JANICE ADAMS

Every year on their wedding anniversary my boss, Woody, and his wife celebrated by staying at the same resort hotel. On their 25th anniversary they booked their usual room. But when the hotel's bell captain escorted them upstairs, they were in for a big surprise.

"There must be some mistake," Woody said. "This looks like the bridal suite."

"It's okay," the bell captain reassured him. "If I put you in the ballroom, that doesn't mean you have to dance."

— CONNIE L. SELLERS

One morning a customer entered my flower shop and ordered a bouquet for his wife. "No card is necessary," he instructed us. "She'll know who sent them."

The delivery truck hadn't even returned to the store when the phone rang. It was the customer's wife. "Who sent the flowers?" she asked.

After explaining that the customer had requested that no card be included, I considered the matter closed—but not so. A bit later, she came rushing in the front door. "You've got to tell me who sent the flowers," she demanded, "before my husband gets home."

— LINDA O. COUCH

"Our credit card was stolen, but I've decided not to report it. The thief is spending less than you did!"

Pregnant with my third child, I was stricken with a bout of morning sickness and lay down on the living-room couch to rest. Just then one of the workmen who was doing repairs in my house walked by and gave me a curious look. "Taking a little break," I explained. "I'm in my first trimester."

"Really?" he said. "What's your major?"

— CARA ANDERSON

When, by means of an at-home early pregnancy test, my wife discovered she was pregnant, she tried to get in touch with me at work. I was out, so she left a message. Later, I found a note on my desk: "E. P. T. —phone home."

— JON RISING

Our dentist recently hired a beautiful young blonde as a dental hygienist. We exchanged small talk for half an hour as she cleaned my teeth and I gazed into her pale-blue eyes. When she finished, she smiled and said, "You have the most perfect mouth." My heart skipped a beat.

Then she continued: "Usually I have a lot of trouble reaching people's wisdom teeth. But your mouth is so big, I can get both hands in easily!"

— PHILLIP B. MURRAY

As a paper salesman, I have a habit of turning over containers and looking for trademarks. This really annoys my wife. After dinner at a pizzeria, we were handed a box for leftovers. I craned my neck to get a better look under it. When she rolled her eyes, I said, "I'm just trying to see who made that box."

"I know," she sighed. "You used to look at me that way."

— CHRIS J. RATTAN

My husband, Mike, and I had several stressful months of financial difficulties. So one evening I was touched to see him gazing at the diamond wedding ring that symbolized our marriage.

"With this ring…" I began romantically.

"We could pay off Visa," he responded.

— DAWN HILL

I realized that the ups and downs of the stock market had become too big a part of our life one night as my husband and I prepared for bed. As we slid beneath the covers, I snuggled up to him and told him I loved him.

Drifting off to sleep, he drowsily whispered back, "Your dividend growth fund went up three days this week."

— SHIRLEY S. DILLON

While in the checkout line at my local hardware store I overheard one man say to another, "My wife has been after me to paint our shed. But I let it go for so long she got mad and did it herself."

His friend nodded. "I like women who get mad like that."

— C.V. MAYNARD

When a woman in my office became engaged, a colleague offered her some advice. "The first ten years are the hardest," she said.

"How long have you been married?" I asked.

"Ten years," she replied.

— TONYA WINTER

When my younger brother and his wife celebrated their first anniversary, they invited the rest of the family to join them for dinner. The conversation focused on the newlyweds and how they happened to meet. Caught up in the romance of the story, one by one the men related how we had met our wives. Eventually everyone had told his story except for my youngest brother.

All eyes were on him when he said, "Oh, Cindy and I met in college. We were matched up by a computer according to compatibility."

"That's the whole story?" my wife asked incredulously.

"Oh, no," he replied with a grin. "They've fixed the computer since then."

— JOHN MORRISSEY

The family was viewing old slides and one flashed on the screen that caught everyone's attention. My father, wearing his favorite golf shirt, was holding me at the tender age of three weeks.

The look on his face told all. "There's my prize possession," my father said.

Touched, I smiled at him as he continued, "I wonder whatever happened to that golf shirt?"

— JEANNE GRAVES

My wife-to-be and I were at the county clerk's office for our marriage license. After recording the vital information—names, dates of birth, etc.—the clerk handed me our license and deadpanned, "No refunds, no exchanges, no warranties."

Albert J. Campbell

My husband, an exercise enthusiast who spends an hour and a half at an athletic club every morning before work, encouraged a middle-aged and quite overweight friend to join him for his morning sessions. The co-worker decided not to tell his wife about his new project until after he had shed the pounds, and he faithfully began meeting my husband at 6 a.m. every day.

At the end of the first week, the friend's wife rolled over in bed and offered this parting advice: "I don't know where you're going, dear, or what you are doing. But just remember: You aren't used to it."

— DEBBIE BEAUCHAMP

Some newly married friends were visiting us when the topic of children came up. The bride said she wanted three children, while the young husband demurred, saying two would be enough for him. They discussed this discrepancy for a few minutes until the husband thought he'd put an end to things, saying boldly, "After our second child, I'll just have a vasectomy."

Without a moment's hesitation, the bride retorted, "Well, I hope you'll love the third one like it's your own!"

— LISA MONGAN

While waiting for a flight, I glanced over at a nearby couple. He was reading the United States Sailing Association's book, *Basic Cruising*. She was reading *Adrift: 76 Days Lost at Sea*.

— BRUCE NEAL

My husband is wonderful with our baby daughter, but often turns to me for advice. Recently I was in the shower when he poked his head in to ask, "What should I feed Lily for lunch?"

"That's up to you," I replied. "There's all kinds of food. Why don't you pretend I'm not home?"

A few minutes later, my cell phone rang. I answered it to hear my husband saying, "Yeah, hi, honey. Uh…what should I feed Lily for lunch?"

— JULIE BALL

Rushing to a bridge tournament, I was pulled over for going 43 in a 35 m.p.h. zone. "What'll I tell my husband?" I worried, explaining to the police officer that he was a self-described "perfect" driver.

The cop took a second look at the name and address on my license. "Did your husband go duck hunting this morning?" he asked.

Baffled, I answered, "Yes."

"I stopped him for going 47."

— ANN ALENE DUNN

Once my divorce was final, I went to the local Department of Motor Vehicles and asked to have my maiden name reinstated on my driver's license. "Will there be any change of address?" the clerk inquired. "No," I replied.

"Oh, good," she said, clearly delighted. "You got the house."

— POLLY BAUGHMAN

To our shock and horror, my sister-in-law and I realized we had each been married nearly 50 years. "That's a long time," I observed.

"A long, long time," she agreed. Then she smiled. "Something just occurred to me."

"What's that?"

"If I had killed your brother the first time I felt like it, I'd be out of jail by now."

— BARBARA MASON

"I'm going to Venus. He's going to Mars."

What Women Want—

▶ BY DAVE BARRY

The other day my son and I were talking about women and I realized that it was time he and I had a Serious Talk, the kind every father should have with his son yet avoids because it's so awkward.

The subject? Buying gifts for women.

This is an area where many men do not have a clue. Exhibit A: my father, a thoughtful man who once gave my mother—on their anniversary—an electric blanket.

He honestly could not understand why, when she opened the box, she gave him That Look. (You veteran men know the one I mean.) After all, this was the deluxe model electric blanket. With automatic thermostat! What more could any woman want?

The mistake that my dad made, and that many guys make, was in thinking that when you choose a gift for a woman, it should do something useful. Wrong! The first rule of buying a gift for a woman is: The gift should not do anything, or if it does, it should do it badly.

Let's consider two possible gifts, both of which, theoretically, perform the same function:

Gift 1: A state-of-the-art gasoline-powered lantern, with electronic ignition and dual mantles, capable of generating 1,200 lumens of light for ten hours on a single tank of fuel.

Gift 2: A scented beeswax candle containing visible particles of bee poop and providing roughly the same illumination as a lukewarm corn dog.

To a guy, Gift 1 is clearly superior because you could use it to see in the dark. To a woman, Gift 2 is much better, because women love to sit around in the gloom with reeking, sputtering candles. Don't ask me why.

All I'm saying is that this is the kind of thing a woman wants. That's why the ultimate gift is jewelry: It's totally useless.

The second rule of buying gifts for women is: You are never finished.

This is the scary part, the part that my son is just discovering. If you have a girlfriend, she will give you, at minimum, a birthday gift, an anniversary gift, a Christmas Hanukkah Kwanzaa gift and a Valentine's Day gift.

Every one of these gifts will be nicely wrapped and accompanied by a thoughtful card. And when she gives you this gift, you have to give her one back. You can't just open your wallet and say, "Here's, let's see…$17!"

And, as I told my son, it only gets worse. Looming ahead are bridal showers, weddings, baby showers, Mother's Day and other Mandatory Gift Occasions that would not even exist if men—as is alleged—really ran the world. Women observe all of these occasions, and more.

My wife will buy gifts for no reason. She'll go into one of those gift stores at the mall that men never enter, she'll find something—maybe a tiny cute box that couldn't hold anything larger than a molecule and is therefore useless—and she'll buy it, plus a thoughtful card.

And she doesn't even know who the recipient is yet!

Millions of other women are out doing the same thing, getting further and further ahead, while we guys are home watching instant replays. We have no chance of winning this war.

That's what I told my son. It was time he knew the truth. ▲

"They said he has a real fear of intimacy."

One night my friend John and I were sitting at a bar where he used to work, when an attractive woman, a former co-worker, came in and sat next to him. She told him she had just had a fight with her husband, a police officer, and needed to get out of the house for a while.

They had been talking for a few minutes when, as a joke, I leaned over to John. "Don't look now," I whispered, "but a guy about six-five just walked in. And he's got a gun."

Without hesitating, John turned to me. "Quick, Ed," he said, "kiss me on the lips."

— E. J. KRAMER

I had taken a rare day off from work and, having shed the corporate uniform, was dressed scruffily, with my hair in rollers. Glancing out my window, I saw a van blocking my driveway.

Incensed, I flew to the door and told the driver to move it immediately.

About an hour later, all dressed up to go shopping, I was backing my car out of the driveway and noticed the driver standing on the sidewalk. A little embarrassed, I smiled and nodded hello.

"Ma'am," he said to me, "I hope your grandmother is only visiting. She is one tough old cookie."

— JEAN HENRY

Driving my friend Steve and his girlfriend to the airport, we passed a billboard showing a bikini-clad beauty holding a can of beer. Steve's girlfriend glanced up at it and announced, "I suppose if I drank a six-pack of that brand, I'd look like her."

"No," Steve corrected. "If I drank a six-pack, you'd look like her."

— JOHN D. BOYD

My boyfriend and I were taking his 19-year-old niece to a weekend festival. When we arrived at her house to pick her up, she appeared in tasteful but very short shorts, and a tank top with spaghetti straps. A debate began immediately about appropriate dress. I took the girl's side, recalling that when we began dating, I dressed the same way.

"Yes," said my boyfriend sternly, "and I said something about it, didn't I?"

Everyone looked at me. "Yeah," I replied. "You said, 'What's your phone number?'"

— CHARNELL WALLS WATSON

For our 20th anniversary my husband and I vacationed in Hawaii, where we went snorkeling. After an hour in the water everyone got back on the boat, except for me and one handsome young man. As I continued my underwater exploring, I noticed that everywhere I swam, he swam. I snorkeled for another 40 minutes. So did he. I climbed back in the boat; so did he.

I felt very flattered and, as I took off my fins, asked him coyly why he had stayed in the water for so long. "I'm the lifeguard," he replied matter-of-factly. "I couldn't get out until you did."

— SHARON FORGUE

One morning I found a beautiful long-stemmed rose lying by the kitchen sink. Even though the flower was plastic, I was thinking how, after all the years we had been married, my husband could still make such a wonderful romantic gesture. Then I noticed a love note lying next to it. "Dear Sue," it read. "Don't touch the rose. I'm using the stem to unclog the drain."

— SUZAN L. WIENER

A woman friend looked at my chest and said, "Of course."

That's when I realized I was wearing a T-shirt I had picked up at the annual biker rally in Sturgis, S.D. It read "If a man says something in the woods where no woman can hear, is he still wrong?"

— RUSS HARGREAVES

My wife and her friend Karen were talking about their labor-saving devices as they pulled into our driveway. Karen said, "I love my new garage-door opener."

"I love mine too," my wife replied, and honked the horn three times. That was the signal for me to come out and open the garage.

— GENE WARD

My husband knows the pitfalls of trying to communicate with the opposite sex—especially me. For instance, I recently tried on a pair of pants and needed a second opinion about how they looked. "Do I look too fat in these pants?" I asked.

"No," he said, pausing, obviously worried about his response. "You look…just fat enough."

— KATHY SEUFERT

For years my sister's husband tried unsuccessfully to persuade her to get a hearing aid. "How much do they cost?" she asked one day after he had pitched the idea to her again.

"They're usually about $3,000," he said.

"Okay, well, if you say something worth $3,000," she replied, "I'll get one."

— EDWIN A. REINAGEL

Timeless Humor from the 50's

A Connecticut chap, an incorrigible practical joker, often makes his long-suffering wife the butt of his painful pranks. But last fall she finally got her chance to even the score. The couple were spending the weekend in a New York hotel. It was a hot night, and when they got back to their room after the theater, the husband peeled off his clothes and stretched out on the bed to cool off. By the time his wife was ready for bed, he was fast asleep and she decided not to disturb him.

Some hours later, he woke up and groped his way in the dark toward the bathroom. By mistake he opened the outside door and, still groggy, was halfway down the hall before he became aware of his predicament. He turned back hastily. Then, to his horror, he realized that he was not only locked out but had forgotten his room number.

Frantic, he rushed to the elevator bank, pressed the button and hid around the corner. When the elevator arrived, he thrust out his arm and beckoned wildly. The operator took one look, slammed the elevator door and went for the house detective.

When the detective arrived, he found the unfortunate guest cowering in a corner. He gave him a sheet from the linen closet, called the desk to check his assertion that he was registered at the hotel with his wife and escorted him to his room.

Pounding on the door until the wife opened it, the detective said, "This man claims to be your husband. Is he?"

For a moment she stared at the sheet-draped figure; then she said icily, "I've never seen him before in my life."

— A. E. TATHAM

167

One evening my husband's golfing buddy drove his secretary home after she had imbibed a little too much at an office reception. Although this was an innocent gesture, he decided not to mention it to his wife, who tended to get jealous easily.

Later that night my husband's friend and his wife were driving to a restaurant. Suddenly he looked down and spotted a high-heel shoe half hidden under the passenger seat. Not wanting to be conspicuous, he waited until his wife was looking out her window before he scooped up the shoe and tossed it out of the car. With a sigh of relief, he pulled into the restaurant parking lot. That's when he noticed his wife squirming around in her seat.

"Honey," she asked, "have you seen my other shoe?"

— JOAN FELDMAN

I spent an afternoon helping my boyfriend move into a new home. In one carton I found a crockpot, with an odd-looking and very dirty metal lid. Later I ushered my boyfriend into the kitchen and asked why he hadn't mentioned this perfectly good pot.

He stared at it, then replied, "Well, after I broke the lid I never thought of replacing it with a hubcap."

— CAROLINE C. JONES

Soon after we were married, my husband, Paul, stopped wearing his wedding band.

"Why don't you ever wear your ring?" I asked.

"It cuts off my circulation," Paul replied.

"I know," I said. "It's supposed to."

MARILYN WARE

After I had taken on a few too many projects, my responsibilities began piling up on me. To keep my forgetfulness to a minimum, I started a daily reminder list, scratching off items as I completed them. Some two weeks later I bragged to my husband, Clarence, "Thanks to that list I have never once overlooked a single important detail."

Not long afterward I returned home from a late-night meeting and picked up my list to check on the next day's activities. There, in my husband's handwriting, wedged between "1:30 hair appointment" and "Clean the linen closet," was the notation: "Seduce Clarence."

— MARY E. HOWELL

For a while my husband and I had opposite schedules. He worked during the day and I worked at night. One morning I noticed he left a note to himself on the kitchen counter that said "STAMPS" in large letters. As a helpful surprise, I bought him some at the post office and put them on the counter before going to work.

The next morning I found the same note. "STAMPS" was crossed out. Underneath he had written, "ONE MILLION DOLLARS."

— STEPHANIE SHELLEY

"I guess I thought if we came to France,
you wouldn't still be

you know, you!"

Night Light Fight

BY MARY ROACH

If my husband, Ed, had his way, you could pop by our place any given night and see me sitting in bed, struggling to hold my head up under the weight of a night-vision headset. Ed is an early-to-sleep sort of chap, who'll announce around 8 p.m., "Just going to change into my pj's and read for a while." Once he becomes horizontal, however, it's pretty much over.

This makes it difficult for yours truly, for I really do read in bed, including the part where you turn the page and read a second one and then a third one. Ed would like for me to do this in a quiet, motionless, pitch-dark manner. Instead, I do it in a chip-crunching, light-on, getting-in-and-out-of-bed-for-more-chips manner. In the spirit of compromise, I bought Ed earplugs and a black satin sleep mask. "It's

dashing," I said of the mask. "You look like Antonio Banderas in *Zorro*." This was a lie. He looked like Arlene Francis in "What's My Line?"

"Zorro didn't wear a sleep mask," countered Ed. "His had eyeholes cut out."

"It was a special fencer's sleep mask. Come on," I said. "That movie is all about sleep. Why do you think he writes Z's everywhere?"

Ed's argument was that as the awake person, I should have to wear the uncomfortable head wear.

We were inching toward the marriage counselor's couch when in the nick of time, I found a product called Light Wedge: "The only personal reading light that has the ability to save the 50 percent of marriages that end in divorce." It's a thin, glowing slice of acrylic that lies on the

page, enabling one to read "in the dark without keeping his or her partner awake with an irksome reflection."

I settled in with my Light Wedge and a bowl of chips. "Happy now?"

"No," said Ed. "You get crumbs in the bed and steal the blankets. I'm still going to want that divorce."

A married couple can best be defined as a unit of people whose sleep habits are carefully engineered to keep each other awake.

I offered to stop eating in bed if Ed would agree to wean himself from his need for multiple pillows. I roll over in the middle of the night and find myself suffocating against a towering mound of goose down.

We call it Pillow Mountain.

Ed has fallen for the great marketing ploy of the decade: the decorative pillow ploy. It is

A married couple can best be defined as a unit of people whose sleep habits are carefully engineered to keep each other awake.

no longer enough to buy one pillow per head. There must be a decorative pillow behind one's normal head-resting variety, and a spray of bolsters and scatter pillows in front. Each of these must be of a unique size and shape, so as to require the purchase of a specially fitted pillowcase.

Ed corrected me. "It's called a sham."

No argument here. It's a total sham. To outfit the modern bed with its indulgence of pillows and their little pillow outfits costs hundreds of dollars. Beds now contain entire pillow families, six or seven of them, all nestled together against the headboard, as though watching

Leno. "That's okay," I tell them, backing out of the room. "I'll go sleep on the couch."

As we were arguing over the pillow issue, Ed got out of bed to open the bedroom door, which I'd closed so as not to hear the odd poppings and clickings of our refrigerator. Our refrigerator is unique among large appliances, in that it appears to suffer from insomnia. Every night around 4 a.m., it begins shifting, fidgeting and cracking its joints. No doubt it wants some warm milk, which, for a refrigerator, is an existential crisis of considerable weight.

Ed claims not to hear these sounds. He says he needs to have the bedroom door open; other-

wise it gets so stuffy he can't sleep. I can't tell him to open a window, because then it'll be too cold. There'll be an all-night struggle for blanket superiority, and no one, to quote Zorro, will catch any Z's. We'll end up out in the kitchen at 4:30, playing cards with the refrigerator.

I know a lot of other couples have similar bedtime issues, and I hope this column has been helpful. I hope this column has the ability to save the 50 percent of marriages that end in divorce. Or that, at the very least, it helps put one of you to sleep. ▲

I was examining can-
taloupes at the
grocery store and
turned to the produce
clerk, who was refilling
the bins. "Choosing a
cantaloupe is a bit like
picking a mate for
marriage," I observed
casually. "A person has
no idea what he's getting
until it's too late."

He said nothing at first, but as I
walked to the next aisle, he called
after me, "I know. I've had three
cantaloupes."

— GLORIA WEGENER

"No one's winning. It's ballet."

As a single, never-married
woman in my 40s, I have
been questioned endlessly about
my status by friends, relatives and
co-workers. Over the years I've
noticed a subtle change in the
nature of their inquiries.

In my teens, friends would ask,
"Who are you going out with this
weekend?"

In my 20s, relatives would say,
"Who are you dating?"

In my 30s, co-workers might
inquire, "So, are you dating
anyone?"

Now people ask, "Where did
you get that adorable purse?"

— MARY A. ELDER

Timeless Humor from the **70's**

Neighbors of ours had a terrible disagreement over a
patio they wanted for their
backyard. The wife had
rather grand ideas, while the
husband wanted costs kept
to a minimum. The wife won
out, and the construction bill
climbed higher and higher.

I dropped by one day,
when the patio was near
completion, and was sur-
prised to find the husband
smiling from ear to ear as
the workmen smoothed over
the surface. I remarked how
nice it was to see a grin
replace the frown he had
been wearing lately.

"You see where they're
smoothing that cement?" he
replied. "I just threw my
wife's credit cards in there."

— R. HORN

My wife, a registered
nurse, once fussed
over every pain or mis-
hap that came my way.
Recently, however, I
got an indication that
the honeymoon is over.

I was about to fix the
attic fan, and as I lifted
myself from the ladder into
the attic, I scratched my
forehead on a crossbeam.
Crawling along, I picked up splin-
ters in both hands, and I cut one
hand replacing the fan belt. On
the way down the ladder, I missed
the last two rungs and turned my
ankle.

When I limped into the kitchen,
my wife took one look and said,
"Are those your good pants?"

— RICHARD J. SCHWIETERMAN

Bird-watching is a passion of
mine, and my wife has always
been impressed by my ability to
identify each species solely by its
song. To help her learn a little bit
about birds, I bought a novelty
kitchen clock that sounds a different bird call for each hour. We
were relaxing in our yard when a
cardinal started singing. "What's
that?" I challenged.

She listened closely. "It's three
o'clock."

— RICH L. PERSHEY

A woman in my office, recently divorced after years of marriage, had signed up for a refresher CPR course. "Is it hard to learn?" someone asked.

"Not at all," she replied. "Basically you're asked to breathe life into a dummy. I don't expect to have any problem. I did that for 32 years."

— PAULETTE BROOKS

After ten years of widowhood, I remarried. Leaving work one wintry evening, I told a colleague that it was very gratifying to once again have someone worry about me if the roads were icy. My new husband would be awaiting my arrival, I said, and would hurry out to meet me at the car.

I couldn't have been more right. As I pulled into the driveway, my husband burst out the door and came up to me. Rubbing our new car, he anxiously queried, "Did you get salt on it?"

— L. CATHERINE FERGUSON

Recently engaged, my brother-in-law Jeff brought his fiancée home to meet the family. When asked if she was enjoying herself, she politely replied yes. "She would say that," Jeff interjected. "She's not the type to say no."

"I see," my husband said after a brief silence. "And that explains the engagement."

— ALLISON BEVANS

When my wife had to rush to the hospital unexpectedly, she asked me to bring her a few items from home. One item on the list was "comfortable underwear." Worried I'd make the wrong choice, I asked, "How will I know which ones to pick?"

"Hold them up and imagine them on me," she said. "If you smile, put them back."

— ROBERT KERCHER

On my way home from a long and stressful day at the office, the phone rang. It was my husband. "Will you be joining me in the whirlpool bath tonight?" he asked.

What a lovely way to spend an evening, I thought. I was about to tell him how considerate he was when he continued, "Because if you're not, I need to start adding more water to the tub."

— SUSAN NELSON

"Don't ask questions, Ralph. Just tell me who you'd rather look like—Sean Connery or Robert Redford."

173

"

No matter what kind of backgrounds two men are from, if you go, "Hey, man, women are crazy," you've got a friend.

— CHRIS ROCK in Us Weekly

Why leave the nut you got for one you don't know?

— LORETTA LYNN in Esquire

My husband is so confident that when he watches sports on television, he thinks that if he concentrates he can help his team. If the team is in trouble, he coaches the players from our living room, and if they're really in trouble, I have to get off the phone in case they call him.

— RITA RUDNER

Love is the answer, but while you're waiting for the answer, sex raises some pretty good questions.

— WOODY ALLEN

Three words strike fear into the hearts of men: Pop the question.

— ROXANNE HAWN
in The Denver Post

Instead of getting married again, I'm going to find a woman I don't like and just give her a house.

— ROD STEWART

According to *Modern Bride* magazine, the average bride spends 150 hours planning her wedding. The average groom spends 150 hours going, "Yeah, sounds good."

— JAY LENO

My wife and I were comparing notes the other day. "I have a higher IQ, did better on my SATs and make more money than you," she pointed out.

"Yeah, but when you step back and look at the big picture, I'm still ahead," I said.

She looked mystified. "How do you figure?"

"I married better," I replied.

— LOUIS RODOLICO

A friend and her husband were participating in a blood drive, and as part of the pre-screening process, an elderly volunteer was asking some questions. "Have you ever paid for sex?" the woman asked my friend's husband sweetly.

Glancing wearily over at his wife, trying to calm a new baby and tend to several other children milling around her, he sighed, "Every time."

— WENDI WOOLF

While in the men's room at a beach park in Florida, I noticed they had a plastic baby-changing table installed on the wall. Apparently, some sportsmen had co-opted this politically correct amenity for their own use. Above the table was a sign saying: "It is unlawful to clean fish on this table."

— CLIFF REVELL

While at a marine-supply store stocking up on equipment for my boat, I also purchased an inflatable life preserver. "It was my wife's idea," I explained to the grizzled salesman at the counter. "She's buying it for me as a gift."

"Lucky you," he said as he started to write up the order. "My wife got me a length of chain and a cement block."

— THOMAS FRONCEK

My friend's mother is a proper Southern lady and a passionate gardener who spends hours outside with her plants. In her neighborhood, where she has lived most of her life, no one has fences and every yard is open to the next. Recently one of her longtime neighbors, an elderly man, moved away. "Are you going to miss him?" my friend asked.

"Actually I'm relieved," her mother replied. "Now I can bend over."

— RENEE WALKER PRITZKER

"There! Now we're getting somewhere."

175

The Guys & Dolls— Syndrome

BY DAVE BARRY

1 You're on a tight deadline for developing a big sales proposal, but you've hit a snag. You want to go one way; a co-worker named Bob strongly disagrees.

To break the deadlock, you:

(a) Present your position, listen to the other side, then fashion a compromise.

(b) Punch Bob.

2 Your favorite team is about to win the championship, but at the last second the victory is stolen away by a terrible referee's call. You:

(a) Remind yourself that it's just a game, that there are far more important things in life.

(b) Punch Bob.

How to Score: If you answered "b" to both questions, then you are a male. I base this statement on an article in *The New York Times* about the way animals, including humans, respond to stress. According to the article, a group of psychology researchers have made the breakthrough discovery that—prepare to be astounded—males and females are different.

The researchers discovered this by studying both humans and rats, which are very similar to humans except that they are not stupid enough to purchase lottery tickets. The studies show that when males are under stress, they respond by either fighting or running away—the so-called "fight or flight" syndrome. Females respond by nurturing others and making friends—the so-called "tend and befriend" syndrome.

This finding is big news in the psychology community, which is apparently located on a distant planet. Here on Earth, we've been aware for some time that males and females respond differently to stress. We know that if two males bump into each other, they'll respond like this:

First Male: Hey, watch it!
Second Male: No, YOU watch it!
First Male: Oh, yeah?
(They deliberately bump into each other again.)

Two females in an identical situation will respond like this:

First Female: I'm sorry!
Second Female: No, it's my fault!
First Female: Say, those are cute shoes!
(They go shopping.)

If the psychology community needs further proof of the difference between the sexes, I invite it to attend the party held in my neighborhood each Halloween.

This party is attended by several hundred small children who are experiencing stress because their bloodstreams—as a result of the

176

When men go ape, women go shopping. And that's all you need to know about gender.

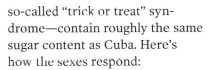

so-called "trick or treat" syndrome—contain roughly the same sugar content as Cuba. Here's how the sexes respond:

- The females, 97 percent of whom are dressed as either a ballerina or a princess, sit in little social groups and exchange candy.

- The males, 97 percent of whom are dressed as either Batman or a Power Ranger, run around making martial-arts noises and bouncing violently off one another like crazed subatomic particles.

Here are some other gender-based syndromes that the psychology community might want to look into:

- The "laundry refolding" syndrome: This has been widely noted by both me and my friend Jeff. The male will attempt to fold a piece of laundry. When he is done, the female, with a look of disapproval, will immediately pick it up and refold it so that it is much neater and smaller. "My wife can make an entire bedsheet virtually disappear," Jeff reports.

- The "inflatable pool toy" syndrome: From the dawn of civilization, the task of inflating inflatable pool toys has fallen to the male. It is often the female who comes home with an inflatable pool toy the size of the *Hindenburg*, causing the youngsters to become very excited. But it is inevitably the male who spends two hours blowing the toy up, after which he keels over, while the kids, who have been helping out by whining impatiently, leap joyfully onto the toy, puncturing it immediately.

I think psychology researchers should find out if these syndromes exist in other species. They could put some rats into a cage with tiny pool toys and miniature pieces of laundry, then watch to see what happens. My guess is that there would be fighting. Among the male researchers, I mean. It's a shame, this male tendency toward aggression, which has caused so many horrible problems such as war and hockey.

It frankly makes me ashamed of my gender.

I'm going to punch Bob. ▲

I was bending over to wipe up a spill on the kitchen floor when my wife walked into the room behind me. "See anything you like?" I asked suggestively. **"Yeah," she said. "You doing housework."**

— MICHAEL SHOCKLEY

One day my housework-challenged husband decided to wash his sweatshirt. Seconds after he stepped into the laundry room, he shouted to me, "What setting do I use on the washing machine?"

"It depends," I replied. "What does it say on your shirt?"

"University of Oklahoma," he yelled back.

— JERRI BOYER

The birth of our second child, a daughter, came after a long and difficult labor. But it was definitely worth it when our beautiful little girl emerged, perfect in every way. Later, in my room, my husband looked at her tenderly, with tears in his eyes.

Then as he glanced up at me, I expected him to utter something truly poetic. Instead he asked, "What's her name again?"

— CHRISTINA L. MILLER

As I was stepping into the shower after an afternoon of yard work, my wife walked into the bathroom. "What do you think the neighbors would say if I cut the grass dressed like this?" I asked.

Giving me a casual glance, she replied, "They'd say I married you for your money."

— JOHN R. BUCO

After four years of separation, my wife and I finally divorced amicably. I wanted to date again, but had no idea of how to start, so I decided to look in the personals column of the local newspaper. After reading through all the listings, I circled three that seemed possible in terms of age and interests, but I put off calling them.

Two days later, there was a message on my answering machine from my ex-wife: "I came over to your house to borrow some tools today and saw the ads you circled in the paper. Don't call the one in the second column. It's me."

— NELSON WORKMAN

I accompanied my husband when he went to get a haircut. Reading a magazine, I found a hairstyle I liked for myself, so I asked the receptionist if I could take the magazine next door to make a copy of the photo.

"Leave some ID—a driver's license or credit card," she said.

"But my husband is here getting a haircut," I explained.

"Yes," she replied. "But I need something you'll come back for."

— MELISSA ANDERSON

"How do you know when you're in love? I don't know. Go ask your mother."

My wife and I were at my high school reunion. As I looked around, I noticed the other men in their expensive suits and bulging stomachs. Proud of the fact that I weighed just five pounds more than I did when I was in high school—the result of trying to beat a living out of a rocky hillside farm—I said to my wife, "I'm the only guy here who can wear the suit he graduated in."

She glanced at the prosperous crowd, then back at me. "You're the only one who has to."

— GEORGE CRENSHAW

At my granddaughter's wedding, the DJ polled the guests to see who had been married the longest. Since it turned out to be my husband and me, the DJ asked us, "What advice would you give to the newly married couple?"

I said, "The three most important words in a marriage are, 'You're probably right.'"

Everyone then looked expectantly at my husband. "She's probably right," he said.

— BARBARA HANCOCK

Mrs. Willencot was very frugal. When her husband died, she asked the newspaper how much it would cost for a death notice. "Two dollars for five words."

"Can I pay for just two words?" she asked. "Willencot dead."

"No, five words is the minimum."

Mrs. Willencot thought a moment. "Willencot dead. Cadillac for sale."

For my fourth Caesarian section I opted for a bikini incision, which, along with the previous scars, would form an arrow on my tummy. "Honey," my husband joked when I told him, "after 13 years and 4 kids, I hardly need directions."

— PATTI CECIL

Timeless Humor from the 70's

About two o'clock one summer morning, my friend and her husband, who likes to sleep in his birthday suit, were awakened by a thunderstorm. They both dashed from the bed and began shutting windows. When her husband got downstairs, he realized the umbrella on the patio table had been left open and gusts of wind were causing the table to teeter precariously near the glass doors. He figured it would take only a moment to run out and take the umbrella down, so he did not waste time fetching a robe.

Once on the patio, however, he found the wind was stronger than he expected. Before he could close the umbrella, the wind lifted the shaft from the table and pulled it and him out into the yard. As he grappled with the umbrella, several flashes of lightning lit up the yard like a Broadway stage. Finally, he accomplished his mission and went back into the house, much to the relief of his wife, who had witnessed the entire episode.

They had no sooner settled in bed than the phone rang. It was their neighbor, who said, "We just wanted to let Mary Poppins know how much we enjoyed the show."

— DOROTHY BRUNI

At the airport check-in counter, I overheard a woman ask for window seats for her and her husband. The clerk pointed out that this would prevent them from sitting together.

"Sweetie," the woman replied. "I just spent ten days of quality time in a compact rental car with this man. I know what I'm requesting."

— CAROL GORES

I was about to leave the house on an errand, and my husband was getting ready for a dental appointment. "I wish we could trade places," I said, knowing how much he dreaded the coming ordeal.

He watched as I gathered our newborn onto my left arm and picked up a package with that hand. I flung a diaper bag and my purse over my right shoulder, grabbed our two-year-old with my free hand and wrestled the car keys from him.

My husband shook his head. "No, thanks," he said. "At least where I'm going they give you anesthesia."

— LINDA CHIARA

Timeless Humor from the **70's**

My mother and I were having a mother-daughter talk about the qualities to look for in a husband. She stressed that husband and wife should be as much alike as possible in interests and backgrounds. I brought up the point that opposites often attract.

"Diane," she said emphatically, "just being man and woman is opposite enough."

— DIANE RENZI

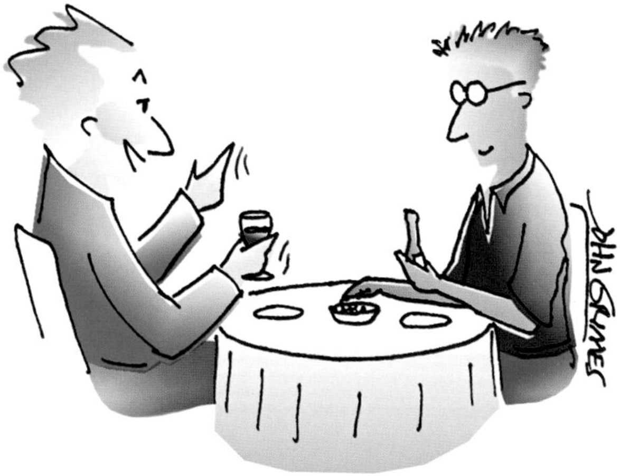

"We're still at that stage where she loves me more than I annoy her."

Humor in Uniform

The trials and tribulations of our sons, daughters, parents, and friends in the military.

"Remember, men, our motto is

Leap before you **look."**

Reservists like myself always had a hard time parking on base, as most spaces were set aside for the brass. My wife never had this problem. I finally found out why after she drove me to the PX and parked in a space marked "Reserved."

"See?" she said. "Just look at all the spaces they've set aside for you Reserves."

— JAMES KLEEMAN

Going over our weekly training schedule one morning at our small Army garrison, we noticed that our annual trip to the rifle range had been canceled for the second time, but that our semi-annual physical-fitness test was still on as planned. "Does it bother anyone else," one soldier asked, "that the Army doesn't seem concerned with how well we can shoot, yet is extremely interested in how fast we can run?"

— THOMAS L. HAMMOND

The colonel who served as inspector general in our command paid particular attention to how personnel wore their uniforms. On one occasion he spotted a junior airman with a violation. "Airman," he bellowed, "what do you do when a shirt pocket is unbuttoned?"

The startled airman replied, "Button it, sir!"

The colonel looked him in the eye and said, "Well?"

At that, the airman nervously reached over and buttoned the colonel's shirt pocket.

— G. DEARING, JR.

When my husband visited our son, Michael, at boot camp, he found him marching smartly with his unit. Michael's father proudly approached the soldiers and began to snap photo after photo. Embarrassed and worried about getting into trouble, Michael looked straight ahead and didn't change his expression.

Suddenly his drill sergeant barked, "Comito, give me 25 push-ups. And the next time your daddy wants your picture, you smile!"

— EDYTHE COMITO

During basic training, our drill sergeant asked for a show of hands of all Jewish personnel. Six of us tentatively raised our hands. Much to our relief, we were given the day off for Rosh Hashanah.

A few days later in anticipation of Yom Kippur, the drill sergeant again asked for all Jewish personnel to ID themselves. This time, every soldier raised his hand. "Only the personnel who were Jewish last week can be Jewish this week," declared the sergeant.

— ALLEN ISRAEL

In a lecture to a group of Korean officers, Lieut. Gen. Bruce C. Clarke, at that time deputy commander of the Eighth Army in Korea, took two or three minutes to tell his favorite joke. His interpreter then quickly translated the joke, using only seven or eight words. Everyone immediately burst into hearty laughter. After the lecture General Clarke asked the interpreter how he had been able to retell such a relatively long joke so quickly.

"Well, sir," the Korean interpreter replied, "I didn't think everyone would get the point, so I said, 'The general has just told a joke. Everyone will please laugh.'"

— ROBERT H. SELLECK

My daughter, Emily, told a friend that her brother, Chris, was training to become a Navy submariner. The friend, who'd just been assigned to a Navy destroyer, good-naturedly called Chris a Bubblehead.

Later I related the story to Chris and asked if he'd heard the term. He said he had, and added, "We also have a name for people who work on destroyers."

"What is it?" I asked.

"Targets."

— JO BARKER

"Support Your Local Coast Guard…Get Lost."

— GRAYCE BARCK

Two days before officer-training graduation, I bragged that my single demerit was the lowest in the company. The next day I saw with chagrin a slip on my bunk, and was thoroughly humbled when I read the list:

1 Demerit: Littering. Penny under bed.

1 Demerit: Lincoln needs a shave and a haircut.

1 Demerit: Trying to bribe an officer.

1 Demerit: Bribe not enough.

— FREDERIC P. SEITZ

After joining the Navy, my husband underwent a physical. During the exam, it was discovered that, due to an abnormality, he couldn't fully extend his arms above his head. Perplexed, the doctor conferred with another doctor.

"Let him pass," suggested the second doctor. "I don't see any problems unless he has to surrender."

— BETTY LEE

Safety is job one in the Air Force. Overstating the obvious is job two, as I discovered when crawling into my military-issue sleeping bag. The label read: "In case of an emergency, unzip and exit through the top."

— KEITH J. WALTERS

One of my jobs in the Army is to give service members and their families tours of the demilitarized zone in South Korea. Before taking people to a lookout point to view North Korea, we warn visitors to watch their heads climbing the stairs, as there is a low overhang. The tour guide, first to the top, gets to see how many people have not heeded his advice.

On one tour I watched almost an entire unit hit their heads one after another as they came up the stairs. Curious, I asked their commander what unit they were from.

"Military intelligence," he replied.

— EDWARD RAMIREZ

While standing watch in the Coast Guard station in Juneau, Alaska, I got a call from the Navy in the nearby city of Adak. They had lost contact with one of their planes, and they needed the Coast Guard to send an aircraft to go find it. I asked the man where the Navy aircraft had last been spotted so we would know where to search.

"I can't tell you," the Navy man said. "That's classified."

— ALFRED MILES

"Don't mind me. It's just the absolute power talking."

Serving as a Marine recruiter in western North Carolina, I found a young man who met all the requirements and was ready to enlist. I explained the importance of being truthful on the application, and he began filling out his paperwork. But when he got to the question "Do you own any foreign property or have any foreign financial interests?" he looked up at me with a worried expression. "Well," he confessed, "I do own a Toyota." We enlisted him the next day.

— PATRICK L. JACKS

To mail a big package of cookies to my two Air Force sons, both of whom were serving in Saudi Arabia, I was required to attach a label describing the contents. I carefully marked the box "Cookies" and sent it off, but after a month my sons said they had yet to receive my package.

Suspicious, I baked another batch, only this time I labeled the contents "Health Food." Within a week my sons reported they had received the goodies.

— WANDA HAMEISTER

After being at sea in the Persian Gulf for 90 straight days, I went to the squadron command master chief to complain. "Chief, I joined the Navy to see the world," I said, "but for the past three months all I've seen is water."

"Lieutenant," he replied, "three-quarters of the earth is covered with water, and the Navy has been showing you that. If you wanted to see the other quarter, you should have joined the Army."

— PAUL NEWMAN

Our division had to repaint our Humvees to a sand color for Desert Storm. The result was a pinkish hue, and the jokes began. One wag renamed us the Pink Panzer Division. But the best was the Humvee bumper sticker "Ask me about Mary Kay."

— DAVID K. DRURY

Having helped prepare the annual budget for my unit of the Seventh Army Special Troops in Heidelberg, Germany, I took the report to the office of the adjutant, who signs all official papers. The adjutant was not in, but his assistant, a young lieutenant, was.

He gasped as I handed him the huge sheaf of charts, figures and explanations. "What am I supposed to do with this?" he asked.

"That's Admiral Blackly.
He drowned in a sea of red tape."

"You have to sign it, sir."

"Thank goodness," he said, sighing with relief. "I thought I had to read it."

— TIMOTHY QUINN

Timeless Humor from the 60's

During my Air Force basic training, I cracked the frames of my eyeglasses. After taping them, I applied for new frames. I didn't get them, so I applied again at each base to which I was sent. After four years, and just before my discharge, I received nine sets of frames—all marked "Rush."

— JOHN C. SOCHER

"He's our most decorated general, although he obviously lost the Battle of the Bulge."

The lieutenant wanted to use a pay phone but didn't have change for a dollar. He saw a private mopping the floors and asked him, "Soldier, do you have change for a dollar?"

"I sure have, buddy," the private answered.

Giving him a mean stare, the lieutenant said, "That's no way to address an officer. Let's try it again. Private, do you have change for a dollar?"

"No, sir," the private replied.

— GEORGE MELLO

My son, Barry, came home from a three-month deployment aboard his submarine, and told us that one of the ways the sailors kept up morale was to make wooden cars out of kits and run derby races. "What do you do for a ramp?" my husband inquired.

"Don't need one," Barry said. "We just put the cars on the floor and then tilt the sub."

— MARY C. RYAN

After years of checking inventories every time we moved, I really thought I knew my way around official Air Force prose. Then I went to work at a toy counter in a PX and found that good old children's favorite, the teddy bear, listed as, "Bears, fur, Edward."

— ALISON KERR

Notice seen on the bulletin board of a Florida air base: "The following enlisted men will pick up their Good Conduct medals in the supply room this afternoon. Failure to comply with this order will result in disciplinary action."

Myra Hayes

My brother and I arrived at boot camp together. On the first morning, our unit was dragged out of bed by our drill sergeant and made to assemble outside. "My name's Sergeant Jackson," he snarled. "Is there anyone here who thinks he can whip me?"

My six-foot-three, 280-pound brother raised his hand and said, "Yes, sir, I do."

Our sergeant grabbed him by the arm and led him out in front of the group. "Men," he said, "this is my new assistant. Now, is there anyone here who thinks he can whip both of us?"

— ROBERT NORRIS

When I was an infantry platoon commander, my Marines trained regularly for nighttime reconnaissance patrol. As we moved along, each of us would whisper the name of any obstacle to the person behind so that no one would be surprised and utter a cry that would disclose our position.

During one exercise, the lead man in the formation occasionally turned around and whispered to me "Log" or "Rock," which I would pass along. Suddenly there was a crash ahead of me and, from several feet down, I heard a single whispered word—"Hole."

— MIKE ROBBINS

Hope and Humor in Uniform

▶ BY JAMIE MALANOWSKI

On the day the United States entered World War II, Bob Hope was 38 years old and as big as any celebrity in America. His breezy, wisecracking persona had proved to be a winner, first in vaudeville, then radio and, beginning in the late 1930s, motion pictures. He was married and had two young children, was earning a half-million dollars a year (a phenomenal amount in those days) and owned a beautiful home in the San Fernando Valley. He would go on to star in television, which further established him as one of the finest performers of his time.

But first, he took up entertaining the troops. Had he not traveled great distances, often perilously close to the fighting, to make American soldiers laugh, it's likely we would remember him less vividly. His image—with his crooked grin, bouncing on the balls of his feet on a stage in front of a thousand men in uniform—is as much a part of Americana as Washington crossing the Delaware.

Hope's initial appearance before a military audience was in May 1941, seven months before Pearl Harbor. A producer of his radio show who had a brother stationed at March Field, an Army base in nearby Riverside, Calif., suggested that Hope perform the show there. With some cajoling, Hope agreed, and for the first time began to adapt his jokes to a military context.

"Well, here we are at March Field…and I want to tell you that I'm thrilled being here.…What a wonderful welcome you gave me. …One rookie came running up and said, 'Are you really Bob Hope?'…They grabbed his rifle just in time."

They were simple, silly gags, but a thousand men ground down by the rigors and monotony of training-camp life are a virtually bombproof audience. Hope cracked up the crowd, which was even more appreciative of singer Frances Langford, a pretty girl-next-door type, who to those men must have seemed like a golden-throated Aphrodite. Both Hope and his sponsor, Pepsodent toothpaste, realized they had discovered a gold mine. For the next five years, with barely an exception, Hope's show originated from a military base.

The entertainer knew how to work an audience. He salted his jokes with GI lingo, dropped in officers' names, mentioned the local watering holes. Hope had always won laughs playing the smart aleck. But the real comic payoff came when he played the biggest chicken of them all.

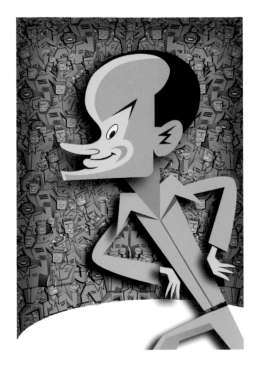

Celebrating the unforgettable funny man

"I just got a new rating from my draft board—Four Z. That means 'Coward.'…One of the aviators here took me for a plane ride this afternoon. I wasn't frightened, but at 2,000 feet, one of my goose pimples bailed out. …But all the fellas here have been great, except for one kid who was doing KP. This fella had been breaking all the rules, going AWOL, running around with women. I said to him, 'What's the big idea, son?' He said, 'Mr. Hope, did you give a pint of blood to the Red Cross last year?' And I said, 'Yes.' He said, 'Well, shake hands with the guy who got it.'"

"I waited in the rain for two hours to see his show," says Ed McMahon, of Johnny Carson's "Tonight Show" fame, then a Marine Corps aviation cadet in Georgia. "In the days before he came, the whole camp was excited. We were in the midst of this rough knock 'em, sock 'em, push 'em out the back door training, and he was just this breath of fresh air, a reminder of the life you used to have."

For his later shows in Vietnam before some 20,000 men, Hope traveled with a large troupe of entertainers and a caravan of television technicians.

But his international World War II trips—some of which Hope underwrote—had a strikingly impromptu quality. In 1942, after a hectic year playing stateside bases and bond rallies (in addition to filming *They Got Me Covered*), Hope persuaded the Army to let him go to Alaska and the Aleutians. Hope, Langford, second banana Jerry Colonna and guitarist Tony Romano piled into an Army cargo plane and flew north, popping from camp to camp.

"I knew it was an old plane when I saw the pilot sitting behind me wearing goggles and a scarf."

Alaska wasn't a fire zone, but it was cold and desolate, and the men, Hope observed, were the loneliest guys in the world. "What we're suffering most is cabin fever," an officer told Hope. "Some of these boys have been stuck up here for a year with old books, old newspapers, old movies and stale relationships."

Hope's company played before crowds of 600 in Quonset huts built for half that number. The laughter—louder, heartier, more appreciative than any he'd ever heard—inspired Hope. One show may have been scheduled, but he'd do another for the fellows who'd been on duty.

After the war, Mort Lachman had a three-decade association with Hope as a writer and director, but during the war was one of those lonely boys in Alaska. "Bob thrived on the laughter," he says.

But something more was at work. The farther from the States the men were stationed, and the more dire the conditions, the more clearly Hope realized what he represented.

"We spelled home to those troops," he later wrote. "When they heard us speak, they were back in the living room in front of the Atwater Kent radio with Mom and Dad."

Even a close call did nothing to temper Hope's enthusiasm. The Army had warned him that air travel in Alaska was inherently dangerous, and advised the troupe's pilot never to fly after dark. But one night, eager to get back to base, Hope persuaded his pilots to skip the planned layover and push on through. It didn't seem that risky a move; after all, the weather was good. But things changed once the party was airborne. Sleet and hail pelted the plane, visibility fell to zero and the radio gave out. Then one of the engines failed.

"We spelled home to those troops," he later wrote. "When they heard us speak, they were back in the living room in front of the Atwater Kent radio with Mom and Dad."

A crew member passed out parachutes and life vests. Suddenly, the plane lurched, smacked by the prop wash from another plane. They were lucky not to have collided, and lucky in another way: The other plane radioed the base about the incident. The men at the airdrome immediately trained every searchlight they had skyward and, with that guidance, Hope's pilots were able to land.

Days later, after returning to California, Hope purchased cigarette cases for the pilots and had them engraved: "Thanks for the memories. Your cargo, Bob Hope and Frances Langford." He then began planning his next campaign. He decided he would follow the front. It was 1943, and American troops had won control of North Africa and begun the invasion of Sicily. Hope and his gypsies went too.

"Hello, fellow tourists!…Well, I'm very happy to be here. Of course, I'm leaving as soon as we finish.…Gosh, it's hot here. I took one look at a pup tent, and it was panting!…But the guys out there are really tough! They don't bother manicuring.…They just stick their hands under a rock and let the cobras bite off the cuticle."

In 11 weeks abroad, Hope put on 250 shows, some of them near the front line. At Palermo, his audience brought their weapons, and fighters patrolled above. "Among the thousands of letters Dad got from GIs," remembers Linda Hope, "was one from a sergeant in charge of a small detail who had trekked miles and miles to see the show, and got there late. They sent up a note that said, 'Sorry we missed the show,' and started trekking back. The next thing they knew, here comes this jeep containing Dad and Frances and Jerry, who delivered a little command performance on the spot."

They made a specific point of playing for the wounded. The troupe crashed into hospital wards like circus clowns, grabbing the nurses and creating an uproar. "They're not interested in your sympathy or how horrified you are," Hope told Langford. "You're there to take their minds off their wounds. That's our job."

"That's all right, fellas, don't get up. Hey, did you see the show, or were you sick before?"

Questions about privilege, about why some stars were in uniform and others were not, percolated during the war years, and Hope was conscious of his civilian status. "Some night," he told a columnist, "some big guy will stand up and yelp, 'Why in hell aren't you in the service?' And that is the $64 question I won't be able to answer."

They may not have enlisted, but Langford recalls the night in Africa they were strafed by fighters and ended up leaping for their lives into a ditch full of sheep droppings. And then there was the night in Palermo when the Germans bombarded Hope's hotel.

"The strafing…the screeching. …We were throwing plenty of stuff at the Germans as well. I joined in. I threw up my dinner."

Inevitably, the day came when a soldier in the audience did challenge Hope. "Draft dodger!" the man yelled. "Why aren't you in uniform?"

Hope defended himself disarm-ingly. "Don't you know there's a war on?" he replied. "A guy could get hurt!"

Those close to Hope say he came home from the 1943 Medi-terranean tour a more serious man. "He had developed a deeper love and respect for people," says his wife, Dolores. He brought back countless messages from the front, and for weeks devoted time each day to calling families to say he'd seen their sons.

Others treated him more seri-ously as well. *Time* put him on the cover, headlining the article "Hope for Humanity." John Steinbeck, writing in the New York *Herald Tribune,* sounded a similar theme. "When the time for recognition of service to the nation in wartime comes to be considered, Bob Hope should be high on the list.…He has caught the soldier's imagination.…It goes beyond how funny he can be. …He has become a symbol."

In 1944 Hope hit the road again, hopping across the South Pacific.

"What an island! You guys aren't defending this place, are you? Let them take it, it'll serve them right!"

One night Hope performed before 15,000 Marines on the island of Pavuvu. Those same Marines went on to take terrible casualties assaulting Peleliu. Months afterward at a hospital ward, Hope saw a man, swathed in bandages, who put out his hand and said, "Pavuvu!"

"I shook his hand and walked away," Hope later wrote. "I couldn't handle it."

The war ended, but Hope's dedication to American service-men and women did not. All the way from the Berlin Airlift to Vietnam through Desert Shield, Hope brought his blend of gags and girls to troops in short supply of both.

The military has recognized his dedication, naming a plane and a ship after him. But perhaps the most meaningful honor accorded Hope was the simplest.

In 1997, Congress named him a veteran.

It's a tribute that no other civil-ian has earned. ▲

Bob Hope died in 2003, less than two months after his 100th birthday.

"This one is for fighting off defense spending cuts."

Whenever I begin to feel a bit smug, I recall my first week at naval officer candidate school in Newport, R.I. I learned quickly, I thought, and was getting adept at giving commands like, "To the rear…", "March" and "Company…Halt."

There is a procedure for stacking rifles in which they end up looking like a small tepee. My bubble of pride was burst when I realized during a drill that I hadn't the faintest idea what the command to stack rifles should be.

With all the dignity I could summon, I called out, "Rifles in little bunches…Put!"

— WILLIAM DUTSON

Pointing to a pan of chicken wings and legs disguised in the classic mess-hall manner, a young airman asked the mess sergeant, "What's for chow?"

"Air Force chicken," replied the sergeant. "You want wings or landing gear?"

— PAUL JAGGER

My wife, Dolores, never quite got the hang of the 24-hour military clock. One day she called the orderly room and asked to speak with me. The person who answered told her to call me at the extension in the band rehearsal hall. "He can be reached at 4700, ma'am," the soldier advised.

With a sigh of exasperation, my wife responded, "And just what time is that?"

— ERIC D. ERICKSON

On a business trip, my father approached a security checkpoint at the airport. The National Guard shift was rotating, and a guard, in full uniform, was in line in front of him. As with everybody else, the soldier was ordered to go through the metal detector. Before doing so, he handed his M-16 rifle to security personnel along with other items such as handcuffs and a flashlight. Still the alarm sounded when he walked through. Further inspection revealed a Swiss army knife inside one of his pockets.

"Sorry, sir," security said to the soldier, "but this item is prohibited." Taking the knife away, the airport worker then handed him back the M-16.

— SAMANTHA COUCHOUD

We had just moved to an Army post from an Air Force base and my young son, an avid fan of GI Joe toys, was excited to see the troops marching in cadence. An even bigger thrill came when he passed the motor pool with its tanks, jeeps and trucks.

"Look!" he squealed with delight. "They have the whole collection!"

— JEREMY THORNTON

My unit at Fort Bliss in Texas was detailed with guard duty. However, since live ammunition was reserved for sensitive locations, our rifles were issued with unloaded magazines. One day while we stood at attention for inspection, the officer in charge confronted a private and barked, "What is the maximum effective range of your M-16, soldier?"

The hapless private glanced down at his empty rifle and replied, "As far as I can throw it, sir."

— JAN GETTING

In helicopter training at Fort Rucker, Ala., I heard a radio transmission between an instructor and his student pilot. They were practicing hovering, a tricky maneuver.

"See if you can keep your helicopter inside the concrete boundary," the instructor said.

A few minutes later, he revised his request. "Hell, Candidate," he shouted, "just keep it in Alabama."

— ANTHONY D. LONG

Our personnel officer, annoyed by the report from his secretary that troops and members of the staff were using the new copying machine for personal documents, posted this notice on the machine: "Troops are not to tamper with the secretary's reproduction equipment without approval of the officer in charge."

— FLOYD G. SEAY

I was a second lieutenant in the Army, learning to fly light aircraft at Fort Sill, Okla. One day I made a perfectly smooth landing—at last. To my horror, when I stepped on the brakes, nothing at all happened.

I shouted to my instructor. "The brakes failed!"

"I'm not surprised," he growled. "We're still two feet in the air."

— DARWIN ADAMS

My Army troop was learning how to parachute from a plane. At 12,000 feet, our drill instructor shouted out instructions for surviving a jump from above the clouds at more than 200 m.p.h. A young recruit raised his hand and asked, "Once we jump out, how much time do we have to pull the cord?"

The instructor looked back, smiled and said, "The rest of your life."

— KEVIN K. HENDRICK

"This Marine Cooking School taught me a great recipe, Mom—you take one hundred pounds of potatoes..."

Bumper sticker:
"To err is human, to forgive divine. Neither is Marine Corps policy."
— TOM FRONCEK

The crew of a fast frigate was practicing the man overboard drill by "rescuing" a bright orange fluorescent dummy dubbed Oscar. The captain watched as a young lieutenant nervously stopped the ship, turned it and maneuvered into place. Unfortunately, he ran right over Oscar.

Surveying the remains of Oscar scattered around the ship, the captain told the lieutenant, "Son, do me a favor. If I ever fall overboard, just drop anchor and I'll swim to you."

— ANTHONY WATSON

One of my first duties as an Air Force officer was to set up a field medical-training program at our hospital. I conducted a class in triage—sorting out battlefield casualties according to the likelihood of survival. We had applied theatrical makeup to several airmen to simulate different wounds. Pointing to one of the "casualties," I said to the group, "This man has severe brain damage. What would you do with him?"

Came this reply from the back of the class: "Make him an officer!"

— THOMAS L. PATTERSON

Newly married, I was en route to Keesler Air Force Base in Biloxi, Miss., to join my husband, a recently commissioned second lieutenant. I arrived at the gate and was motioned in. Gripping a map he had given me, I drove on, looking for the Base Exchange.

After turning onto one road, I heard a siren and was startled to see two airmen in a jeep, motioning me over. One got out and ran toward me. "Please follow us," he said.

Timeless Humor from the **70's**

Approaching a GI who had just arrived in South Vietnam, I asked him how long he expected to be here. "Well," he replied, "the sergeant told us we'd be here for 12 months and two Bob Hope specials or one Purple Heart, whichever comes first."

— JOHN O. HOUCHENS

"Why?" I asked.

"Well, ma'am," he politely replied, "that plane down there would like to take off."

— DIANE SMITH

As a department head stationed on a Navy vessel, I was concerned about one of my senior enlisted men. He was a superb technician, but he had a problem taking orders. One day I took him aside and suggested he try something that had worked for me. "Whenever an officer gives you a directive that you think is stupid," I told him, "just say, 'Yes, sir.' But in your mind, think, 'You're an idiot!' Will this work for you?"

He smiled at me and replied, "Yes, sir!"

— LEO KING

All Creatures

Great and Small

▶

Dogs, cats, and countless common critters are all part of our everyday lives. Here's the funny stuff that happens when animals cross paths with us humans.

"I'd get so much more done if only I could get by
on seventeen hours of sleep."

A man is standing on the curb, getting ready to cross the street. As soon as he steps down onto the pavement, a car comes screaming straight at him. The man picks up speed, but so does the car. So the man turns around and heads back, but the car changes lanes and keeps coming. Now the vehicle is so close and the pedestrian is so scared that he freezes in the middle of the intersection. The car closes in on him—then swerves at the last possible moment and screeches to a halt.

The driver rolls down the window. Behind the wheel is a squirrel. "See," sneers the squirrel, "it's not as easy as it looks, is it?"

One beautiful morning, my husband and I decided to go for a drive in the country. Unfortunately, no matter which road we took, we kept seeing dead possums lying on the shoulder.

After several miles of this, my husband turned to me and said, "Now I think I know the answer to the age-old question 'Why did the chicken cross the road?'"

"What is it?" I asked.

"Well," he replied, "it was to prove to the possums that it could be done."

— JUANITA PAGE

My father's secretary was visibly distraught one morning when she arrived at the office and explained that her children's parrot had escaped from his cage and flown out an open window. Of all the dangers the tame bird would face outdoors alone, she seemed most concerned about what would happen if the bird started talking.

Confused, my father asked what the parrot could say.

"Well," she explained, "he mostly says, 'Here, kitty, kitty.'"

— TERRY WALKER

A man walks into a pub with a salamander on his shoulder and takes a seat at the bar.

"Nice pet," the bartender says. "What's his name?"

"I call him Tiny," the man replies.

"Why's that?"

"Because he's my newt."

— BARNEY WELLS

In good weather, my friend Mark always let his yellow-naped Amazon parrot, Nicky, sit on the balcony of his tenth-floor apartment. One morning, Nicky flew away, much to Mark's dismay. He searched and called for the bird, with no luck.

The next day when Mark returned from work, the phone rang. "Is this Mark?" The caller asked. "You're going to think this is crazy, but there's a bird outside on my balcony saying, 'Hello, this is Mark.' Then it recites this phone number and says, 'I can't come to the phone right now, but if you will leave a message at the tone, I will call you back.'"

Nicky's cage had been kept in the same room as Mark's answering machine.

— ANNE R. NEILSON

sign language

I was editing classified ads for a small-town newspaper when a man called to place an ad. "It should read," he said,

"'Free to good home. Golden retriever. Will eat anything, loves children.'"

— ELLEN YOUNG

At a workshop on dog temperament, the instructor noted that a test for a canine's disposition was for an owner to fall down and act hurt. A dog with poor temperament would try to bite the person, whereas a good dog would lick his owner's face or show concern.

Once, while eating pizza in the living room, I decided to try out this theory on my two dogs. I stood up, clutched my heart, let out a scream and collapsed on the floor.

The dogs looked at me, glanced at each other and raced to the coffee table for my pizza.

— SUSAN MOTTICE

Once while riding the bus to work, I noticed a man at a stop enjoying a cup of coffee. As we approached the stop, he finished drinking and set the cup on the ground. This negligence surprised me, since it seemed to be a good ceramic cup.

Days later I saw the same man again drinking his coffee at the bus stop. Once again, he placed the cup on the grass before boarding. When the bus pulled away, I looked back in time to see a dog carefully carrying the cup in his mouth as he headed for home.

— VALERIE A. HUEBNER

My neighbor's son picked up a stray dog and named it Sam. Some time later, I was having coffee at their house and inquired about Sam.

"Oh, the dog is fine," my neighbor said. "She had a litter of puppies, and so we fixed the problem. Now we call her Sam Spayed."

— JUDY CHRISTENSEN

A snake slithers into a bar and the bartender says, "Sorry, buddy. I can't serve you."

"Why not?" the snake asks.

"Because you can't hold your liquor."

— LYNDELL LEATHERMAN

When my daughter and I caught only one perch on our fishing trip—not enough for even a modest lunch—we decided to feed it to her two cats. She put our catch in their dish and watched as the two pampered pets sniffed at the fish but refused to eat it.

Thinking quickly, my daughter then picked up the dish, walked over to the electric can opener, ran it for a few seconds, then put the fish back down. The cats dug right in.

— SUSAN WARD

"I wasn't chewing it, I was editing it."

"George! NO!
Your cholesterol."

"Have someone force one of these down your throat every six hours."

My son is an avid listener to our city's police frequency, and he leaves the scanner on all the time. One morning while making his bed, I heard the dispatcher say, "Car 34, there is a five-foot boa constrictor in a front yard. The resident wants a policeman to come and remove it."

There was a long pause, then some static. Slowly, a voice said, "We can't get the car started."

— JANET R. SMITH

Living in a household with eight indoor cats requires buying large amounts of kitty litter, which I usually get in 25-pound bags—100 pounds at a time. When I was going to be out of town for a week, I decided to go to the supermarket to stock up. As my husband and I both pushed shopping carts, each loaded with five large bags of litter, a man looked at our purchases and queried, "Bengal or Siberian?"

— JUDY J. HAGG

According to the Internet: The inscription on the metal bands used by the U.S. Department of the Interior to tag migratory birds has been changed. The bands used to bear the address of the Washington Biological Survey, abbreviated as "Wash. Biol. Surv."—until the agency received the following letter from an unhappy camper: "Dear Sirs: While camping last week, I shot one of your birds. I think it was a crow. I followed the cooking instructions on the leg tag and want to tell you it tasted horrible."

The bands are now marked "Fish & Wildlife Service."

— CHRISTOPHER DEFFENBAUGH

When a rattlesnake got loose in the second-floor hall of the science building at my university, it created quite a furor. Fortunately, one of the professors was an expert on snakes. An agitated student ran to fetch him, urging him to come quickly, as a dangerous snake was loose, terrorizing everyone in the building.

The professor leisurely strolled out into the hall, examined the snake from head to tail, and calmly returned to his office. "It's not one of mine," he said, and closed the door.

— CARL ADKINS

A truck ran a red light, almost sideswiping our car. As my husband veered away, he threw his arm across me, protecting me from a possible collision. I was ready to plant a big kiss on my hero's cheek when he apologized.

In his haste, he admitted, he had forgotten it was me in the front seat and not our black Labrador, Checkers.

— APRIL COLE

I worked at a boarding kennel where people leave their dogs and cats while on vacation. One morning I had taken a cat out of his cage, and after playing with him and replenishing his food and water, I put him back in.

A few minutes later, I was surprised to see the feline at my feet, since the cage doors lock automatically when they're shut. I couldn't figure out how the cat escaped, until I bent down to pick him up and spied his nametag: "Houdini."

— BARBARA ROHRSSEN

On a recent trip to the post office, I took a few minutes to read the notices posted on the public bulletin board in the lobby. One in particular caught my eye.

It read "Lost in post-office parking lot, small boa constrictor, family pet, will not attack. Reward."

Below the notice someone had written, in what appeared to be very shaky handwriting: "Please, would you mind posting another notice when you find your boa? Thank you."

— SUSAN ESBENSEN

In his younger days our golden retriever, Catcher, often ran away when he had the chance. His veterinarian's office was about a mile down the road, and Catcher would usually end up there. The office staff knew him well and would call me to come pick him up.

One day I called the vet to make an appointment for Catcher's yearly vaccine. "Will you be bringing him?" asked the receptionist. "Or will he be coming on his own?"

— LAURA STASZAK

"How can I ever live up to all this hype?"

If dogs could talk, it would take a lot of fun out of owning one.

— ANDREW A. ROONEY, from "Not That You Asked" (Random House)

You know why fish are so thin? They eat fish.

— JERRY SEINFELD

I feel strongly that the visual arts are of vast importance. Of course I could be prejudiced. I am a visual art.

— KERMIT THE FROG

Does it ever amaze and delight you that of all the places in the world—cold grassy nests under hedgerows, warm patches of sun on a carpet—the cat chooses to sit on your lap?

— NEVADA BARR, Seeking Enlightenment (Putnam)

A racehorse is an animal that can take several thousand people for a ride at the same time.

— MARJORIE JOHNSON

The cat could very well be man's best friend but would never stoop to admitting it.

— DOUG LARSON, United Feature Syndicate

The turkey is living proof that an animal can survive with no intelligence at all.

— HARVEY D. COMSTOCK

At the end of a visit to Amsterdam, a friend borrowed an old suitcase from his hosts to carry home his souvenirs. At the airport, however, a customs officer subjected our friend's luggage to a thorough search and even sent for a drug-sniffing dog. Sure enough, the dog entered the area, headed straight for the borrowed bag and went into a frenzy. The customs officer now intensified his search, but ultimately he found nothing.

After arriving home, the young man immediately phoned his hosts and told them how puzzled he'd been by the dog's behavior.

"Perhaps," the owner of the suitcase said, "it was because that's the bag our cat usually sleeps in."

— J. RIETDIJK-SHEPHERD

I like hunting fossils, a hobby that isn't exactly my wife's favorite. On one excursion, I found the petrified bones of a squirrel-like mammal. When I brought them home and told my wife what they were, she squelched my excitement.

"I've heard of many a squirrel bringing a nut home," she remarked, "but this is the first time I've heard of a nut bringing a squirrel home."

— J. H. HILL

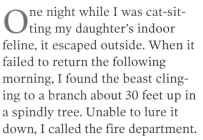

One night while I was cat-sitting my daughter's indoor feline, it escaped outside. When it failed to return the following morning, I found the beast clinging to a branch about 30 feet up in a spindly tree. Unable to lure it down, I called the fire department.

"We don't do that anymore," the woman dispatcher said. When I persisted, she was polite but firm. "The cat will come down when it gets hungry enough."

"How do you know that?" I asked.

"Have you ever seen a cat skeleton in a tree?" she said.

Two hours later the cat was back, looking for breakfast.

— TERRY CHRISTIANSEN

The drive-up window at the bank where I'm a teller has an outside drawer to accept customer transactions. A woman once drove up with her dog in the front passenger seat, and the pet eagerly jumped over onto the driver's lap when the car reached my window. He looked excited to see me.

"Your dog is so friendly!" I said to the owner.

"He thinks he's at McDonald's," she replied.

— MARILYN BOURDEAU

I always scoffed when my sister insisted that our three dogs are computer literate. Then one day when I was signing on to AOL, I noticed that when the "welcome" voice came on, the dogs immediately settled down. Later, when they heard the "good-bye" sign-off, all three dogs rushed to the door expecting to be walked.

— MARGUERITE CANTINE

sign language

In the Moreno Valley (Calif.) *Recycler:*

"Homing pigeons free to good home. Must live far, far away."

— CHRISTY SELTER

Chicken Delight

▶ BY WILLIAM GRIMES

She came, she clucked, she conquered our New York City backyard.

One day in the dead of winter, I looked out my back window and saw a chicken.

It was jet-black with a crimson wattle, and it seemed unaware that it was in New York City. In classic barnyard fashion, it was scratching, pecking and clucking.

I shrugged off the apparition. Birds come and go. Usually they're pigeons, not chickens, but like other birds, this one had wings and it would probably use them. Or so I thought.

The protagonist of this story is known simply as the Chicken. How it came to a small backyard in Astoria, Queens, remains a matter of conjecture. The chicken made its first appearance next door, at the home of a multitude of cabdrivers from Bangladesh. My wife, Nancy, and I figured they had bought the chicken and were fattening it for a feast. That hypothesis fell into doubt when the chicken hopped the fence and began pacing the perimeter of our yard with a proprietary air.

Eating it was out of the question. As a restaurant critic and an animal lover, I subscribe to a policy of complete hypocrisy. Serve fish or fowl to me, but don't ask me to watch the killing. Once I meet it, I don't want to eat it.

Nancy and I next theorized that the chicken had escaped from a live-poultry market about four blocks away and was on the run. Our hearts went out to the brave little refugee. We had to save it.

Of course we knew nothing about raising chickens. For starters, we didn't know whether our chicken was male or female. Moreover, what do chickens eat? A colleague put me in touch with a farmer, Steve Townley of Milford, N.J. He poured balm over my many and various anxieties. "Chickens will eat just about anything," he said. Cold would not kill them off. "They just fluff their feathers," Townley told me. And if there are no predators, there's really no need for a coop.

Chickens were beginning to sound like the ideal pet.

The chicken took to its new surroundings easily. Its main social task was to integrate into the local cat society—a group of about five strays we feed. How would the two species deal with each other?

One morning I looked out the window and saw four cats lined up at their food bowls, and, right in the middle, eating cat food with gusto, was the chicken.

Occasionally it would push a cat aside to get a better position.

The cats, for their part, regarded the chicken warily. To the extent that it was a bird, it was prey. But big prey. From time to time they would stalk, press their bodies to the ground, swish their tails and give every sign of going for the kill. Then they would register the chicken's size and become gripped by second thoughts. A face-saving, halfhearted lunge would follow.

The two sides soon achieved parity. Sometimes I'd look out back and see a cat chasing the chicken. Ten minutes later I'd see the chicken chasing a cat. I like to think they reached the plane of mutual respect. Perhaps affection.

Although it was nice to know the chicken could eat anything, cat food didn't seem right. When the pet-store staff couldn't help, I did what any mature adult male would do in a crisis. I called my mother.

Mom drove to the local feed store in La Porte, Texas, and picked up a 25-pound bag of scratch grains, a blend of milo, corn and oats. She began shipping the grain in installments. The chicken seemed to appreciate the feed, and I certainly preferred seeing it eat grain, especially after the grisly evening when I set out a treat for the cats—leftover shreds of chicken—and saw the chicken happily join in.

Our care paid off. One morning, Nancy spied an egg on the patio. At the base of the pine tree, where the chicken slept, was a nest containing four more eggs.

They were small, somewhere between ecru and beige, but this was it. The blessed event.

Soon we could count on five or six eggs a week.

After I wrote about the chicken in the *New York Times*, my mailbag was bursting with letters offering advice on the proper care and feeding of chickens.

Disturbed that she did not have a name, fans wrote with suggestions. Vivian had a certain sultry appeal; Henrietta seemed cute. But Henny Penny?

The media jumped in. National Public Radio quizzed me about the chicken for one of its weekend programs. "My producer wants to know, could you hold the telephone up to the chicken so we can hear it?" the interviewer asked.

Unfortunately, I don't have a 100-foot cord on my telephone. The Associated Press sent a photographer to capture the chicken's many moods. (She had two.)

Then one morning I looked out my kitchen window, and my heart stopped. No chicken—not in my pine tree or the tree next door. Nor was she pecking and scratching in any of the nearby yards. There were no signs of violence, only a single black feather near the back door.

She was definitely missing. But why?

Spring was in the air. Could she be looking for love? Or perhaps she was reacting badly to the burdens of celebrity? Or maybe she was simply looking for a place to lay her eggs in peace.

Like Garbo retiring from motion pictures, she left at the height of her popularity, well on her way to becoming the most photographed, most talked about chicken of our time.

And I am left cherishing the memories. Nancy and I had grown to love our chicken.

If anyone happens to see a fat black hen, tell her this for me: There's a light in the window, and a warm nest at the base of the pine tree. ▲

I saw two dogs walk over to a parking meter. One said to the other, "How do you like that? Pay toilets."

My father-in-law had prostate surgery. We brought him to the hospital at 7:30 a.m., and he was operated on at eight. We were amazed when the hospital called at noon to tell us he could go home. Two months later our beagle, Bo, also had prostate surgery. When I brought him in, I asked the veterinarian what time I should pick him up. The vet told me Bo would remain overnight. "Overnight?" I said. "My father-in-law came home the same day." The vet looked at me and said, "Bo's not on Medicare."

— CLYDE DYAR

"I'll negotiate, Stan, but I won't beg."

An adorable little girl walked into my pet shop and asked, "Excuse me, do you have any rabbits here?"

"I do," I answered, and leaning down to her eye level I asked, "Did you want a white rabbit or would you rather have a soft, fuzzy black rabbit?"

She shrugged. "I don't think my python really cares."

— CINDY PATTERSON

Each morning at 5:30, I take my Lhasa Apso, Maxwell, for a walk. He has the bad habit of picking up bits of paper or other trash along the way. When he does, I command him to "drop it," and he usually complies. One morning, though, he absolutely refused to drop a piece of litter. So I told him to "sit" and then approached him to see what his treasure was. It was a $10 bill.

— ELSA BOGGS

Lost in the woods, a hiker spends two days wandering around with no food. Finally, he spots a bald eagle, hits the bird with a big rock and eats it. A park ranger stumbles on the scene and arrests the man for killing an endangered species. In court, the hiker explains that he was on the edge of starvation and had no choice.

"Considering the circumstances, I find you not guilty," says the judge. "But I have to ask—what did the eagle taste like?"

"Well, Your Honor," the hiker replies, "it tasted like a cross between a whooping crane and a spotted owl."

— ERIC FLEMING

A French poodle and a collie were walking down the street. The poodle turned to the collie and complained, "My life is such a mess. My owner is mean, my girlfriend is having an affair with a German shepherd and I'm as nervous as a cat."

"Why don't you go see a psychiatrist?" asked the collie.

"I can't," replied the poodle. "I'm not allowed on the couch."

— JOHN W. GAMBA

We visited our newly married daughter, who was preparing her first Thanksgiving dinner. I noticed the turkey thawing in the kitchen sink with a dish drainer inverted over the bird. I asked why a drainer covered the turkey.

Our daughter turned to my wife and said, "Mom, you always did it that way." "Yes," my wife replied, "but you don't have a cat!"

— A. C. STOKERS, JR.

"I could swear that box of frozen fish sticks was here a minute ago."

My friend's husband, Ray, is a state trooper and enjoys sharing the excuses people use when stopped for speeding. One day, however, the tables were turned. Ray maintains an aquarium of exotic fish, and a prized specimen had threatened to turn belly up. The off-duty officer called a pet store, and they advised him to immediately purchase a special additive that would correct the water's pH.

Ray and his wife jumped into the car and rushed to the store. A state trooper signaled them to pull over. "Go ahead," Ray's wife said. "Tell him you've got a sick fish!"

— DEBRA MCVEY

A couple of dog owners are arguing about whose dog is smarter. "My dog is so smart," says the first owner, "that every morning he waits for the paper boy to come around. He tips the kid and then brings the newspaper to me, along with my morning coffee."

"I know," says the second owner.
"How do you know?"
"My dog told me."

"Nice dog. What's its name?" I asked my friend's 10-year-old son.
"Bob," he said.
"And your cat?"
"Bob."

"How do you keep them straight?"
"Well one is Bob Cat and the other is Bob Barker," the boy answered.
"Tell him your rabbit's name," his father suggested.
The kid smiled and said, "Dennis Hopper."

— MIKE HARRELSON

After our dog died, my parents had her cremated, and they placed the ashes in a special box on the fireplace mantel. One day the boy next door came over to play and noticed the fancy container. "What's in the box?" he asked.

"That's our dog," my mom replied.

"Oh," the boy simply said. A minute later he remarked, "He's awfully quiet, isn't he?"

I was at a yard sale one day and saw a box marked "Electronic cat and dog call—guaranteed to work." I looked inside and was amused to see an electric can opener.

— BRET SOHL

207

Enclosed with the heartworm pills my friend received from a veterinarian was a sheet of red heart stickers to place on a calendar as a reminder to give her pet the medication. She attached these stickers to her kitchen calendar, marking the first Saturday of every month. When her husband noticed the hearts, he grinned from ear to ear, turned to his wife and asked, "Do you have something special in mind for these days?"

— MARY LOUISE RUSSO

A friend of mine is a deputy with the sheriff's department canine division. One evening, the deputy was dispatched to the scene of a possible burglary, where he discovered the back door of a building ajar. He let the dog out of his patrol car and commanded it to enter and seek.

Jumping from the back seat, the dog headed for the building. After lunging through the doorway, the dog froze and backed out. My friend was puzzled until he investigated further. Then he noticed the sign on the building: "Veterinarian's Office."

— ELIZABETH BENNETT

Snake 1:
Are we poisonous?

Snake 2:
I don't know. Why?

Snake 1:
I just bit my lip.

FAITH LACKEY

My niece bought her five-year-old daughter, Kayleigh, a hamster. One day he escaped from his cage. The family turned the house upside down and finally found him. Several weeks later, while Kayleigh was at school, he escaped from his cage again. My niece searched frantically but never found the critter. Hoping to make the loss less painful for Kayleigh, my niece took the cage out of her room.

When Kayleigh came home from school that afternoon, she climbed into her mother's lap. "We've got a serious problem," she announced. "Not only is my hamster gone again, but this time he took the cage."

— PATSY STRINGER

When my kid sister and my mother bought three exotic birds, they named them This, That and The Other. After a few months, This died, and they buried the bird in the backyard. A few more months later, The Other passed away and they buried it next to This. Then the last bird died.

Mom called my sister and tearfully announced, "Well, I guess that's That."

— GLORIA VITULANO

"Maybe aerobics wasn't such a good idea."

"You have just one more wish. Are you sure you want *another* belly rub?"

The Great Hamster Caper

▶ BY JIM GROVE

No pint-size rodent would ruin my daughter's reputation.

Friday. The weekend beckoned. But when I walked through the door, I heard a traumatized child. Amy, our eight-year-old, was sobbing. Hammie the hamster was inside our bathroom wall.

One major complicating factor: Hammie was not ours. He was the class hamster. He had come to our house as part of the great second-grade pet cultural exchange, having survived more than a dozen home visits with the kids in Mrs. Blackwell's class. A hamster with peer pressure attached.

Now, though he had been in our house only a few hours, Hammie was where no paw should tread—on and under pipes, stirring up drywall dust, munching on whatever looked tasty.

As great tragedies often do, this one started with a small act of kindness. Amy had uncaged Hammie in the bathroom for an early evening romp as she guarded the door. Unfortunately there was the teeniest hole where the sink cabinet meets the wall. We'd never known it was there, but to Hammie, it must have looked like the Florida Turnpike. A quick sprint and he was gone: down the linoleum, over the baseboard and into the wall. And now the little squirt's telltale scratching seemed to move in rhythm to the sobs outside.

Midnight. The family was fast asleep while I maintained the hamster watch. Poking my finger into the hole, I felt a hamster paw. I bent over and, startled, gazed right into Hammie's eyes. He seemed to be smiling.

At first I thought that by baiting Hammie with some hamster fast food—carrots, apple, a huge piece of lettuce—the little guy would pitter-patter back into the bathroom. He went for the lettuce. Unfortunately, he took it right back into the hole.

After a restless night we swore one another to a tell-and-you-die oath. We had 48 hours to capture Hammie. It would be bad enough without kick-starting the second-grade rumor mill.

Saturday afternoon. The plan of attack: Lure Hammie into the Mice Cube, a small plastic rectangle. Bait it, and the hungry rodent goes in the trapdoor, but he doesn't come out.

This night brought less sleep—more scratch, scratch,

scratch　no Hammie. I guessed he still had plenty of lettuce.

Sunday morning. We prayed for Hammie. Amy said that under no circumstances would she ever attend school again if we didn't catch him. The pressure was on.

A key to successful parenting, I'm told, is having a complete support network. A visit to Dad's secret weapon, The Pet Store Guy, now seemed crucial.

When I told him of our crisis, he barely batted an eye. Clearly he knew a lot about hamster psychology. In his opinion, Hammie was either a) on the lam and loving it, b) playing a game of catch-me-if-you-can or c) lost in the wall. But he would come out. Hunger would win.

The Pet Store Guy told me to take a two-gallon bucket and place an apple inside. Douse a towel in apple juice. Put the bucket a few hamster steps from the hole and drape the towel over the side—a kind of hamster ramp, if you will. Just enough towel should stick into the bucket to allow the hamster to fall in but not crawl out.

Bedtime Sunday. The trap was in place, but the bathroom wall was eerily quiet. Was Hammie alive in there? I sat in a chair, feeling defeated. I had been beaten by a pint-size rodent.

Then, in what seemed like one of those slow-motion *Chariots of Fire* moments, my hamster-loving, sweet-hearted girl was motioning to us from the door. Amy had heard the hamster drop in the bucket.

She looked first. Her anxiety as she peered over the edge of the bucket, followed by the sheer euphoria of her realization that he was there, was indescribable. My wife and I savored every second, as a living page of our family journal unfolded.

Hugs and kisses. Hero Dad. Hero Mom. Hamster high-fives.

There are moments in your children's lives when your heart bounces through your throat—the first step, the first bike ride, the first sentence read, the first hamster drop.

I never did win a stuffed animal at the carnival for my sweetheart. But now I know how it feels. ▲

My father and a friend were talking about the doors they had installed so their animals could let themselves in and out of the house. My dad asked his friend, who had two massive Great Danes, "Aren't you afraid that somebody might crawl through the dogs' door and steal something?"

"If you saw an opening that big," said his friend, "would you crawl through it?"

— HORST JENKINS

Squirrels had overrun three churches in town. After much prayer, the elders of the first church determined that the animals were pre-destined to be there. Who were they to inter-fere with God's will? they reasoned. Soon, the squirrels multiplied.

The elders of the sec-ond church, deciding they could not harm any of God's creatures, humanely trapped the squirrels and set them free outside of town. Three days later, the squirrels were back.

It was only the third church that succeeded in keeping the pests away. The elders baptized the squirrels and registered them as members of the church. Now they only see them on Christmas and Easter.

— E. T. THOMPSON

"It's my way of showing support."

I bought my sons a pet rabbit after they promised they would take care of it. As expected, I ended up with the responsibility. Exasperated, one evening I said, "How many times do you think that rabbit would have died if I hadn't looked after it?"

"Once," my 12-year-old son replied.

— L. BARRY PARSONS

One day while we were doing yard work, my nine-year-old daughter found a baby snake, and I encouraged her to catch it and put it in a jar. Later she found a huge bullfrog and got another jar to put it in.

After dark I told her she would have to set them free. With the frog in one hand and the snake in the other, she started down the porch steps. Suddenly she screamed wildly, dropped both the snake and the frog, and ran into the house.

"What happened?" I asked, my heart thumping.

"Did you see that?" she replied. "That moth almost got me."

— CASSANDRA DALZELL

One afternoon I was walking on a trail with my newborn daughter, chatting to her about the scenery. When a man and his dog approached, I leaned into the baby carriage and said, "See the doggy?"

Suddenly I felt a little silly talking to my baby as if she understood me. But just as the man passed, I noticed he reached down, patted his dog and said, "See the baby?"

— CATHERINE REARDON

As I was walking through a variety store, I stopped at the pet department to look at some parakeets. In one cage a green bird lay on his back, one foot hooked oddly into the cage wire.

I was about to alert the saleswoman to the bird's plight when I noticed a sign taped to the cage: "No, I am not sick. No, I am not dead. No, my leg is not stuck in the cage. I just like to sleep this way."

— JOAN DEZEEUW

A hypnotist was visiting the aquarium during feeding time. "You know," the hypnotist said to the man feeding the fierce shark, "I could hypnotize that shark."

"You're crazy! He'll rip you limb from limb," the feeder said, laughing. "But, hey, if you're so brave, be my guest."

The hypnotist jumped in, swam to the shark and stared it in the eye for a full minute. The animal paused, blinked, and then tore into him. The bleeding man slowly made his way out of the tank.

"I thought you could hypnotize him," sneered the feeder.

"I did," the hypnotist said, holding his arm. "Now he thinks he's an alligator."

— JOHN CASON

My brother adopted a snake named Slinky, whose most disagreeable trait was eating live mice. Once I was pressed into going to the pet store to buy Slinky's dinner.

The worst part of this wasn't choosing the juiciest-looking creatures or turning down the clerk who wanted to sell me vitamins to ensure their longevity. The hardest part was carrying the poor things out in a box bearing the words "Thank you for giving me a home."

— JOANNE MITCHELL

"How many times have I told you— No coffee after September!"

"Oh, yeah, like the stripes help."

One of the highlights of the freshman biology class at New Mexico Highlands University was the monthly feeding of a caged rattlesnake kept in the laboratory. One time, the entire class gathered around the cage and, in complete silence, watched as the feeding took place.

"I'm jealous of the snake," the instructor said. "I never get the class's undivided attention like this."

A student answered matter-of-factly, "You would if you could swallow a mouse."

— DIANE TALBOTT-MOSIER

Dave's parrot was always using bad language, so he asked the vet how he could stop it. "Every time the bird swears, put it in the freezer for 15 seconds," advised the vet.

The next time the parrot uttered an expletive, Dave did as the vet said. Then, feeling guilty, Dave opened the freezer.

Shivering, the parrot came out saying, "I'm sorry for all the bad language I've been using." Dave was astounded at the sudden change. Then the parrot said, "By the way, what did the chicken do?"

— PAUL IRWIN

My sister-in-law, a truck driver, had decided to get a dog for protection. As she inspected a likely candidate, the trainer told her, "He doesn't like men."

Perfect, my sister-in-law thought, and took the dog.

Then one day she was approached by two men in a parking lot, and she watched to see how her canine bodyguard would react. Soon it became clear that the trainer wasn't kidding. As the men got closer, the dog ran under the nearest car.

— DANNY ARIAIL

The vet prescribed daily tablets for our geriatric cat, Tigger, and after several battles my husband devised a way to give her the medication. It involved wrapping Tigger in a towel, trapping her between his knees, forcing her mouth open and depositing the pill on the back of her tongue.

David was proud of his resourcefulness until one hectic session when he lost control of both cat and medicine. Tigger leaped out of his grasp, paused to inspect the tablet—which had rolled across the floor—and then ate it.

— MADI LEGERE

The Truth About Cats

JERRY H. SIMPSON, JR., AND LOUIS M. BUZEK

Broadway's longest-running show, *Cats,* brought audiences a romanticized view of these well-loved pets. Despite the elaborate costumes, popular songs and lively dancing, the play didn't quite capture the essence of our feline companions. Here is what *Cats* should have done:

▲ Audience members should have entered the theater only to find their seats had been clawed and covered with fur.

▲ Sometimes the actors would have performed, but sometimes not—depending on their mood.

▲ The show would have had to stop several times to allow cast members to bathe and groom themselves.

▲ When certain audience members opened their playbills, cast members should have attempted to lie down on them.

▲ For no apparent reason, the actors should have randomly run to the lobby and then back to the stage at top speed. They then should have continued as if nothing had happened.

▲ A special audience member might have found a headless bird in his or her seat after intermission.

▲ Most of the final act should have consisted of the cast just staring at the audience.

Our cat, Figaro, comes home between 10 or 11 at night to eat. If he's late, I turn on the carport light and call him until he appears.

One day my daughter was explaining to a friend where we live, and her friend said, "Is that anywhere near the house where the woman stands on her steps late at night and sings opera?"

— MARGARET MATHES

Sounds of crashing and banging in the middle of the night sent me and my husband out to our garage. There we spotted three raccoons eating out of the cat dish. We shooed them away and went back to bed.

Later that week we were driving home and I noticed three fat raccoons ambling down the road. "Do you think those are the same ones we chased off?" I asked.

"Hard to tell," said my husband. "They were wearing masks."

— CHERIE KONVICKA

"He likes you!"

Jim strolls into the paint section of a hardware store and walks up to the assistant. "I'd like a pint of canary-colored paint," he says.

"Sure," the clerk replies. "Mind if I ask what it's for?"

"My parakeet," says Jim. "See, I want to enter him in a canary contest. He sings so sweet I know he's sure to win."

"Well, you can't do that, man!" the assistant says. "The chemicals in the paint will almost certainly kill the poor thing!"

"No, they won't," Jim replies.

"Listen, buddy, I'll bet you ten bucks your parakeet dies if you try to paint him."

"You're on," says Jim.

Two days later he comes back looking very sheepish and lays $10 on the counter.

"So the paint killed him?"

"Indirectly," says Jim. "He seemed to handle the paint okay, but he didn't survive the sanding between coats."

As spring migration approached, two elderly vultures doubted they could make the trip north, so they decided to go by airplane.

When they checked their baggage, the attendant noticed that they were carrying two dead armadillos.

"Do you wish to check the armadillos through as luggage?" she asked.

"No, thanks," replied the vultures. "They're carrion."

— FRED BRICE

"Botox"

Word Play

Is English the easiest language to mangle? It sure seems so. Here are silly word plays, ridiculous euphemisms, hysterically flawed utterances, and other fun language twists and plays.

When our air conditioner broke down, we called for a serviceman to come and take a look at it. It turned out to be a high school classmate of my husband's named Love. He said next time we needed any repairs to ask for him. The next year when we needed service again, we requested Mr. Love. I took the day off from work and waited for him to arrive.

After he had worked on our air conditioner, he left his work order behind. It had my name and said: "Wants Love in afternoon."

— DONNA MELLER

A pregnant woman lapses into a deep coma. She awakens and frantically calls for the doctor. "You had twins. A boy and a girl. They're fine," he says. "Your brother named them."

Today was the day. I was going to get a tattoo. I walked into a local shop to check out their designs. But I had second thoughts when I noticed the two "artists" working there had the last names of **Pane and Burns.**

— LINDSAY HALVERSON

Oh no, the new mother thinks. He's an idiot. Expecting the worst, she asks, "What's the girl's name?"

"Denise," the doctor says. Not bad, she thinks. Guess I was wrong about him.

"And the boy?"

"DeNephew."

Pity the poor insomniac dyslexic agnostic. He stays up all night wondering if there really is a dog.

While I was driving through a seedy area of San Diego, I noticed that sandwiched between a strip bar and a liquor store sat a storefront with all of its windows suspiciously blacked out. Over the door was a sign that proudly declared, "Welcome to Kink-o's. We have nothing to do with office supplies."

— DARLENE BENAVIDEZ

Our regimental sergeant major was well known for his abuse of the English language, and we all joked about it. At parade one morning, he announced in a stentorian voice, "Certain people have been making allegations about me. If I catch these alligators, they will be in for a hard time."

— C. G. MALEY

Can you be a closet claustrophobic?

GINA FADELY   **COSMIC QUESTION**

My son, a student at West Springfield High School in Massachusetts, asked me to quiz him on material he had been studying for a history exam. When I asked him to name three famous defenders of the Alamo, he correctly identified Davy Crockett and William Travis, but he was at a loss for the third man, Jim Bowie.

"They named a knife after him," I hinted.

"Jack?" he asked hopefully.

— CONNIE GILBERT

New definitions to add to your vocabulary:

Arbitrator: A cook that leaves Arby's to work at McDonald's.

Bernadette: The act of torching your mortgage.

Parasites: What you see from the top of the Eiffel Tower.

Primate: Removing your spouse from in front of the TV.

Subdued: A guy that works on submarines.

— EDWARD THOMPSON

A Harley rider eating in a restaurant is checking out a gorgeous redhead. Suddenly she sneezes and her glass eye comes flying out of its socket. The biker reaches up, snatches it out of the air, and hands it back to her. "I am so embarrassed," the woman says. "Please join me for dinner."

They enjoy a wonderful meal together and afterwards she invites him to the theater, followed by drinks. She pays for everything. Then she asks him to her place for a nightcap, and to stay for breakfast.

The next morning the guy is amazed. "Are you this nice to every biker you meet?" he asks.

"Not usually," she replies. "But you just happened to catch my eye."

— FROM THE INTERNET

"Do you have the root of all evil?"

There were only two people in line ahead of me at the electronics store, yet the wait was dragging on forever. Finally the customer behind me muttered, "Mr. Hare must be on vacation."

Only then did I notice the name tag on the man at the register. It read: "Mr. Turtle, sales associate."

— BRON WRIGHT

Hear about the guy who went to the library and checked out a book called *How to Hug?* He got home and found out it was volume seven of the encyclopedia.

Freshmen in the general-science class at Mark Twain Middle School in Mar Vista, Calif., were studying astronomy. "What do we call a group of stars that makes an imaginary picture in the sky?" the teacher asked.

"A consternation," one student replied.

— RALPH E. HEDGES

At the end of a long, hard day, I found myself standing in line at a fast-food restaurant with my husband, Stan, and our three-year-old daughter. The service was painfully slow, and my husband's temper began to mount.

"Look, honey, it's been a long day," I said, trying to console him. "You're tired, I'm tired, she's tired."

Before I could say another word, Stan interrupted me, smiling. "You conjugate well," he said.

— SHERRY DEPASSE

sign language

The New York-New Jersey Trail Conference was preparing to move from its longtime home in New York City to Mahwah, N.J. The day before the big move, the following sign appeared on the door:

"Here today, gone to Mahwah."

— JANICE CECHONY

220

For anyone who gets confused about proper grammar and style in writing, we offer, from the Internet, the following tip sheet, "How to Write Good":

- It is wrong to ever split an infinitive.
- Contractions aren't necessary.
- The passive voice is to be avoided.
- Prepositions are not the words to end sentences with.
- Be more or less specific.
- Who needs rhetorical questions?
- Exaggeration is a billion times worse than understatement.

What do fish say when they hit a concrete wall?…Dam!

What do you get from a pampered cow?…Spoiled milk.

What do you call cheese that isn't yours?…Nacho cheese.

What do you call four bullfighters in quicksand?…Quattro sinko.

What do you get when you cross a snowman with a vampire?…Frostbite.

— DUSTIN GODSEY

I went to the butcher's the other day and I bet him fifty bucks that he couldn't reach the meat on the top shelf.

He said, "No, the steaks are too high."

— ED THOMPSON

The state trooper pulled up alongside a speeding car and was shocked to see that the little old lady behind the wheel was knitting. The officer switched on his lights and sounded his siren, but the driver was oblivious. So the trooper cranked up the bullhorn and yelled to the woman, "Pull over."

"No," the old lady shouted back. "Cardigan."

Sitting at a stoplight, I was puzzling over the meaning of the vanity plate on the car in front of me. It read "Innie."

Then I got it. The make of the car was Audi.

— KATHY JOHNSON

If someone is addicted to eating Thanksgiving leftovers, can he quit cold turkey?

MICHAEL MORSE   **COSMIC QUESTION**

Most of my English literature classmates thought reading Melville's *Billy Budd* would be an easy task because the novel is only 90 pages long. One boy, however, complained that the text was heavy and hard to comprehend.

"Hey," another student suggested, "maybe you should try reading Budd Light."

— CARRIE L. BENSON

"The labs are back."

In our software-applications class at Williamsville East High School in upstate New York, we were running through a list of common computer lingo, which included "Pentium," "motherboard" and "gigabyte." Skimming the list, one girl noticed the term "RAM."

"Isn't that a kind of truck?" she asked without thinking.

"Sure," replied another student. "You can rent them at a megahertz."

— HEATHER LESSIG

Danny was hard to miss at our school. A Civil War buff who forever wore his Confederate overcoat, he was a friend to all. When he was passed over during the vote for senior superlatives, many of us were disappointed; surely there must have been some category suitable for him.

The whole school was pleased, therefore, when the yearbook adviser surprised us with an additional photo. There was Danny, decked out in his gray coat, with the caption: "Most Likely to Secede."

— MICHAEL G. STEWART

When someone offers you a penny for your thoughts, and you put in your two cents' worth, what happens to the other penny?

COSMIC QUESTION

According to the Internet: Students in a Harvard English 101 class were asked to write a concise essay containing four elements: religion, royalty, sex and mystery. The only A+ in the class read: "'My God,' said the Queen, 'I'm pregnant! I wonder who did it.'"

— E.T. THOMPSON

News that her third child was going to be a girl thrilled my cousin, who already had two boys. "My husband wants to call her Sunny," she told me, "and I want to give her Anna as her middle name in memory of my mom."

I thought they might want to reconsider their decision, since their birth announcement would herald the arrival of Sunny Anna Rainey.

— CAROLYN WALLIS

Police are investigating the murder of Juan Gonzalez. "It looks like he was killed with a golf gun," one detective observes.

"A golf gun?" asks his partner. "What in the world is a golf gun?"

"I don't know. But it sure made a hole in Juan."

Two boll weevils grew up in Alabama. One moved to Hollywood and became a famous actor. The other stayed in the cotton field and never amounted to anything. He became known as the lesser of two weevils.

— DUSTIN GODSEY

"You have to admire the way she juggles family and career."

"We request low bail as my client is not a flight risk."

Wit by Wire

Scrolling through my e-mail the other day, I saw half a dozen messages, none really urgent and none fewer than 100 words long. One, from someone I had just met, clocked in at 1,286 words.

Back in the days when electronic messages were truly urgent, every word counted—literally. I remember trying to cut a telegram down to the 15-word economy rate. Those Western Union operators were great editors, sticklers who wouldn't let you get away with reducing multiple words into one by adding hyphens. "Love-and-kisses? That's three words, sir."

It has been a long time since I have gotten or sent a telegram. Cheap long distance, faxes and e-mail have made it possible to be as wordy as we want. And in our rush to communicate instantly, we barely pause to mourn the passing of the telegram as a literary genre. As those distinctive yellow forms disappear from our lives, so too do poetry, drama and wit.

When I was growing up, a knock on the door from a Western Union messenger always marked a significant moment. The generation before mine trembled at the approach of a telegram, dreading the words THE SECRETARY OF WAR DESIRES ME TO EXPRESS HIS DEEP REGRET. In my day, the Vietnam era, we trembled at telegrams from the President that began with a maddeningly upbeat greeting.

Telegrams had their own code words—STOP, SOONEST, PROCEEDING, ADVISE—representing freeze-dried sentences. The form itself was built for concision.

In his introduction to *Barbed Wires,* Joyce Denebrink's collection of funny telegrams, Marvin Kitman wrote that the U.S. inventor of the telegraph, Samuel Morse, "pruned the deadwood out of the language." Morse's first official telegraph message, sent on May 24, 1844, from the U.S. Capitol, was only four words long: WHAT HATH GOD WROUGHT.

Between those taps on Morse's telegraph key and the playing of taps for the telegram 130-odd years later, the wires have vibrated with bons mots. There was no medium as perfect for telling someone off. The best may have been one sent to Lord Home, British foreign secretary: TO HELL WITH YOU. OFFENSIVE LETTER FOLLOWS.

Two titans of repartee got going when George Bernard Shaw invited Winston Churchill to the opening of his new play: AM RESERVING TWO TICKETS FOR YOU FOR MY PREMIERE. COME AND BRING A FRIEND— IF YOU HAVE ONE. Churchill's reply: IMPOSSIBLE TO BE PRESENT FOR THE FIRST PERFORMANCE. WILL ATTEND SECOND—IF THERE IS ONE.

▶ BY CHRISTOPHER BUCKLEY

The telegram traffic between war correspondents and their editors back home provided great moments. When Italy invaded Ethiopia in 1935, a false rumor circulated in London that an American nurse had been killed in an air raid. Field correspondent Evelyn Waugh received this from his editor: REQUIRE EARLIEST STORY AMERICAN NURSE UPBLOWN. Waugh cabled back NURSE UNUPBLOWN.

When an illustrator in Havana in 1898 cabled to William Randolph Hearst THERE WILL BE NO WAR, Hearst cabled back: YOU FURNISH THE PICTURES AND I'LL FURNISH THE WAR. The Spanish-American War soon followed.

Concision sometimes led to confusion. In 1933 the U.S. embassy in Bulgaria cabled home as follows: A DAUGHTER WAS BORN TO QUEEN IOANNA. SHALL PRESENT CONGRATULATIONS TO THE PRIME MINISTER.

What you read in a telegram depended on where you stood. A lawyer who unexpectedly won a difficult case for a client wired JUSTICE HAS TRIUMPHED. The client replied: APPEAL CASE AT ONCE!

In a medium that depended on brevity, the smallest error could be a Freudian blip. The wife of a Hollywood director who was on location with a foxy leading lady received this: HAVING A WONDERFUL TIME, WISH YOU WERE HER.

The military, as a rule, doesn't try to be funny in its cables, but sometimes they turn out that way. Back in the days of the British Grand Fleet, a sailor wanting to make sure his admiral had fresh clothing after a tour at sea cabled to shore: WHO DO YOU RECOMMEND FOR ADMIRAL'S WOMAN? That was quickly followed by PLEASE INSERT WASHER BETWEEN ADMIRAL AND WOMAN.

The most concise military message of all was sent in the mid-19th century when the British captured the Indian province of Sind, now in Pakistan. Gen. Charles Napier's dispatch was reportedly one word long: PECCAVI. In Latin that means "I have sinned." (Say "Sind" and "sinned" out loud, and there you have it.)

It seems a while since there's been a neatly worded dispatch from the field. Maybe if General Schwarzkopf had been allowed to go all the way, Operation Desert Storm would have ended with a cabled flourish: BAGHDAD IN BAG. On the other hand, when you live in the age of machines that can transmit *Moby Dick* in three seconds, who's got time to be brief? ▲

My friend John came into French class one Monday with a pillow that he placed on his seat. Over the weekend he had been skiing and mildly fractured his tailbone. Our teacher promptly asked him to explain, *en français,* why he was sitting on a pillow.

To our amusement, John answered, "Sorbonne."

— GEORGE B. SHUPING

Today in the markets, helium was up; feathers were down. Paper was stationary. Elevators rose, while escalators continued their slow decline. Mining equipment hit rock bottom. The market for raisins dried up. Coca-Cola fizzled. Balloon prices were inflated. And Scott Tissue reached a new bottom.

— ERIC CAMPBELL

According to John Steinbeck, "Texas has its own private history based on, but not limited by, facts." Texas also has its own language, based on, but not limited by, English. Here's a primer on Tex-ish:
- The engine's running, but ain't nobody drivin' (not too smart)
- Tighter than bark on a tree (stingy)
- We've howdied, but we ain't shook yet (we've met, but haven't been formally introduced)

- She's got tongue enough for ten rows of teeth (she's a talker)
- This ain't my first rodeo (I've been around).

— FROM THE INTERNET

Did you hear that NASA is planning to send a group of Holsteins into orbit? Apparently they're calling it the herd shot round the world.

My high-school basketball team was scheduled to play in the district tournament, and when we got there we were all excited to find our pictures and

our stats published in the glossy program. My friend Brian Bird, a senior who was having a great season, eagerly searched for his name. But then he threw the program down in disgust, and I figured that there must be some error in his entry.

Sure enough, his name appeared as "Bird, Brain."

— DARREN JOHNSON

As a fund-raiser, the chemistry club designed and sold T-shirts. Written across the front were our top "Stupid Chemistry Sayings":
- Have yourself a Merry Little Bismuth
- What do you do with dead people? Barium
- You stupid boron!
- We hope your year is very phosphorous.

— SHANE HART

Stuck in rush-hour traffic, I couldn't help but stare when a burly biker wearing black leather jacket and chaps pulled up next to me on a shocking pink Harley Davidson. My first thoughts were, "Is that really a pink Harley? I wonder if he's…"

Just then the traffic cleared and he pulled in front of me. On the back of his helmet were stenciled the words "Yes it is. No I'm not."

— AMY CARPENTER

Shortly after my son started college, the president of the university had an assembly for the new students. "Welcome to Johns Hopkins," he began, "And please note that it's Johns, not John."

Then he told how one of his predecessors, Milton Eisenhower, had been invited to talk at the University of Pittsburgh. After he was introduced as the president of "John Hopkins," Eisenhower said, "Thank you. It's great to be in Pittsburgh."

— JOSEPH B. MIRSKY

Driving through Southern California, I stopped at a roadside stand that sold fruit, vegetables and crafts. As I went to pay, I noticed the young woman behind the counter was painting a sign. "Why the new sign?" I asked.

"My boyfriend didn't approve of the old one," she said. When I glanced at what hung above the counter, I understood. It declared: "Local Honey Dates Nuts."

— THEODORE BOLOGNA

I took my high-school government class on a field trip to the county jail. Near the end of the tour, we passed through the prison's recreation room. There I spotted two board games sitting on a table, selections that I thought were particularly appropriate to a correctional facility: Life and Sorry.

— CHRISTINA GUERLAND

While waiting in line at the Department of Vehicle Services for my new license plate, I heard the clerk shout out, "E I E I O." "Here," the woman standing next to me answered.

Curious, I asked if she was married to a farmer, or maybe taught preschool.

"Neither," she replied. "My name is McDonald."

— JIM PIERCE

A favorite beach restaurant of ours has a simple way of advertising its hours. During the day, the window panes sport large letters spelling "Open."

After hours, the "N" is moved forward to spell "Nope."

— PHIL TRIPP

Three vampires walk into a bar. "What can I get ya?" asks the bartender.

"Blood," orders the first vampire.

"Make it two," says the second.

The bartender looks at the third. "What about you, buddy?"

"Plasma," says the vampire.

"Okay," replies the barman. "Let me make sure I've got this straight. Two bloods and a blood light."

— WESTON DAVIS

If you arrest a mime, do you still have to tell him he has the right to remain silent? **?**

MICHAEL MORSE **COSMIC QUESTION**

PAINT THINNER

227

I believe in an open mind, but not so open that your brains fall out.

— ARTHUR HAYS SULZBERGER

Polite conversation is rarely either.

— FRAN LEBOWITZ, Social Studies (Random House)

As far as I'm concerned, "whom" is a word that was invented to make everyone sound like a butler.

— CALVIN TRILLIN in The Nation

Baseball, it is said, is only a game. True. And the Grand Canyon is only a hole in Arizona.

— GEORGE F. WILL in Fast Company

If truth is beauty, how come no one has their hair done in the library?

— LILY TOMLIN

The problem with people who have no vices is that they're pretty sure to have some annoying virtues.

— ELIZABETH TAYLOR

My early choice in life was either to be a piano player in a whorehouse or a politician. And to tell the truth, there's hardly any difference.

— HARRY S. TRUMAN

I looked up the word *politics* in the dictionary. It's actually a combination of two words: *poli,* which means many, and *tics,* which means bloodsuckers.

— JAY LENO on "The Tonight Show"

My wife and I were on the Ohio Turnpike, stuck behind a car going under the speed limit in the passing lane. The car, which sported an Indiana Hoosier basketball bumper sticker, refused to move over. Exasperated, I finally shouted out, "Hoosier idiot!"

My wife turned to me and said quietly, "You are, dear."

— GEORGE COX

Hoss drove over to the next county to buy a new bull for the farm. It cost more than expected, and he was left with only one dollar. This was a problem, since he needed to let his wife, Sue, know that he'd bought the bull so she could come get it with the truck—and telegrams cost a dollar per word. Hoss thought hard for a minute. Finally he said, "All right. Here's my dollar. Go ahead and just make it this one word: Comfortable."

"How's that going to get your point across?" the clerk asked, scratching his head.

"Don't worry," Hoss said. "Sue's not the greatest reader. She'll say it real slow."

— RICHARD H. SCHEUB

Did you hear about the satellite dishes who married?

The ceremony was awful, but the reception was great.

— SANDRA CORONA

The gladiator was having a rough day in the arena—his opponent had sliced off both of his arms. Nevertheless, he kept on fighting, kicking and biting as furiously as he could. But when his opponent lopped off both feet, our gladiator had no choice but to give up, for now he was both unarmed and defeated.

— TEDDEM YEE

"I think I'll just stay in tonight, maybe open a can of worms."

Our son recently married a Russian woman. During the reception, Russian and American guests proposed toasts. As someone translated, my sister-in-law said, "Good health, good fortune. Go and multiply."

I couldn't help noticing that some of the guests looked confused. We found out later that this had been translated as, "Good health, good fortune. Go and do math."

— DAVID A. MACLEOD

Nancy was Catholic, but her fiancé, Chris, was not. Since my friends were planning to be married in the Catholic Church, Chris made sure to listen carefully throughout their prenuptial sessions. At one meeting the priest turned to Chris and told him, "Since you are not Catholic, we shall have the ceremony without Eucharist."

Later that day, Chris was noticeably upset, so Nancy asked what was wrong. "I don't understand," he said. "How can we have the ceremony without me?"

— KURT SHELLENBACK

People Who Become Words

▶ BY JAY HEINRICHS

There once was an original Maverick—Samuel A. Maverick, mayor of San Antonio in the mid-1800s—who, despite the name, was no maverick. He was just a small-town politician whose name lives on not because he was a great gunfighter—apologies to you, James Garner, and you, Mel Gibson—but because he was lazy. When Maverick bought a herd of cattle in 1847, he allowed the steers to roam on his ranch, unbranded. From then on, unbranded cattle—and, eventually, independent-minded humans—became known as mavericks.

As a household word, Mayor Maverick has some distinguished, if not always appreciative, company, including the likes of Mr. Boycott, Ms. Bloomer and Monsieur Leotard. There was a real guy named Silhouette and, for that matter, a real Guy. All of these people achieved a sort of immortality when their names were turned into everyday words called eponyms (from the Greek "upon a name").

Some 35,000 have made their way into English.

Murphy's Law is one of the most famous eponyms—the legacy of one very picky Air Force officer. In the late 1940s, Capt. Ed Murphy, an aircraft engineer by training, complained about an incompetent technician on his team. "If there is any way to do it wrong, he will," Murphy said. His co-workers began calling the captain's pessimism Murphy's Law, and mentioned it in a press conference. As long as people keep on making mistakes, Murphy will live.

More distant, but still enduring, is the memory of the original Guy, an Englishman named Guy Fawkes. On November 5, 1605, Fawkes attempted to blow up Parliament and King James I. The English still remember the date by burning stuffed dummies in effigy, and for years any bizarrely dressed person was known as a guy. Over time, and after crossing the Atlantic, the term picked up a less humbling connotation.

The British have a knack for punishing memorable characters with eponyms.

Charles Cunningham Boycott was an English estate manager who refused to lower rents for poor Irish tenant farmers, inspiring a rent strike and the first boycott. Thomas Derrick, another unpopular Brit, worked as executioner at London's Tyburn gallows, hanging hundreds of convicts before being convicted of rape and condemned to die. The Earl of Essex pardoned him, only to be executed in 1601 for treason—by Derrick. A derrick was once a gallows; now the word refers to any equipment used to hang something. (Mr. Derrick did not live long enough to hang any Hooligans, members of a rowdy Irish clan who, legend has it, terrorized a London neighborhood in the 1890s.)

Meet the Cobb in salad, the Bloomer in underwear and the Derrick in crane.

Also achieving dubious fame was Etienne de Silhouette. A deficit-fighting finance minister of France in 1759, he had the nerve to suggest raising taxes.

His name became a synonym for cheapness. There's debate among linguists about just how we got the contemporary usage of silhouette: Some say the black-on-white cut paper portraits then popular were named after the skinflint finance minister, while others insist he was known for making the cut-out portraits.

Shirley Temple has never liked Shirley Temples. ("Too sweet," she says).

Nonetheless, during the more than 60 years since a bartender at the Brown Derby restaurant in Hollywood mixed 7-Up and grenadine in her honor, people have pressed Shirley Temples on her. The retired diplomat Shirley Temple Black might well wish her name were Cobb. At least then she'd get a stick-to-your-ribs salad. That concoction began with Bob Cobb, owner of the Brown Derby restaurant in Los Angeles, who invented his salad in 1926.

If you're ambitious to become an eponym yourself, the fashion world might be a good start. Amelia Bloomer, an American feminist of the 1800s, championed the undergarment known as bloomers. And the French aerialist Jules Leotard, creator of the flying trapeze, popularized the even more daring tights.

The newest eponyms come from mass media and politics. People already talk about gumping through life—getting by on dumb luck, the way Forrest Gump did in the movie. "Doing a Homer" means smacking your head and saying, "D'oh!" Homer Simpson-style, either in frustration, or because you've done something dumb—or both.

Among the wonks in Washington, "to bork" is to viciously attack a candidate or appointee. That's in honor of Robert Bork, the Reagan nominee to the Supreme Court whose career was torpedoed in the Senate. One day we may find that people use marthastewart as a single word to mean to arrange with excruciatingly good taste. (As in "I'm marthastewarting his party.")

Over time, eponyms may change meaning dramatically. That was the happy outcome for Bertha Krupp, a German military manufacturer during World War I. Her firm made a giant howitzer that British soldiers dubbed Big Bertha. But the hefty arms merchant has been redeemed through sport: Contemporary golfers refer to her fondly as they swing the innovative driver named—what else?—Big Bertha. ▲

After a long career of being blasted into a net, the human cannonball was tired. He told the circus owner he was going to retire. "But you can't!" protested the boss. "Where am I going to find another man of your caliber?"

Searching in my library for two books by communications expert Deborah Tannen turned into an Abbott and Costello routine. "What's the first book?" the librarian asked.

"*That's Not What I Meant,*" I said.

"Well, what did you mean?"

"That's the title of the book," I explained.

"Okay." She looked at me a little skeptically. "And the other book?"

"*You Just Don't Understand.*"

"Excuse me?"

I got both books. Eventually.

— NORM WILLIAMS

Tiffany adopts two dogs, and she names them Rolex and Timex. "Where'd you come up with those names?" asks her friend Mandy. "HellOOOOOO," Tiffany replies. "They're watchdogs!"

— GUSTAVO YEPES

Aoccdrnig to rscheearch at an Elingsh uinervtisy, it deosn't mttaer in waht oredr the ltteers in a wrod are, the olny iprmoetnt tihng is taht teh frist and lsat ltteer is at the rghit pclae. The rset can be a toatl mses and you can sitll raed it wouthit a porbelm. Tihs is bcuseae we do not raed ervey lteter by istlef but the wrod as a wlohe.

Johnathan Powell

"I'm sorry."

Coincidences were flying when a man was arrested and charged with stealing a bird feeder from Cornell University's ornithology laboratory. According to the Associated Press, police charged James Buzzard, 44, who lives on Cardinal Drive in Ithaca, N.Y., with stealing the feeder from the lab on Sapsucker Woods Road.

— GEROLENE E. SNAVELY

When my wife and I were vacationing in the eastern part of our state, our car's license plate was stolen. We planned to go to a local office for a replacement, but then we discovered that our registration had expired. The new one was at home in a pile of mail.

After much thought, we came up with a solution. Taping a sign over the empty license-plate space on the rear of the vehicle, we made the eight-hour trip home safely. Not a single state trooper stopped us, but many passing motorists took great pains to honk and wave at us.

Our sign read "Just Married!"

— GARY FROEHLICH

"Try double **clucking** on it."

My wife walked into a coffee shop on Halloween to find the woman behind the counter with a bunch of sponges pinned to her uniform.

"I'm assuming this is a costume," said my wife. "But what are you supposed to be?"

The waitress responded proudly, "I'm self-absorbed."

— SCOTT PIPER

Rick, a banker, is showing off his fancy new boat to his friend Jim. But the boat sinks, and Rick can't swim. So Jim starts pulling him to shore.

Finally, with only 50 feet to land, Jim says, "So do you think you could float alone?"

Rick gasps back, "This is a heck of a time to be asking for money!"

If a pig loses its voice, is it disgruntled?

One day, the president of the company came upon a young man who was expertly counting out a large wad of the firm's cash. The boss asked, "Where did you get your financial training, young man?"

"Yale," the young man answered proudly.

"Ah, a fellow Ivy Leaguer! What's your name?"

"Yack Yackson."

— ADAM JOSHUA SMARGON

The zoo keeper needed to purchase some new animals, so he started composing a letter: "To whom it may concern, I need two mongeese." That doesn't look right—too bad I don't have a dictionary, thought the zoo keeper.

So he started over: "To whom it may concern, I need two mongooses." That doesn't look right either, he thought.

Finally he got an idea: "To whom it may concern, I need a mongoose. And while you're at it, make it two."

"Honey, I'm taking the dog out to do his business."

The new composers' dictionary:

Adagio Frommagio—
To play in a slow and cheesy manner.

Angus Dei—
To play with a divine, beefy tone.

A Patella—
Unaccompanied knee-slapping.

Frugalhorn—
A sensible, inexpensive brass instrument.

Dill Piccolino—
A wind instrument that plays only sour notes.

Approximento—
A musical entrance that is somewhere in the vicinity of the correct pitch.

— E. T. THOMPSON

Did you hear about the self-help group for compulsive talkers? It's called On & On Anon.

— SALLY DAVIS

A policeman looked up to see a woman racing down the center of the road at 100 m.p.h. He pulled her over and said, "Hey, lady, would you mind telling me why you're going so fast down the middle of the road?"

"Oh, it's okay, Officer," she replied. "I have a special license that allows me to drive like that."

"Oh, yeah?" Let's see it." The cop looked at the license and then concluded, "Ma'am, there's nothing special about this. It's just a temporary license."

"Look at the very bottom, though," the woman insisted. "See? It says 'Tear along the dotted line.'"

— ROCKY MEYERSON

Eye halve a spelling chequer
It came with my pea sea
It plainly marques four my revue
Miss steaks eye kin knot sea
Eye strike a key and type a word
And weight four it two say
Weather eye am wrong oar write
It shows me strait a weigh
As soon as a mist ache is maid
It nose bee fore two long
And eye can put the error rite
Its rarely ever wrong
Eye have run this poem threw it
I am shore your pleased two no
Its letter perfect in it's weigh
My chequer tolled me sew.

— SAUCE UNKNOWN

Rev up your engines and tell the crabgrass to look out. The 12th annual Mow Down, Show Down Lawn Mower Championship was held in Avon Park, Florida, bringing out the best and fastest in lawn-mower racing. It also brought out some colorful names.

Entrants included: Weedy Gonzales, Blading Saddles, Turfinator, Sodzilla and Mr. Mowjangles.

— JOHN DRATWA

"I fear that one day I'll meet God, he'll sneeze, and I won't know what to say."

— RONNIE SHAKES,
SUBMITTED BY SHARON KANSAS

What's in a Name?

▶ BY JOSEPH F. WILKINSON

Just ask King Fisher, Robin Banks and Minnie Vann——

I first became interested in memorable names while listening to *The Barber of Seville.* I wondered if there was a woman somewhere named Barbara Seville.

I checked my library, which has telephone directories on CD-ROM. I discovered there are actually two Barbara Sevilles—in Ketchum, Idaho, and Fairfield, Calif.

An electronic treasure chest had been opened for me. I felt in this great country there should be a woman named Rosetta Stone. I found six (Pflugerville, Texas; Morris Plains, N.J.; Ellicott City, Md.; Leavenworth, Kan.; Beckley, W. Va.; Miami). They're probably daughters of archeologists, linguists and historians.

A memorable name is a head start. Imagine this salesman's cold call.

"There's someone here to see you," the receptionist tells the company president. "His name is Frank N. Stein."

"Send him right up."

Frank N. Stein (Miami; Taylors, S.C.; Castro Valley, Calif.; Rindge, N.H.; Rockville, Md.; Norman, Okla.) is a name that gets attention.

My search was limited mostly by my imagination. I found a score of Robin Banks, as well as Georgia Peach (Belcourt, N.D.), M. T. Head (Durham, N.C.) and Minnie Vann (Jackson, Tenn.; Fort McCoy, Fla.). There were many listings for Pearl Harper. Everyone remembers Pearl Harper.

There are several women listed as Sunny Day, one as Happy Day (Graysville, Pa.) and another as Summer Day (Derby, N.Y.). There are lots of June Days but not many May Days—possibly because parents don't want their daughters sounding as though they are calling for help whenever they identify themselves.

Guys make a good showing too. A little work turned up Phil Harmonic (New York City; Beaumont, Texas), King Fisher (Miami) and Lance Boyle (Bath, N.H.; Hayward, Wis.). James Dandy—there were several of them—must be Jim to everyone. Then there are the old show-biz favorites: Laurel Hardy (Irvine, Ky.; Flushing, N.Y.; San Francisco) and Stephen Eady (Chattanooga, Tenn.; Alexander City, Ala.).

Some names are only distinctive in telephone directories or other listings where last names appear first. For example, Cracker, Jack (Wilkes-Barre, Pa.); Dollar, Bill (there were eight of them!); Wise, Guy (Magnolia, Ark.; Quinlan, Texas; Middletown, Pa.; Marianna, Fla.). Dozens of women are named West, Virginia, and there are two North, Carolinas (Oxford, N.C.; Keysville, Va.).

If only my parents had named me Sword, my phone-book listing might have given me an edge. ▲

Why did the French train derail?

Toulouse-Lautrec.
JOHN KELL

What do you call a Far Eastern monk who
sells reincarnations?

A used karma dealer.
RICHARD SELTZER

How many ears did Davy Crockett have?

Three—his left ear, his right ear, and his wild front ear.
MUZAMMIL PATEL

Why did the cowboy buy a dachshund?

Someone told him to get a long little doggy.
SAVANNA SMITH

What do you call someone who has just
printed 1,000 puns off the Internet?

Well e-quipped.
J. C. PICKETT

What did the scientist say to his stubborn,
argumentative clone?

"Why can't you be a reasonable facsimile?"
MARK SOLOMON

What do you call a rap star who has
studied classical music?

Yo Yo Ma Ma.
FRANK J. PLAZA

MUELLER

LAUGHINGSTOCK

While redecorating my bathroom, I phoned a shop to see if it stocked a particular model of toilet. "We haven't got one here," said the clerk.

"Oh, no!" I said, crestfallen. His number had been the fourth one I'd called.

"Don't worry," he added helpfully. "I'll contact our other outlets to see if there's anybody out there sitting on one."

— DOUG BINGHAM

Things you need to know if your son wants to quit school and become a rock star:

- What do you call a guitar player who breaks up with his girlfriend? Homeless.
- What's the difference between a rock musician and a 16-inch pizza? The pizza can feed a family of four.
- What's the definition of an optimist? A rock musician with a mortgage.
- How do you define perfect pitch? It's when you throw your son's guitar into the dumpster and it lands right on top of his amplifier.

I was waiting to board a plane in Houston when a flight attendant stopped a woman in front of me to question her about the number of carry-on bags she had. The woman vehemently defended herself, claiming the extra bag was really her purse. It was the size of a large briefcase, but she insisted that it shouldn't count as a carry-on item. The flight attendant finally let the woman pass.

As the next man stepped up, the flight attendant's gaze settled on his bags. Immediately, he held up his briefcase and exclaimed, "This is my wallet."

— KIMBERLEY LEVACY

Everything is expensive in the upscale resort town where we live, and part of what you pay for is attitude. I realized this after I bought a couple pounds of hamburger at the fancy market on Main Street.

When I was taking the meat out of the bag at home, I noticed the label, "Ground Charles."

— FRAN COPELAND

If athletes get athlete's foot, do astronauts get mistletoe?

E. T. THOMPSON   **COSMIC QUESTION**

Did you ever notice: When you put the two words "The" and "IRS" together, they spell "THEIRS"?

— D. F. SPELLMAN

Sitting in the first row of coach class during a lengthy flight, my wife and I were able to hear a flight attendant as he pushed a wine cart down the aisle in the first-class section. "Would you care for chardonnay or burgundy?" he asked the high-paying passengers.

A few minutes later the attendant opened the curtain between the two sections, offered wine to one final first-class patron, then wheeled the same cart forward to our aisle. "Excuse me," he said, looking down at us, "would you care for a glass of wine? We have white and red."

— WILLIAM V. COPELAND

Following months of marijuana drug busts, the DEA took the contraband into a remote region to burn. The fire was blazing brightly when an agent noticed that a flock of terns was flying around the area. Concerned about the effects of the smoke on the birds, they called the National Audubon Society.

Their worst fears were confirmed. There was not one tern left unstoned.

— JOHN ARENDS

Fear factor. Are you scared of heights? Cramped spaces? If so, you've got plenty of company. Some people, though, have to wrestle with phobias that may surprise you.

- Automatonophobia = fear of ventriloquist dummies
- Ecclesiophobia = fear of church
- Aulophobia = fear of flutes
- Selenophobia = fear of the moon
- Venustraphobia = fear of beautiful women
- Logizomechanophobia = fear of computers.

Reporter: "Brzinlatowskiczinina is the name of the guy on the west side who was struck by lightning."

City editor: "What was his name before he was struck?"

Did you hear about the Buddhist who refused his dentist's Novocaine? He wanted to transcend dental medication.

Did you hear about the college professor who was involved in a terrible car wreck? He was grading papers on a curve.

— JACK R. KISER

Seattle has a reputation for rainy weather, so it wasn't surprising when Wang's Chinese Buffet restaurant started advertising "Dim Sun on Weekends."

— MARGUERITE POUGH

Does Santa call his elves "subordinate clauses"?

DOUG HECOX · COSMIC QUESTION

A man called the phone company to complain about his listing in the directory. "I told you that my last name is Sweady," he said, "but you have it listed as Cyirwu."

"I'm sorry, sir," the phone-company rep said. "I'll fix it so it'll be correct the next time we publish the directory. Now how do you spell your name?"

"Just like I told you before," the customer said. "It's S as in sea, W as in why, E as in eye, A as in are, D as in double-u and Y as in you."

— BILL GAULEY

Psychiatry students were in their Emotional Extremes class. "Let's set some parameters," the professor said. "What's the opposite of joy?" he asked one student.

"Sadness," he answered.

"The opposite of depression?" he asked another student.

"Elation," he replied.

"The opposite of woe?" the prof asked a young woman from Texas.

The Texan replied, "Sir, I believe that would be giddyup."

Words that aren't in the dictionary but should be:

Bozone—n.
The substance surrounding stupid people that stops bright ideas from penetrating.

Decafalon—n.
The grueling event of getting through the day consuming only those things that are good for you.

Maypop—n.
A bald tire.

Pajangle—n.
Condition of waking up with one's pajamas turned 180 degrees.

Snackmosphere—n.
The empty but explosive layer of air at the top of a potato chip bag.

— BERT CHRISTENSON

"Doc, you've got to help me. Every time I drive down a country lane, I find myself singing 'Green Green Grass of Home.' Every time I see a cat I sing 'What's New Pussycat?' And last night I sang 'Delilah' in my sleep. I tell you, Doc, my wife was not at all amused."

"I wouldn't worry. It seems you have the early symptoms of Tom Jones syndrome."

"I have never heard of that. Is it common?"

"It's not unusual."

The fur began to fly when my fellow airplane passengers learned there was a chance they might miss their connecting flights out of Aspen. When we finally landed, I found out just how nasty things got.

Over the intercom, a harried flight attendant announced, "Those of you continuing on to L.A., please wait outside next to the boarding ramp and we will have a shuttle run you over."

— ALAINA WAGNER

"His personals ad said he was solid."

240

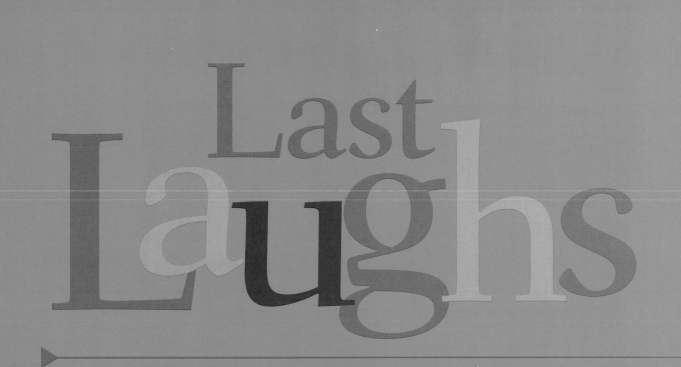

Last Laughs

Jest the facts: Laugh-out–loud humor we couldn't resist, plus the funniest one-liners of all time.

Did you hear about the doctor who went on a ski trip and got lost on the slopes? He stamped out "help" in the snow, but nobody could read his writing.

— HAROLD ZUBER

An older father noticed his son's Viagra tablets in the medicine cabinet. "Could I try one?" he asked. "Sure," his son said, "but make the most of it. Each of those pills costs ten bucks."

His dad was shocked by the price. "Don't worry," he promised, "I'll pay you back."

The next morning the son found an envelope under his breakfast plate. Inside was $110.

"Dad," he said, "that pill only cost $10."

"I know," his father said, smiling. "The ten is from me. The hundred is from your mother."

— DON KELLY

It's Tuesday. Three in the afternoon. Los Angeles police pick up a con artist on a section 872, the old Fountain of Youth scam. The con artist is selling bottles filled with a liquid that he claims slows the aging process.

The detective tells his partner,

"Frank, check his record. My gut tells me that our boy has played this game before."

Frank reports back. "You're right, he's got priors. He was busted for the same thing in 1815, 1887, 1921…"

— RON DENTINGER

Joe and Dave are hunting when Dave keels over. Frantic, Joe dials 911 on his cell phone and blurts, "My friend just dropped dead! What should I do?"

A soothing voice at the other end says, "Don't worry, I can help. First, let's make sure he's really dead."

After a brief silence the operator hears a shot ring out. Then Joe comes back to the phone. "Okay," he says nervously to the operator. "What do I do next?"

When the patrolman saw the man speed past, he pulled him over and asked for his license and registration. "I lost my license after my fifth DWI," the guy replied calmly. "I'll give you the registration, but don't freak out when I open the glove box because I've got a couple of guns in there. And if you should search the car, don't be surprised if you find a some drugs and illegal aliens in the trunk."

Alarmed, the patrolman went back to his car and called for backup. Moments later a SWAT team swept down on the car. The

driver was handcuffed as the team searched the vehicle.

"There's no drugs or guns in this car, buddy'" the SWAT leader said to the driver.

"Of course there aren't," the driver replied. "And I suppose that cop told you I was speeding, too."

— DARRELL ELMORE

Vacationing in Arizona, a group of British tourists spots a cowboy lying by the side of the road with his ear to the ground. "What's going on?" they ask. "Two horses—one gray, one chestnut—are pulling a wagon carrying two men," the cowboy says. "One man is wearing a red shirt, the other a black shirt. They're heading east."

"Wow!" says one of the tourists. "You can tell all that just by listening to the ground?"

"No!" replies the cowboy. "They just ran over me."

— JOHN GAMBA

Timeless Humor from the 50's

"For 20 years," mused the man at the bar, "my wife and I were ecstatically happy."

"Then what happened?" asked the bartender.

"We met."

On business in Mexico, three men get drunk and wake up in jail to learn they will be executed, though none of them can recall what they did to deserve it. The first man put in the electric chair is asked for his last words. "I'm from Yale Divinity School, and believe in the power of God to intervene on behalf of the innocent." The switch is thrown, but nothing happens. The jailers figure God wants the man alive and let him go.

The second man is strapped in. "I'm from Harvard Law School, and believe in the power of justice to intervene on behalf of the innocent." The switch is thrown; again, nothing. The jailers think the law is on this man's side, so they let him go.

The last man says, "Well, I'm an electrical engineer from MIT, and you're not electrocuting anybody if you don't connect those two loose wires down there."

"When I press my forehead with my finger, it really hurts," a patient complained to his doctor. "And when I do the same to my cheek, it's also painful. Even if I press on my stomach, I suffer. What can it be?"

"If I've only got two weeks to live, I'll take the last week in July and first week in August."

Stumped, the physician sent the patient to a specialist. The man returned to his doctor the following week.

"What did the specialist say?" the doctor asked.

"I have a broken finger."

— GEORGE RUSSELL

The 16th tee featured a fairway that ran along a road fenced off on the left. The first golfer in a foursome teed off and hooked the ball. It soared over the fence and bounced onto the street, where it hit the tire of a moving bus and ricocheted back onto the fairway.

As they all stood in amazement, one of his partners asked, "How did you do that?"

The golfer shrugged. "You have to know the bus schedule."

The police officer pulled over a guy driving a convertible because he had a penguin riding in the passenger seat. "Hey, buddy, is that an actual penguin?"

"Yeah. I just picked him up."

"Well, why don't you take him to the zoo?"

The guy agreed, but the very next day the cop saw him drive by again with the penguin sitting beside him. "I thought I told you to take that thing to the zoo," said the officer.

"I did," the guy replied. "And we had such a good time, tonight we're going to a hockey game."

A woman goes to the drugstore and asks for arsenic. "What do you want that for?" the pharmacist asks.

"I want to kill my husband," she replies. "He's having an affair with another woman."

"I can't sell you arsenic to kill your husband," says the pharmacist, "even if he is cheating."

244

The woman pulls out a picture of her husband with the pharmacist's wife. The druggist turns pale and replies, "Oh, I didn't realize you had a prescription."

— MARSHA SCHAUER

Six things you never want to hear at the tattoo parlor:
- "'Eagle'? I thought you said 'beagle.'"
- "Boy, I hate it when I get hiccups."
- "Hey, buddy, we ran out of red, so I used pink."
- "Two O's in 'Bob,' right?"
- "I bet you can't tell I've never done this before."
- "Anything else you want to say? You've got all kinds of room back here."

An old man living alone on a farm wrote to his only son, Bubba, in prison. "Dear Bubba: I'm feeling pretty bad because it looks like I won't be able to plant my potato garden this year. I'm just getting too old to be digging up a garden plot. Wish you were here—I know you would take care of it for me. Love, Dad."

About a week later, the farmer received this letter. "Dear Dad: Don't dig up the garden! That's where I buried the bodies. Love, Bubba." The next day, FBI agents stormed the property and dug up the entire garden. They didn't find any bodies, though, so they apologized to the old man and left.

Soon the farmer received another letter. "Dear Dad: Go ahead and plant the potatoes now. It's the best I could do under the circumstances. Love, Bubba."

"Where did you get that great motorcycle?" the engineering student asked his friend.

"I was minding my own business," his fellow engineer replied, "when a gorgeous woman rode up on it, jumped off, threw the bike to the ground, tore off her clothes and said, 'Take what you want.'"

The first engineer nodded his approval. "Good choice," he said. "The clothes probably wouldn't have fit."

— ED PERRATORE

I got thrown out of a mime show the other day for having a spasm. They thought I was heckling.

— JEFF SHAW

CALDWELL

Nancy offers her friend Veronica a ride home from work. During the drive, Veronica notices a brown paper bag on the front seat between them. "It's a bottle of wine," says Nancy. "I got it for my husband."

Veronica nods. "Good trade."

— ALAN E. OWENS

One day a genie appeared to a California man and offered to grant him one wish. The man said, "I wish you'd build a bridge from here to Hawaii so I could drive over there anytime."

The genie frowned. "I don't know. It sounds like quite an undertaking," he said. "Just think of the logistics. The supports required to reach the bottom of the ocean, the concrete, the steel! Why don't you pick something else?"

The man thought for a while and then said, "Okay, I wish for a complete understanding of women—what they're thinking, why they cry. I wish I knew how to make a woman truly happy."

The genie was silent for a minute, then said, "So how many lanes did you want on that bridge?"

— LISA FREDERICK

A priest, a nun, a rabbi, a lawyer and a doctor walk into a bar. The bartender takes one look at them and says, "What is this? A joke?"

— SEAN MORRISON

A pair of cows were talking in the field. One says, "Have you heard about the mad cow disease that's going around?"

"Yeah," the other cow says. "Makes me glad I'm a penguin."

His wife was going into labor, and a man dialed 911 in a panic. When the dispatcher came on the line, he cried, "My wife is having a baby. Her contractions are only two minutes apart. What am I supposed to do?"

The dispatcher said, "Calm down, sir. Is this her first child?"

"No," the frantic man replied. "This is her husband!"

Up in heaven, the pastor was shown his eternal reward. To his disappointment, he was given only a small shack. But down the street he saw a taxi driver being shown a lovely estate with gardens and pools.

"I don't understand it," the pastor said. "My whole life, I served God with everything I had and this is all I get, while a mere cabby is given a mansion?"

"It's quite simple," St. Peter said. "When you preached, people slept; when he drove, people prayed."

— JOEL BERGMAN

Timeless Humor from the **60's**

Breathless scientist, to returning spaceman: "Is there any life on Mars?"

Spaceman: "Well, there's a little on Saturday night, but it's awfully dead the rest of the week."

"This Heimlich instructional video just won't stay in the VCR."

A local charity had never received a donation from the town's most successful lawyer. The director called to get a contribution. "Our records show you make $500,000 year, yet you haven't given a penny to charity," the director began. "Wouldn't you like to help the community?"

The lawyer replied, "Did your research show that my mother is ill, with medical bills several times her annual income?"

"Um, no," mumbled the director.

"Or that my brother is blind and unemployed?"

The stricken director began to stammer out an apology.

"Or that my sister's husband died in an accident," said the lawyer, his voice rising in indignation, "leaving her penniless with three kids?"

The humiliated director said simply, "I had no idea."

"So," said the lawyer, "if I don't give any money to them, why would I give any to you?"

The dying penny pincher told his doctor, lawyer and pastor, "I have $90,000 under my mattress. At my funeral I want each of you to toss an envelope with $30,000 into the grave." And after telling them this, he died.

At the funeral, each threw his envelope in the grave. Later, the pastor said, "I must confess. I needed $10,000 for my new church, so I only threw in $20,000."

The doctor admitted, "I needed $20,000 for new equipment at the hospital, so I only had $10,000 in the envelope."

"Gentlemen, I'm shocked that you would blatantly ignore this man's final wish," said the lawyer. "I threw in my personal check for the full amount."

In the hospitality suite at a bar association convention, a young lawyer meets the Devil. The Devil says, "Listen, if you give me your soul and the souls of everyone in your family, I'll make you a full partner in your firm."

After mulling this over, the lawyer says, "What's the catch?"

Jim's doctor tells him he has only one day to live. When Jim goes home to share the bad news with his wife, she asks what he wants to do with the little bit of time he has left. "All I want," Jim tells his beloved wife, "is to spend my last few hours reliving our honeymoon." Which is exactly what they did.

But after four hours of blissful romance, she announces that she's tired and wants to go to sleep.

"Oh, come on," Jim whispers in her ear.

"Look," his wife snaps, "I've got to get up in the morning. You don't!"

The Japanese eat little fat and suffer fewer heart attacks than the British or Americans. The French eat a lot of fat and also suffer fewer heart attacks than the British or Americans. The Italians drink a lot of red wine and also suffer fewer heart attacks than the British or Americans.

Conclusion: Eat and drink what you like. Speaking English is apparently what kills you.

— IRWIN KNOPF

Jake: "Why are cowboys' hats turned up on the sides?"

Bill: "I don't know, Jake. Why?"

Jake: "So that three people can fit in the pickup."

— DONNA L. ANDERSON

Proudly showing off his new apartment to a friend late one night, the drunk led the way to his bedroom, where there was a big brass gong. "What's that big brass gong for?" asked the friend.

"It's not a gong. It's a talking clock," the drunk replied.

"A talking clock? How's it work?"

"Watch," said the drunk. He picked up a hammer, gave the gong an ear-shattering pound and stepped back.

Someone on the other side of the wall screamed: "Hey, you jerk. It's three in the morning!"

— E. T. THOMPSON

These two green beans are crossing the freeway when one of them is hit by an 18-wheeler. His friend scrapes him up and rushes him to the hospital. After hours of surgery, the doctor says, "I have good news and bad news."

The healthy green bean says, "Okay, give me the good news first."

"Well, he's going to live."

"So, what's the bad news?"

"The bad news is he'll be a vegetable for the rest of his life."

A junior manager, a senior manager and their boss were on their way to a lunch meeting. In the cab, they found a lamp. The boss rubbed it and a genie appeared. "I'll grant you one wish each," the genie said.

Grabbing the lamp from his boss, the eager senior manager shouted, "I want to be on a fast boat in the Bahamas with no worries." And, poof, he was gone.

The junior manager couldn't keep quiet. He shouted, "I want to be in Miami, with beautiful girls, food and cocktails." And, poof, he was gone.

Finally, it was the boss's turn. "I want those idiots back in the office after lunch."

— ASHFAQ AHMED

249

Two doctors and an HMO manager die and line up together at the Pearly Gates. One doctor steps up and tells St. Peter, "As a pediatric surgeon, I saved hundreds of children." St. Peter lets him enter.

The next doctor says, "As a psychiatrist, I helped thousands of people live better lives." St. Peter tells him to go ahead.

The last man says, "I was an HMO manager. I got countless families cost-effective health care."

St. Peter replies, "You may enter. But," he adds, "you can only stay for three days. After that, you can go to hell."

God populated the earth with vegetables of all kinds, so that Man would live a long and healthy life. And Satan created the 99-cent double cheeseburger. And Satan said to Man, "Want fries with that?"

And Man said, "Supersize them!" And Man gained pounds.

And God created healthful yogurt, and Satan froze the yogurt, and brought forth chocolate, nuts and brightly colored candy to put on top. And Man gained more pounds.

And God brought forth running shoes, and Man resolved to lose

/ SMELTZER

those extra pounds. And Satan brought forth cable TV, remote control and potato chips. And Man clutched his remote and ate his chips. Satan saw this and said, "It is good."

And Man went into cardiac arrest. And God sighed and created quadruple bypass surgery.

And Satan created HMOs...

A thug and his girlfriend were strolling down the street late at night, holding hands and gazing into shop windows. Passing a jewelry store, the girlfriend spotted a shiny ring. "Oh!" she exclaimed. "I'd just love to have that."

The thug looked around, and without a word threw a brick through the window, reached in and grabbed the ring. "There you go, baby," he said. The girl was impressed.

They walked on until she spotted a leather jacket in another

window. "Wow," she said. "It sure is beautiful."

"Hold on," said the thug. He threw another brick through the window and handed her the coat.

A few blocks later she spotted an attractive pair of boots. "Oh—" she began, but the thug interrupted.

"C'mon, baby," he said. "You think I'm made of bricks?"

— STEPHEN McCULLOUGH

The blind man walks into a bar and says, "Wanna hear a blond joke?"

The bartender tells him, "Well, I'm blond and I won't appreciate it. The man sitting next to you is 265 pounds, and is also blond. The man behind you is 285 pounds, and he's a blond too. Do you still want to tell that joke?"

"No way," says the blind man. "Not if I have to explain it three times."

— PAT PATEL

Timeless Humor from the 60's

Did you hear they are putting a clock in the Leaning Tower of Pisa? Because what's the good if you have the inclination and don't have the time?

Reporter interviewing a 104-year-old woman: "What is the best thing about being 104?" She replies, **"No peer pressure."**

— SYLVIA R. SHINER

A biologist assigned to work in deepest Africa hired a guide to take him upriver to the remote site where he would do his study. As they were making their way into the jungle, the scientist heard the sound of drums. "What is that drumming?" he asked his guide nervously.

The guide, who spoke little English, replied, "Drums okay, but very bad when they stop." The drumming continued for two weeks while the biologist conducted his fieldwork. Finally, on the last day, the drums suddenly stopped, and the forest fell eerily silent.

Alarmed, the scientist called out to his guide, "The drums have stopped! What happens now?"

The guide crouched down, covered his head with his hands and, with despair in his voice, answered, "Bass solo."

Phoning a patient, the doctor says, "I have some bad news and some worse news. The bad news is that you have only 24 hours left to live."

"That is bad news," the patient replies. "What could be worse?"

The doctor answers, "I've been trying to reach you since yesterday."

Lou sees a sign in front of a house: "Talking Dog for Sale." Intrigued, he rings the bell and the owner shows him the dog. "What's your story?" Lou asks.

The dog says, "I discovered I had this gift when I was just a pup. The CIA signed me up, and soon I was jetting around the world, sitting at the feet of spies and world leaders, gathering important information and sending it back home. When I tired of that lifestyle, I joined the FBI, where I helped catch drug lords and gunrunners. I was wounded in the line of duty, received some medals, and now a movie is being made of my life."

"How much do you want for the dog?" Lou asks the owner.

"Ten dollars," says the owner.

Lou is incredulous. "Why on earth would you sell that remarkable dog for so little?"

"Because he's a liar. He didn't do any of that stuff."

— STEVE DERIVAN

So... which one is yours?

Everything is changing. People are taking their comedians seriously and the politicians as a joke.

— WILL ROGERS

Humor is a rubber sword—it allows you to make a point without drawing blood.

— MARY HIRSCH

Inviting people to laugh with you while you are laughing at yourself is a good thing to do. You may be the fool, but you're the fool in charge.

— CARL REINER, My Anecdotal Life (St. Martin's)

You know there is a problem with the education system when you realize that out of the three R's, only one begins with an R.

— DENNIS MILLER, "Dennis Miller Live," HBO

No matter what happens, somebody will find a way to take it too seriously.

— DAVE BARRY,
Dave Barry Turns 50 (Crown)

Humor is always based on a modicum of truth. Ever heard a joke about a father-in-law?

— DICK CLARK

How come if you mix flour and water together you get glue? And when you add eggs and sugar you get cake? Where does the glue go?

— RITA RUDNER

A scoutmaster asks his troop to list three important things to bring in case they get lost in the desert. Food, matches, a bandana are all mentioned. Then Timmy suggests a compass, a canteen of water, and a deck of cards.

"I get the first two items," says the leader. "But what good are the cards?"

"Well, as soon as you start playing solitaire, it's guaranteed someone will come up to you and say, 'Put the red nine on top of the black ten.'"

John told the mortician to spare no expense for his father's funeral. So when a bill for $3,200 arrived after the funeral, John paid it next month, he received a bill $85. He paid it, figuring it had been left off the original tally. But a month later, after receiving another bill for $85, John called the funeral director.

"You said you wanted the best funeral we could arrange," the director told him. "So I rented him a tuxedo."

— RICHARD REYNOSA

Last night I played a blank tape at full blast. The mime next door went nuts.

— STEVEN WRIGHT

"Knock, knock."

"Who's there?"

"Control freak. Now you say, 'Control freak who?'"

"Quit complaining! I was the hammock last week!"

On the way home from work, Tom is stopped on the street by an attractive woman in a suggestive outfit.

"For $100, I'll do anything you ask in three words or less," she whispers.

"Okay," agrees Tom, handing over the cash. "Paint my house."

— BILL UPDIKE

At a convention of blondes, a speaker insisted that the "dumb blonde" myth is all wrong. To prove it he asked one cute young volunteer, "How much is 101 plus 20?"

The blonde answered, "120."

"No," he said, "that's not right." idience called out, "Give her chance."

o the speaker asked the blonde, "How much is 10 plus 13?"

Slowly the blonde replied, "16."

"Sorry," he said, shaking his head.

Once again the crowd oared, "Give her another chance."

"This is your last try," warned the speaker. "How much is 2 plus 2?"

Carefully she ventured, "Four?"

And the crowd yelled, "Give her another chance!"

— JAMES T. DORSEY

253

A farmer on a tractor approached a driver whose car was stuck in a mud hole. "For ten bucks, I'll pull you out of there," the farmer said.

"All right," the driver agreed. After the farmer had pocketed the money, he said, "You know, yours is the tenth car I've rescued today."

"Wow," the driver said incredulously. "When do you have time to work on your land? At night?"

"No," the farmer replied. "Night is when I fill the hole with water."

— RODRIGO CAMARGO

This duck walks into a store one day and asks the clerk, "Do you have any grapes?"

The clerk replies, "Sorry, no."

The next day the duck walks into the same store and again asks, "Do you have any grapes?"

The clerk says, "No."

The next day the duck walks into the store and asks, "Do you have any grapes?"

This time the clerk says: "No. And if you ask me one more time, I'll staple your feet to the floor."

The next day the duck walks into the store and asks, "Do you have any staples?"

The clerk says, "No."

So the duck says, "Do you have any grapes?"

— GREG WILKEY

Overheard: "I hate talking cars. A voice out of nowhere says things like, 'Your door is ajar.' Why don't they say something really useful, like 'There's a state trooper hiding behind that bush.'?"

A businesswoman is sitting at a bar. A man approaches her. "Hi, honey," he says. "Want a little company?"

"Why?" asks the woman. "Do you have one to sell?"

— CAROLYN A. STRADLEY

So this neutron walks into a bar and orders a beer. "How much will that be?" the neutron asks.

"For you," replies the bartender, "no charge."

— LYNDELL LEATHERMAN

The man auditioning for the circus was confident, even though he'd been told the impresario had seen it all. "I have the most unusual act," the man said before he began. "Just watch. I'm sure you'll be amazed."

He proceeded to climb a tall tower, and then jumped off, his arms flapping wildly. Nearing the ground, the man's fall suddenly slowed and he soared upward. He swooped past the impresario twice and then fluttered gently to the ground, where he beamed triumphantly at his audience.

The impresario stood there for a moment staring at the man. Finally he said, "So is that all you've got? Bird impressions?"

Two attorneys walk into a diner, order drinks and pull their lunches from their briefcases. "Sorry," the bartender says, "but you can't eat your own food in here."

The guys look at each other, shrug their shoulders and swap sandwiches.

— LYDIA PRINCE

A man approaches the Gate of Heaven and asks to be let in. "Tell me one good thing you did in your life," St. Peter says to him.

"Well," replies the fellow, "I saw a group of punks harassing an elderly woman, so I kicked their leader in the shins."

"When did this happen?"

"About 40 seconds ago."

— MICHAEL S. COFFEY

In Nevada two men were shutting down their small casino at about 2 a.m. when a beautiful woman came in and said she wanted to gamble $2,000 on one roll of the dice. They said they were closed, but she insisted that one roll would only take a minute. The men figured why not, the odds were in their favor.

So the woman put her money down, and they put theirs down. Then she said, "Wait just a moment," and went to the rest room.

She came out a minute later, stark naked, and rolled the dice. "Seven," she said, and picked up the money, returned to the rest room, dressed and left.

"Did you see that seven?" one man asked the other.

"No," he replied. "I thought you did."

— BOYCE D. KESTERSON

Phil visits his doctor after weeks of not feeling well. "I have bad news," says the doctor. "You don't have long to live."

"How long have I got?" asks a distraught Phil.

"Ten," the doctor says sadly.

"Ten? Ten what? Months? Days?"

Suddenly the doctor interrupts, "Nine…"

"The first thing you have to understand is that when they throw your ball, they're not trying to get rid of you."

255

It was the annual grudge match football game between the large animals and the small animals. In the first half, the big animals crushed the little critters. But by the second half, things had turned around. The big animals' stars—the elephant, rhino and hippo—were all tackled for huge losses. "Who's making all those tackles?" asked the small critters' coach.

"I am," said the centipede.

"Why weren't you here earlier when we needed you?" the coach yelled. The centipede replied,

"I was having my ankles taped."

A scrawny little fellow showed up at the lumber camp looking for work. "Just give me a chance to show you what I can do," he said to the head lumberjack.

"All right," said the boss. "Take your ax and cut down that redwood tree."

Five minutes later the skinny guy was back. "I cut it down," he said, "and split it up into lumber."

The boss couldn't believe his eyes. "Where did you learn to cut trees like that?"

"The Sahara," the man answered.

"The Sahara Desert?"

"Desert? Oh, sure, that's what they call it now!"

— KUMIKO YOSHIDA

Mother Teresa arrives in Heaven. "Be thou hungry?" God asks. Mother Teresa nods. He serves them each a humble sandwich of tuna on rye bread. Meanwhile, the sainted woman looks down to see gluttons in Hell devouring steaks, lobsters and wine.

The next day God invites her to join him for another meal. Again, it's tuna on rye. Again, she sees the denizens of Hell feasting.

The next day, as another can of tuna is opened, Mother Teresa meekly says, "I am grateful to be here with you as a reward for the pious life I led. But I don't get it: All we eat is tuna and bread while in the other place they eat like kings."

"Let's be honest," God says with a sigh, "for just two people, does it pay to cook?"

Two dogs were out for a walk. One dog says to the other, "Wait here a minute. I'll be right back." He walks across the street and sniffs a fire hydrant for about a minute, then rejoins his friend.

"What was that all about?" the other dog asks.

"Just checking my messages."

Alice and Ted went snowboarding, and Ted brought along a quart-size thermos. Alice had never seen one, and asked what it was. "It's a thermos," replied Ted. "The guy at the store told me it's used for keeping hot things hot and cold things cold."

"Sounds great," said Alice. "What do you have in it?"

"Three coffees and a Popsicle."

— JEANNE STANTON

Do you know what you get when you play a country-and-western song backward? You get your job back, you get your house back, your wife back, your truck back . . .

The husband came home unexpectedly and found his wife in the arms of another man.

"What do you think you're doing?" he shouted.

"See?" the woman said to her companion. "I told you he was stupid."

I went on a 45-day diet. It's going great. I've already lost 30 days.

A guy goes on vacation to the Holy Land with his wife and mother-in-law. Halfway through their trip, the mother-in-law dies. So the guy goes to an undertaker, who explains that they can ship the body home, but it'll cost $5,000. Or they can bury her in the Holy Land for $150.

"We'll ship her home," says the son-in-law.

"Are you sure?" asks the undertaker. "That's an awfully big expense. And I can assure you we do a very nice burial here."

"Look," says the son-in-law, "two thousand years ago they buried a guy here, and three days later he rose from the dead. I just can't take that chance."

— JASON TUTHILL

Two guys were discussing modern trends on sex and marriage. "I didn't sleep with my wife before we got married," Roy said. "Did you?"

"I'm not sure," Bobby replied. "What was her maiden name?"

— JONATHAN DURIA

"It's chilly in here," the wealthy customer sniffed. "Will you please turn down the air conditioner?"

"No problem, sir," said the waiter.

After a few minutes, the man flagged the server again. "Now I'm too warm."

"All right," said the waiter. But soon the customer was chilly again.

Finally a patron at a nearby table whispered to the waiter, "I commend you for your patience. That guy is certainly keeping you busy."

"No, he's not," the waiter said with a shrug. "We don't even have an air conditioner."

"Billy's opinions do not reflect the views of the Andersons, their affiliates or subsidiaries."

Lou, Sam and Joe walk into a bar and each order a pint. Just as they're about to take their first sip, flies land in each of their drinks.

Lou, the most squeamish of the trio, pushes his beer away in disgust.

Sam, the thrifty one, fishes the fly out and drinks his beer.

And Joe, the lush, drags the fly out, holds it over the beer and yells, "C'mon, spit it out! Spit it out!!"

Overheard: "If Batman is supposed to be so smart, how come he wears his underwear outside his clothes?"

— ASHLEY COOPER

"May I try on that dress in the window?" the gorgeous young woman asks the manager of the designer boutique.

"Go ahead," the manager replies. "Maybe it'll attract some business."

— HARRY BUCK

The nurse said to the doctor, "There's an invisible man in the waiting room."

The doctor replied, "Tell him I can't see him now."

— PAUL W. REGENESS

The devout cowboy lost his favorite Bible while he was mending fences out on the range. Three weeks later a cow walked up to him carrying the Bible in its mouth. The cowboy couldn't believe his eyes. He took the book out of the cow's mouth, raised his eyes heavenward and exclaimed, "It's a miracle!"

"Not really," said the cow. "Your name is written inside the cover."

— ROMAN WILBERT

"You've got to help me, Doc," the Irishman said. "It's me ear. There's somethin' in there."

"Let's have a look. Why, my goodness, it's true. You've got money lodged up in there." The doctor proceeded to pull out a $100 bill. "Wow," he said, "and there's still more." Out came a few more hundreds, then some fifties and some tens. Finally the doctor said, "Well, that seems to be it."

"How much was there, all told?"

"One thousand, nine hundred and ninety dollars."

"Ah, yes, that'd be right," said the Irishman. "I knew I wasn't feeling two grand."

"Every time I drink a cup of coffee, doctor, I have a stabbing pain in my right eye. What should I do?"

"Take the spoon out of your cup."

— STEVE JARRELL

Shelley, a talent scout for a large recording studio, was walking by a convent when he heard someone singing in a voice so beautiful he couldn't believe his ears. He rang the bell and asked to speak to the woman with the amazing voice. Soon a young nun appeared.

"Sister," Shelley said, "I represent Euphonics, Inc., and I'd like you to make a tape of hymns. Your fee could be donated to charity."

"I'd be delighted," she replied, "but first I must get written permission from our mother superior."

"Okay, Sister, just give me a call." Shelley rushed back to the office and described his find to his boss. Then he asked for a raise.

Replied the boss, "Wait till the nun signs, Shelley."

— STEVE KEUEBEL

A doctor answered the phone and heard the familiar voice of a colleague on the other end of the line say, "We need a fourth for poker."

"I'll be right over," the doctor answered.

As he was putting on his coat, his wife asked, "Is it serious?"

"Oh, yes," the doctor answered gravely. "In fact, there are three doctors there already."

— DOROTHEA KENT

"I think Mary is getting suspicious about all the long walks."

Timeless Humor from the 70's

Then there's the story about the gossip columnist who asked comedian George Burns, 74, if he planned to marry the 19-year-old UCLA student he was dating. George took a long puff on his cigar and quipped, "I told her I might think it over if she gets all A's on her report card."

How many country-western singers does it take to change a lightbulb?

Five. One to put in the new bulb, and four to sing about how much they long for the old one.

LESLIE R. TANNER

Who invented copper wire?

Two tax attorneys fighting over a penny.

EARLE HITCHNER

Why did the Pope cross the road?

He crosses everything.

TOM FLITTER

Why do some testing labs prefer to use lawyers instead of mice?

Because there are more lawyers than mice, the scientists don't get as attached to the lawyers, and there are some things mice won't do.

How many lawyer jokes are there?

Only three. The rest are true stories . . .

What do you get when you cross a librarian and a lawyer?

All the information you want, except you can't understand it.

PRADHAN NAGESH

Ralph was on his way home from work one night when, to his horror, he suddenly realized that he'd completely forgotten his daughter's birthday. He rushed to the toy store and asked the manager, "How much is the Barbie in the window?"

"Which one?" the manager replied. "We have Workout Barbie for $19.95, Malibu Barbie for $19.95, Soccer Barbie is $19.95, Cinderella Barbie $19.95, Retro '70s Barbie $19.95, and Divorced Barbie is $375."

"Hold on," Ralph said. "Why is Divorced Barbie $375 when all the other Barbies are only $19.95?"

"Well," said the store manager, "Divorced Barbie comes with Ken's car, Ken's house, Ken's boat, Ken's dog, Ken's cat, Ken's furniture…"

Jack walked into his house breathless and exhausted. "What happened?" his wife asked. "It's a great idea I had," he gasped, smiling proudly. "I ran all the way home behind the bus and saved myself fifty cents."

His wife frowned. "That's just like you, Jack, always thinking small," she said, shaking her head disapprovingly. "Why couldn't you have run behind a taxi and saved yourself six dollars?"

One day, the general noticed one of his soldiers behaving oddly. He would pick up every piece of paper he saw, read it, frown and say, "That's not it," and drop it.

After a month of this, the general finally arranged to have the soldier tested. The psychologist found that the soldier was deranged, and wrote out his discharge from the Army.

The soldier picked it up, smiled and said, "That's it."

Ten men and one woman are hanging on to a rope that extends down from a helicopter. The weight of 11 people is too much for the rope, so the group decides one person has to jump off. No one can decide who should go, until finally the woman volunteers.

She gives a touching speech, saying she will sacrifice her life to save the others, because women are used to giving up things for their husbands and children.

When she finishes speaking… all the men start clapping.

— MARGARET PITMAN

Babs couldn't understand why she was losing so badly at Trivial Pursuit. Nevertheless, she persevered, rolling the dice and landing on green—Science & Nature. Her question was, "If you are in a vacuum and someone calls your name, can you hear it?"

Babs mulled over the question for a minute, and then asked, "Is it on or off?"

A guy walks into a bank, points a gun at the teller and says, "Give me all your money, lady, or you're geography."

"Don't you mean 'history'?" the teller asks.

"Hey, lady," the thug replies. "Don't change the subject."

— MIRIAM HARTILL

261

50 Funniest One-Liners

As *Tonight Show* writer Dave Hanson points out, if you're a master of the one-liner, your audience will never drift—even for a split second. There's too much of a chance they might miss something. We combed the comedy archives to find the funniest short takes out there, from classic to current. Like your own personal stand-up show!

"Women don't want to hear what you think. Women want to hear what they think, in a deeper voice."

— BILL COSBY

Cupid's Arrow

"A guy knows he's in love when he loses interest in his car for a couple of days."

— TIM ALLEN

Cupid's Arrow Sharpened

"The quickest way to a man's heart is through his chest."

— ROSEANNE BARR

"When I eventually met Mr. Right, I had no idea that his first name was Always."

— RITA RUDNER

"A man in love is incomplete until he has married. Then he's finished."

— ZSA ZSA GABOR

"I always wanted to be the last guy on earth, just to see if all those women were lying to me."

— RONNIE SHAKES

Financial Genius

"A bank is a place that will lend you money, if you can prove that you don't need it."
— BOB HOPE

"Money won't buy friends, but you get a better class of enemy."
— SPIKE MILLIGAN

In Sum…

"I really didn't say everything I said."
— YOGI BERRA

Unfathomable

"Imagine if there were no hypothetical situations."
— JOHN MENDOZA

"I don't consider myself bald. I'm simply taller than my hair."
— THOM SHARP

"You know the world is going crazy when the best rapper is a white guy, the best golfer is a black guy and the tallest guy in the NBA is Chinese."
— CHRIS ROCK

It's a Zoo

"Time's fun when you're having flies."
— KERMIT THE FROG

"The trouble with the rat race is that even if you win, you're still a rat."
— LILY TOMLIN

"Give a man a fish and he has food for a day; teach him how to fish and you can get rid of him for the entire weekend."
— ZENNA SCHAFFER

"Outside of a dog, a book is man's best friend; inside of a dog, it's too dark to read."
— GROUCHO MARX

"Cats are smarter than dogs. You can't get eight cats to pull a sled through snow."
— JEFF VALDEZ

Miss Manners

"If you haven't got anything good to say about anyone, come and sit by me."
— ALICE ROOSEVELT LONGWORTH

"The first thing I do in the morning is brush my teeth and sharpen my tongue."
— DOROTHY PARKER

Deadly Serious

"It's not that I'm afraid to die; I just don't want to be there when it happens."
— WOODY ALLEN

Women on the Edge

"I have my standards. They may be low, but I have them."

— BETTE MIDLER

"I've been on a calendar, but I've never been on time."

— MARILYN MONROE

"I used to be Snow White, but I drifted."

— MAE WEST

"Deep down, I'm pretty superficial."

— AVA GARDNER

Men on the Edge

"I just recently had my Visa card stolen. Now it's everywhere I want to be."

— SCOTT WOOD

"A cynic is a man who, when he smells flowers, looks around for a coffin."

— H.L. MENCKEN

"I drink to make other people interesting."

— GEORGE JEAN NATHAN

"If God meant us to be naked, he would have made our skin fit better."

— MAUREEN MURPHY

Keeping Score

"If a woman has to choose between catching a fly ball and saving an infant's life, she will choose to save the infant's life without even considering if there are men on base."

— DAVE BARRY

"Football combines the two worst features of American life: violence and committee meetings."

— GEORGE WILL

"I went to a fight the other night and a hockey game broke out."

— RODNEY DANGERFIELD

"The trouble with jogging is that the ice falls out of your glass."

— MARTIN MULL

Highly Questionable

"What's another word for thesaurus?"

— STEVEN WRIGHT

"If winning isn't everything, why do they keep score?"

— VINCE LOMBARDI

"If mini-marts are open 365 days a year, 24 hours a day and 7 days a week, why do the doors have locks on them?"

— GALLAGHER

Fashion Plates

"Men who have pierced ears are better prepared for marriage. They've experienced pain and bought jewelry."

— RITA RUDNER

Health Nuts

"I told my doctor I broke my leg in two places. He told me to quit going to those places."

— HENNY YOUNGMAN

"Housework can't kill you, but why take a chance?"

— PHYLLIS DILLER

Wisdumb

"Never ask the barber if you need a haircut."

— WARREN BUFFETT

"We've all heard that a million monkeys banging on a million typewriters will eventually reproduce the entire works of Shakespeare. Now, thanks to the Internet, we know this is not true."

— ROBERT WILENSKY

"It's so simple to be wise. Just think of something stupid to say and then don't say it."

— SAM LEVENSON

A Comedy of Heirs

"When you're eight years old, nothing is your business."

— LENNY BRUCE

"If your parents never had children, chances are you won't, either."

— DICK CAVETT

"When I was born, I was so surprised I couldn't talk for a year and a half."

— GRACIE ALLEN

"Never lend your car to anyone to whom you've given birth."

— ERMA BOMBECK

"This is a strange country we live in. When it comes to electing a President, we get two choices. But when we have to select a Miss America, we get 50."

— JAY LENO

Odds-on Favorites

"I figure you have the same chance of winning the lottery whether you play or not."

— FRAN LEBOWITZ

Speed Traps

"Have you noticed that anyone driving slower than you is an idiot and anyone driving faster than you is a maniac?"

— GEORGE CARLIN

"Why do they call it rush hour when nothing moves?"

— ROBIN WILLIAMS

"Instant gratification takes too long."

— CARRIE FISHER

The teacher asks, "If you had one dollar and you asked your father for another, how many dollars would you have?"

Vincent raised his hand and answered, "One dollar."

The teacher shook her head. "You don't know your math."

Vincent said, "You don't know my father."

Walking into the local chamber of commerce, the stranger obviously looked desperate. He approached the guy at the counter and asked, "Is there a criminal attorney in town?" The guy behind the counter replied, "Yes, but we can't prove it yet!"

— JOHN G. STEEN

Louise came home and found Henry stalking around with a fly swatter. "Killed any yet?" she asked. "Yep," Henry answered. "Two males and a female."

"How could you tell?"

"Well," said Henry, "two were on a beer can and one was on the telephone."

Two friends were beginning a game of golf. The first man stepped up to the tee, hit the ball and got a hole in one. The other man said, "Now I'll take my practice swing, and then we'll start the game."

— EDWARD W. STRICKLER

Shakey said to the psychiatrist, "Doc, every time I get into bed, I think there's somebody under it. You gotta help me!"

"Come to me three times a week for two years and I'll cure your fears," said the shrink. "And I'll only charge you $200 a visit."

"I'll think about it," said Shakey.

Six months later the doctor met Shakey on the street and asked why he never came to see him.

"For two hundred bucks a visit? A bartender cured me for ten dollars."

"Is that so! How?"

"He told me to cut the legs off the bed."

"I got this great new hearing aid the other day. It really works fantastically."

"Are you wearing it now?"

"Yep. Cost me a small fortune, but it's really top of the line."

"What kind is it?"

"Twelve thirty."

A pastor, known for his lengthy sermons, noticed a man get up and leave for part of the service. After church, the pastor asked the man where he had gone. "To get a haircut," the guy said.

"But," asked the pastor, "why didn't you do that before the service?"

"Because," the gentleman replied, "I didn't need one then."

— RUBEN QUEZADA

"It's number two! That's the man who stole my identity."

Albert comes home, plops down in front of the TV and says to his wife, "Quick! Get me a beer before it starts." She rolls her eyes and brings him a beer.

Fifteen minutes later he says, "Get me another beer. It's going to start any minute now."

His wife is furious. "Is that all you're going to do tonight? Sit in front of that television drinking beer? You have to be the world's laziest, most—"

He interrupts her with a heavy sigh. "Well," he says. "It's started."

Two atoms are walking down the sidewalk when they accidentally bump into each other. "I'm really sorry!" the first atom exclaims.

"Are you all right?"

"Actually, no," the second atom replies. "I lost an electron."

"Oh, no! Are you sure?"

"I'm positive!"

— VYAS SARWESHWAR PRASAD

Bill walked into a bar with a lump of Tarmac under his arm. "What can I do for you?" asked the bartender, looking him up and down. "A beer for me," Bill replied, "and one for the road."

— NIGEL PENN

A homeless beggar walked up to a well-dressed woman shopping in Beverly Hills and moaned, "I haven't eaten anything in four days."

The woman looked at him, sighed and said, "I wish I had your willpower."

— PAUL SILVEIRA

Clementine is driving home one night when her car is hit by a bad hailstorm, leaving hundreds of dents. The next day she goes to a body shop for a repair estimate. The repairman winks at his buddy and tells Clementine that if she blows into the tailpipe really hard, the dents will just pop out.

After she arrives home, she blows with all her might into the exhaust pipe. Her roommate asks what she's doing. Clementine explains the repairman's tip. "But it doesn't work," she says, pausing to catch her breath.

"Duh!" replies her friend. "You have to roll up the windows first!"

— MINDY VAUGHAN

The curvy redhead limped into the doctor's office complaining about a trick knee. The doctor stooped down, peering at the knee, and asked, "Now what's a joint like you doing in a nice girl like this?"

— JOHN DRATWA

Late one night the political candidate came home and gave his wife the glorious news: "Darling, I've been elected!"

"Honestly?" she replied.

"Hey," the politician said, frowning, "why bring that up?"

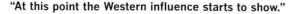

"At this point the Western influence starts to show."

Did you hear about the guy who froze to death at the drive-in? He went to see Closed for the Winter.

On their first date, a man asked his companion if she'd like a drink with dinner. "Oh, no, what would I tell my Sunday school class?" she said.

Later, he offered her a cigarette. "Oh, no, what would I tell my Sunday school class?" she said again.

On the drive home, he saw a motel. Figuring he had nothing to lose, he asked if she wanted to stop in there.

"Okay," his date replied.

"What will you tell your Sunday school class?" he asked, shocked.

"The same thing I always tell them. 'You don't have to drink or smoke to have a good time.'"

— GEORGE NORDHAM

A businessman taking an efficiency seminar presented a case study on his wife's routine for cooking breakfast: "After a few days of observation, I determined what was slowing her down and suggested ways to speed up the process."

"Did it work?" the teacher asked.

"It sure did. Instead of taking her 20 minutes to cook my breakfast, it takes me only seven."

Then there was the 85-year-old woman who found her husband in bed with another woman. She was so enraged that she dragged him to the balcony of their Miami high-rise and pushed him to his death. When she appeared in court, the judge asked if she had anything to say in her own defense.

"Well, Your Honor," she replied, "I figured if at 92 he could make love, he could fly too."

— ROB MARSHALL

Bob and Bill fly to Alaska for a fishing trip. They hire a bush pilot and rent a boat, rods and tackle. After two weeks, they've caught only one small salmon.

"Man, Bill," Bob says. "Do you realize this lousy fish cost us about $2,000 apiece?"

"Wow," Bill replies. "At that rate, it's a good thing we only caught one."

Howard dies and waits in line for judgment. He notices that some souls go right into heaven, while Satan throws others into a burning pit. But every so often, instead of hurling a poor soul into the fire, the devil tosses it aside.

Curious, Howard asks Satan, "Excuse me, but why are you tossing them aside instead of flinging them into hell with the others?"

"They're from Seattle," Satan replies. "They're too wet to burn."

— ANNETTE JOHNSON

Jason showed his buddy the beautiful diamond ring he had bought his girlfriend for her birthday. "I thought she wanted a four-wheel-drive vehicle," ventured his friend.

"She did," Jason said. "But where am I going to find a fake Jeep?"

— ZHANG WENPENG

sign language

Church bulletin bloopers, courtesy of the Internet.

"Morning sermon: Jesus Walks on the Water. Evening sermon: Searching for Jesus."

"Ladies, don't forget the rummage sale. It's a chance to get rid of those things not worth keeping around the house. Don't forget your husbands."

A young woman was describing her date to a friend. "After dinner," she said, "he wanted to come back to my apartment, but I refused. I told him my mother would worry if I did anything like that."

"Then what happened?" asked her friend.

"He kept insisting, and I kept refusing," the young woman responded.

"He didn't weaken your resolve, did he?" the friend asked.

"Not a bit. In the end, we went back to his apartment. I figured, let his mother worry."

Sunday a minister played hooky from church so he could enjoy a round of golf, leaving his assistant to conduct the service. He drove to a faraway golf course to avoid bumping into any parishioners.

Looking down, St. Peter said to God, "You're not going to let him get away with this, are you?" The Lord shook his head.

The minister took his first shot, and scored a 420-yard hole in one. St. Peter was outraged. "I thought you were going to punish him!" he said to the Lord.

The Lord looked at St. Peter and replied, "So who's he going to tell?"

— CLAIRE PARKER

"Young man, where do you work?" the judge asked the defendant.

"Here and there," said the man.

"What do you do for a living?"

"This and that."

"Take him away," said the judge.

The man said, "Wait a minute! When will I get out?"

The judge replied, "Sooner or later."

So a guy walks into a bar with a pair of jumper cables hanging around his neck. The bartender gives him a look and says gruffly, "All right, pal, I'll let you stay, but don't start anything."

— SCOTT HOFFMAN

text credits

art credits

Have a funny joke or anecdote of your own?

We want to hear it! Log on to rd.com and click on "Submit a Joke."